Beethoven

Symphony No. 4 in B-Flat Major
Op. 60

Creation, Origins and Reception History
Incorporating
Contextual Accounts of Beethoven and His Contemporaries

BEETHOVEN

As depicted by the life mask taken by Franz Klein in 1812
(derived from a copy in the author's possession)

BEETHOVEN
SYMPHONY NO. 4
IN B-FLAT MAJOR
OP. 60

CREATION ORIGINS
AND
RECEPTION HISTORY

Incorporating contextual accounts of
Beethoven and his contemporaries

Terence M. Russell

Jelly Bean Books

The right of Terence Russell to be identified as the
Author of the Work has been asserted by him in accordance
with the Copyright, Designs and Patents Act 1988.

Copyright © Terence M. Russell 2024

Published by
Jelly Bean Books
136 Newport Road
Cardiff
CF24 1DJ

ISBN: 978-1-917022-76-7

www.candyjarbooks.co.uk

All rights reserved.
No part of this publication may be reproduced, stored in a
retrieval system, or transmitted at any time or by any means,
electronic, mechanical, photocopying, recording or otherwise
without the prior permission of the copyright holder. This book is
sold subject to the condition that it shall not by way of trade or
otherwise be circulated without the publisher's prior consent in any
form of binding or cover other than that in which it is published.

CONTENTS

AUTHOR'S NOTE	I
INTRODUCTION	IX
EDITORIAL PRINCIPLES	XIV
BEETHOVEN'S FINANCIAL TRANSACTIONS	XVII
SYMPHONY NO. 4: SELECTED WRITINGS	1
Beethoven House, Digital Archives	1
(Sir) George Grove	3
Ernest Markham Lee	5
Donald Francis Tovey	6
Donald Nivison Ferguson	8
Robert Simpson	9
Louise Elvira Cuyler	11
Joseph Braunstein	12
Michael Broyles	14
William Drabkin	15
Alec Harman, Anthony Milner and Wilfrid Mellers	16

Richard Osborne	17
Elizabeth Schwarm Glesner	19
Theodor Adorno	20
Michael Steinberg	21
Barry Cooper	23
Alfred Peter Brown	24

BEETHOVEN AND VIENNA: GESTATION OF THE B-FLAT MAJOR SYMPHONY — 26

Portraits of Beethoven	28
Personal Impressions of Beethoven	29
Post Heiligenstadt	33
Achievement Amidst Insecurity	35
Jérôme Bonaparte: offer of post of Kapellmeister	38
Beethoven's Annuity Contract	40
Vienna: Concert Venues and Music-Making	42
Beethoven's Orchestra	47

CREATION ORIGINS — 54
RECEPTION HISTORY — 85
LATER RECEPTION: MUSICOLOGY — 140

Heinrich Friedrich Rellstab	141
Hector Berlioz	142
Clara Schumann	145
Sir George Grove	147
Ernest Markham Lee	150
Romain Rolland	152
Paul Bekker	154
Donald Francis Tovey	158
Marion Scott	160
Arturo Toscanini	162
Richard Strauss	166
Donald Nivison Ferguson	168
Wilfrid Howard Mellers	171

Robert Simpson	172
Igor Stravinsky	174
Louise Elvira Cuyler	176
Basil Deane	177
Joseph Braunstein	179
William Preston Stedman	181
Anthony Hopkins	183
Denis Matthews	186
Michael Broyles	188
Alec Harman, Anthony Milner and Wilfrid Mellers	190
Richard Osborne	191
Peter Hauschild	192
William Kinderman	194
Theodore W. Adorno	196
Michael Steinberg	198
Alfred Peter Brown	199
Terry Barfoot	202
BIBLIOGRAPHY	204
INDEX	239
ABOUT THE AUTHOR	244

AUTHOR'S NOTE

I have cherished the idea of making a study of the life and work of Beethoven for many years. This statement requires a few words of personal reflection. I first encountered Beethoven in my early piano lessons – Minuet in G major, WoO 10, No. 2. At the same time I became acquainted with his piano pupil Carl Czerny – *Book One, Piano Studies*. My heart sank when I discovered the rear cover advertised a further *99* books in the same series – scales, arpeggios studies for the left hand, studies for the right hand – all the way to his Op. 824! By coincidence, my *Czerny Book One* was edited by Alec Rowley – who had the same surname as my music teacher. In my childish innocence, I often wondered why *he himself* never appeared to give me a lesson!

In my teenage years I found myself drawn ever closer to

Beethoven's music in the manner that ferromagnetic materials are ineluctably held captive in the sway of a magnetic field. The impulse to which I yielded is well described in words the conductor Bruno Walter gave in one of his rare public addresses:

> 'It is my belief that young people at that age are more easily impressed by what is heroic and grandiose; that they more easily understand works of art in which passionate feelings are violently uttered in raised accents, and that the lighter sounds of cheerfulness are less impressive to them.'

I do indeed recall the stirring effect made on me on first hearing the Overture *Egmont*, the unfolding drama of the Fifth Symphony and the declamatory opening chords of the *Emperor* Piano Concerto.

I resolved to read everything I could about Beethoven, starting with Marion Scott's pioneering English-language study of the composer in *The Master Musicians series*. My father took out a subscription for me for *The Gramophone* magazine, enabling me to read reviews of the new 'LP' recordings – none of which though I could afford! The LP was then – 1950s – beginning to supplant the 78 rpm shellac records, stacks of which could be purchased for as little as six pence each in 'old' money. I listed to the radio to hear Anthony Hopkins 'Talking about music' and to other musicological luminaries including Howard Fergusson, Hans Keller, Paul Hamburger, Denis Matthews, and Peter Stadlen.

At this same time, I had the privilege of hearing Beethoven's music performed by the *Hallé Orchestra* under the baton of Sir John Barbirolli, and experienced the *Carl*

Rosa Opera Company perform the composer's only opera *Fidelio*, I borrowed the piano-reduction score from the City Library to become better acquainted with this moving work — only to find the score's fists full of notes were well beyond my capabilities. Nonetheless, since then *Fidelio's* every note has been woven into my DNA. I also recall the period when the *London Promenade Concerts* were designated 'Friday night is Beethoven night'.

Through these influences I resolved to visit Vienna to see where Beethoven had lived and worked. But how? The support for such travel was beyond the means of my family. Fortunately, in my final year at school (1959), an opportunity presented itself. I saw a poster that stated *WUS — World University Service* — required volunteers to work in the Austrian town of Linz to help relocate refugees who were living there in improvised wooden shacks — displaced and dispossessed victims of the Second World War. To those participating all expenses would be paid together with free accommodation — in one of the crumbling wooden shacks! From Linz, I planned to make my way to Vienna.

I applied to *WUS* and, despite being a mere school-leaver, I was accepted. The *WUS* authorities doubtless reasoned the building-trade skills I had acquired during my secondary education in the building department of a technical school would be useful. This proved to be the case. At the refugee camp I dug trenches and was allowed to assist as a bricklayer. All about me were wide-eyed children eager to help but mostly getting in the way. I recall one afternoon when a reporter from *The Observer* newspaper paid a visit to our construction site to gather material for an article he was writing on European post-war recovery — he generously admired my trenches and brickwork!

Of lasting significance was another visit, this time from a Belgian priest. He took a group of us to the nearby

Mauthausen Concentration Camp, recently opened as a silent and solemn memorial to those who had perished there. It was a deeply moving experience. Years later I learned of the views of the ardent Beethovenian Sir Michael Tippet. After the horrors of the *Holocaust*, he posed the question for mankind: 'What price Beethoven now?' He posited: 'Could we any longer find solace in Beethoven's setting of Schiller's *Ode to Joy* and its utopian vision – "Be embraced you Millions"?'

My refugee contribution duly came to end and Vienna beckoned. On arrival there I found scenes reminiscent of *The Third Man* and *Harry Lime*. I recall, for example, encountering cobblestones piled high in the streets waiting to be replaced after having been disturbed by the heavy armoured vehicles that had so recently passed over them. But Vienna was welcoming. I visited the houses where Beethoven had lived and worked and paused outside others associated with him that were identified by a commemorative plaque and the Austrian flag. A particularly memorable occasion was attending a recital in the great salon within the palace of Beethoven's noble patron Prince Lobkowitz – the very one where the *Eroica* Symphony had been premiered. Ultimately, my steps led me to the composer's first resting place in the *Währinger Ortsfriedhof*. I paid silent homage to the great man and, as I did so, discovered nearby the resting place of Franz Schubert to whom Beethoven was an endless source of admiration and inspiration.

I felt a youthful impulse to discover yet more about Beethoven and his music. But absorption in musicology would have to take second place. My chosen career beckoned in the guise of architecture – 'the mother of the arts' and 'the handmaid of society'. There was room though for Beethoven's music and from that time on it has been my constant companion through attendance at recitals, in concerts and music-making in the home. And at home a reproduction of Franz Kline's 1812 study of the composer has greeted me each day for more than half a century.

On my retirement from a career in architectural practice, research and university teaching, the opportunity finally presented itself for me to devote time to researching Beethoven musicology. Having attained my eightieth year also emboldened me to make progress with my good intentions!

With these autobiographical remarks outlined I will say a few remarks about my working method— see also the comments made in *Editorial Principles*.

As a member of staff of The University of Edinburgh, I had the good fortune to have access to the *Reid Music Library*, formed from a nucleus of books bequeathed by General John Reid and augmented over the years by such custodians as Sir Donald Francis Tovey, sometime *Reid Professor of Music* and renowned Beethoven scholar. Over a period of three years, I made a survey of the many works in the Reid collection. I consulted each item in turn making records on paper slips — many hundreds — that I deemed to be relevant for my researches. I confined my searches to book-publications, as reflected in my accompanying bibliography. All of this was quite some years ago, the cut-off date for my researches being 2007. Beyond this date I have not surveyed any further works. I am mindful though that Beethoven musicology and related publication continue to be a major field of endeavour in the manner of the proverbial 'ever rolling stream'.

In the intervening years since completing my archival researches, personal tribulations associated with family illness and bereavement slowed my progress in giving expression to my projected intentions. Latterly, however, with renewed energy, and more time at my disposal, I have been able to make progress. My studies take the form of a set of monographs. The first set of these, trace the creation origins and reception history of each of Beethoven's piano sonatas and string quartets. The resulting texts also incorporate contextual accounts of Beethoven and his contemporaries. Also included in my musicological surveys are two related Beethoven anthologies. The set of monographs in question, identified by short title, are:

Beethoven: An anthology of selected writings.
Beethoven: The piano sonatas: An anthology of selected writings.

The Piano Sonatas:
Op. 2–Op. 28
Op. 31–Op. 81a
Op. 90–Op. 111

The String Quartets:
Op. 18, Nos. 1–6
Op. 59, Nos. 1–3 (Razumovsky); Op. 74 (The Harp); Op. 95 (Quartetto serioso)
Op. 127, Op. 132 and Op. 130 (Galitzin)
Op. 131, Op. 135; Grosse Fuge, Op. 133 and Op. 134 (Fugue transcription)

I provide further information about these studies in the introduction to each individual monograph. Suffice it for me to state here the basic premise upon which my work is founded. I believe it is rewarding, concerning the life of a great artist, to find connections between who he *was* and what he *did*; in Martin Cooper's words 'between his personality, as expressed on the one hand in human relationships, and on the other in artistic creation'. (*Beethoven, The Last*

Decade) That is not to say I consider it essential to the enjoyment of Beethoven's music to know this or that fact about it. His music can be enjoyed, as millions do, with — in Robert Simpson's apt phrase — 'an innocent ear', for what it is and how it reaches out to us in purely musical terms without any prejudging of its merits based upon extra-musicological facts. Maynard Solomon expresses similar thoughts:

> 'It is doubtless true that we need have no knowledge whatever of a composer's biography, or knowledge of any other motivating factor of any kind, to appreciate the artwork on some fundamental level.' (*Beethoven Essays*, 1988, p. 116)

I must make a further point. I am mindful that a scholar who ventures into a field of study that is not rightly his may be regarded with some suspicion. In this regard I can but ask the reader to place his or her trust in me in the following way. I have attempted to bring to my work the care which publishers and their desk editors have required of me in my book writings relating to architecture — listed elsewhere.

As inferred, it is now more than sixty years since I paid homage to Beethoven in Vienna's *Währinger Ortsfriedhof* and my warmth of feeling towards the composer and his music have grown with the passing of the years. My studies are not intended to be propaedeutic — that would be pretentious. However, if in sharing with others what I have to say contributes to their knowledge and understanding of the composer, and thereby increases their own feelings towards him and his works, my own pleasure in bringing my work to completion will be all the more enhanced.

When Beethoven arrived in Vienna, he was unknown. He was armed though with a note of encouragement from his youthful friend and benefactor Count Ferdinand Waldstein. It contained the often-quoted words: 'Receive Mozart's spirit from Haydn's hands.' Some forty years later Beethoven passed away in the House of the black-robed Spaniards at 200 *Alservorstädter*, the *Glacis* where he had lived since the autumn of 1825. Soldiers had to be called to secure the doors to the inner courtyard of the house from the pressure of onlookers. His body was blessed in the *Alservorsttädt Parish Church*, schools were closed and perhaps as many as 10,000 people formed a funeral procession — an honour ordinarily reserved for monarchs. The *Marcia Funebre* from the composer's Op. 26 Piano Sonata was performed at the funeral ceremony. Franz Grillparzer read the funeral oration. Franz Schubert, who, as remarked in life so admired Beethoven, was one of the pallbearers. The composer's mortal remains were lowered into a simple vault. Beethoven now belonged to history.

Dr Terence M. Russell
Edinburgh 2020

To the foregoing I am pleased to add the following works:

The Piano Concertos
The Symphonies: An Anthology of Selected Writings
Symphony No. 1 In C Major, Op. 21
Symphony No. 2 in D Major, Op. 36
Symphony No. 3 in E-flat Major, Op. 55 (*Eroica*)
Symphony No. 4 in B-flat Major, Op. 60

TMR
2024

INTRODUCTION

1806 was a creative period for Beethoven. In addition to the composition of the Symphony in B-flat major, Op. 60, he worked on the Piano Concerto in G major, Op. 58, the three String Quartets, Op. 59 (*Razumovsky*), the Violin Concerto in D major, Op. 61, and his Opera *Leonora* (*Fidelio*), Op. 72. For the latter he composed the Overture *Leonora* No. 3, Op. 72b — one of the work's *four* overtures. After completing the *Eroica* Symphony, Beethoven did not commence work directly on the Fourth Symphony. Instead, he began work on what would become the celebrated Symphony No. 5 in C minor, Op. 67. However, he set this aside for various reasons. Beethoven's biographer Alexander Wheelock Thayer suggested, with the work comparatively advanced, Beethoven felt disposed to take his next symphony 'in a different direction'— one having a more relaxed mood and character. (Elliot Forbes editor, *Thayer's life of Beethoven*, Princeton University Press, 1967)

Beethoven arranged the order of his nine symphonies with considerable thought and care. Richard Osbourne remarks:

> 'Beethoven [showed] characteristic genius in differentiating between works which he worked on more or less simultaneously: the Fourth and Fifth Symphonies and, later on, the Seventh and Eighth. The contrast between the gamesome and lyrical Fourth and the fearsomely dramatic Fifth ... is particularly interesting since the two works have a certain amount in common. In the Fourth Symphony, for example, we first meet the idea of Beethoven bringing the third movement Trio round twice, an effect he was also inclined to use in the Fifth ... [in addition] The drum-led finale of the Fifth Symphony is one of music's most celebrated instrumental inspirations, but no less remarkable in the preparation for the recapitulation of the first movement of the Fourth Symphony where the drum single-handedly reasserts the tonic in B flat.' (Richard Osborne, *Beethoven* in: Robert Layton editor. *A Guide to the Symphony.* 1995)

The Fourth Symphony returns to the more classical style of the First and Second Symphonies and, in contrast, stands between two dramatic and expansive companions, namely, the Third Symphony (*Eroica*) and the Fifth Symphony (C minor). This disposed Robert Schuman to liken the B-flat major Symphony to 'a slender (*schlanke*) Greek maiden between two Norse giants'. However, notwithstanding

Schuman's well-intended simile, authorities today consider his imagery has rendered a disservice to the Fourth Symphony. Though it is much shorter than the *Eroica*, and certainly less dramatic than the Fifth, the Fourth Symphony continues some of the expansive tendencies of the composer's larger works. In its defence, it has been described as possessing 'a glow of passion' (Donald Nivison Ferguson, *Masterworks of the Orchestral Repertoire: A Guide for Listeners*. Minneapolis: University of Minnesota Press, 1954) and 'muscles of steel beneath [its] silken skin [that] sometimes tense and flex with sudden force' (Robert Simpson, *Beethoven Symphonies*. London: British Broadcasting Corporation, 1970)

Beethoven's normal method of working was to jot down ideas and fragments of themes in a pocket notebook that he always carried with him when he was outdoors walking in the countryside. When back home he would develop these at his writing desk in a sketchbook, often turning from one work to another. In the case of the Fourth Symphony, no sketches have survived. Terry Barfoot believes: '[The] absence of surviving sketches for the Symphony No. 4 would suggest, like the music itself, that it was a spontaneous outpouring.' (*Symphony No.4 in B-flat major, Op. 60: Notes to the BBC Radio Three Beethoven Experience,* Tuesday 7 and Wednesday 8 June 2005, www.bbc.co.uk/radio3/Beethoven)

Notwithstanding the genial warmth and musical accessibility of the Fourth Symphony, its early performances earned the censure of some music critics. Following performances in 1807, the music correspondent of the *Journal des Luxus und der Modem* complained:

> 'Richness of ideas, bold originality and fullness of power, which are the particular merits of Beethoven's muse were very much in evidence

> to everyone at these concerts; yet many found fault with the lack of a noble simplicity and the all too fruitful accumulation of ideas which on account of their number were not always adequately worked out and blended, thereby creating the effect more often of rough diamonds.'

In 1807, the twenty-one years old Carl Maria von Weber heard a play-through of the Fourth Symphony and did not find it to his liking:

> 'I have just come from the rehearsal of a symphony [the B-flat major] by one of our newest composers [Beethoven]; and though ... I have a tolerably strong constitution, I could only just hold out, and five minutes more would have shattered my frame and burst the sinews of my life ... First a slow movement full of short disjointed ideas, at the rate of three or four notes per quarter of an hour; then a mysterious roll of the drum and passage of the violas, seasoned with the proper quantity of pauses and *ritardandos*; and to end all a furious *finale*, in which the only requisite is that there should be no ideas for the hearer to make out, but plenty of transitions from one key to another – on to the new note at once! never mind modulating! – above all things, throw rules to the winds, for they only hamper a genius.' (As quoted in: George Grove, *Beethoven and his Nine Symphonies*, 1896)

In fairness to Weber, in his later years, he modified his headstrong opinions of Beethoven's music and became an admirer, for example, of the composer's Opera *Fidelio* — that he championed with enthusiasm.

Reflecting on the eventual reception of the Fourth Symphony by the Viennese critics, present-day authorities consider they may have subsequently been favourably disposed to accept it because of many of the work's Haydnesque characteristics, not least the adoption of the key of B-flat major that Haydn had made familiar to the public in his own Symphony No. 98 (1792) and Symphony No. 102 (1794). One such authority remarked in more general terms:

> 'In a deepening trend which began in 1806 with the Fourth Symphony, the Fourth Piano Concerto, and the Violin Concerto, [Beethoven] now settled to imbue many of his works with a sense of inner repose that no longer required turbulent responses to grand challenges. A new lyrical strain enters his music, along with a pre-Romantic freedom of harmonic motion and of structural design.' (Maynard Solomon, *Beethoven*, 1977)

At the close of Beethoven's lifetime (he died in 1827), the Fourth Symphony was well-established in the concert repertoire — certainly in Vienna, Beethoven's adopted hometown. This is evident in an article that appeared in 1825 in the *Berliner Allgemeine musikalische Zeitung* — a journal dedicated to reviews of contemporary music. It had been founded the year before by the music theorist Adolf Bernhard Marx in collaboration with the Berlin music publisher Adolph Martin Schlesinger. The article in question was written by the poet and respected music critic Ludwig Rellstab — known to Schubertians for contributing the texts to the first seven songs of the composer's

Schwanengesang. Rellstab's hearing a performance of the Fourth Symphony disposed him to enthuse in a manner that forms a fitting introduction to our own survey of this elevating and innovative composition:

> 'If I were called upon to give an opinion on this long-familiar work, I would undertake to point out that practically no other work of Beethoven's shows so effective control of the overall form as in this Symphony. The individual movements are so beautifully juxtaposed, everything develops so naturally, as only the most accomplished master would be able to bring about, for: "Only from perfected powers can grace step forth" [quoting Corinthians 2].'

TMR

EDITORIAL PRINCIPLES

By its very nature a study of this kind draws extensively on the work of others. Every effort has been made to acknowledge this in the text by indicating words quoted or adapted with single quotation marks. Wherever possible, for the sake of consistency, I have retained the orthography of quoted texts making only occasional silent changes of spelling and capitalization. Deleted words are identified by means of three ellipsis points ... and interpolations are encompassed within square brackets [ ]. Quoted words, phrases and longer cited passages of text remain the intellectual property of their copyright holders.

I address the reader in the second person, notwithstanding that the work is my own — produced without the benefit of a desk editor. It follows that I must bear the responsibility for any errors of misunderstanding or misinterpretation for which I ask the reader's forbearance. A collaboration I must acknowledge is the help I received from the librarians of the *Reid Music Library* at the University of Edinburgh. Over the three-year period it took me to compile my reference sources, they served me with unfailing courtesy, often supplying me with twenty or more books at a time. In converting my manuscript into book-format, I wish to thank my editorial coordinator, William Rees, for his support and painstaking care. I would also like to thank Shaun Russell (no relation) for his work designing the covers for each of the volumes.

My admiration for Beethoven provided the initial impulse to commence this undertaking and has sustained me over the several years it has taken to bring my enterprise to completion. That said, I am no Beethoven idolater. I am mindful of the danger that awaits one who ventures to chronicle the work of a great artist. I believe it was Sigmund Freud who suggested that biographers may become so disposed to their subject, and their emotional involvement with their hero, that their work becomes an exercise in idealisation. In response to such a putative charge let me say. First, I am no biographer. I do however make occasional reference to Beethoven's personal life and his relationships with his contemporaries. Second, I acknowledge Beethoven has his detractors. Accordingly, I have not shrunk from allowing dissentient voices, critical of Beethoven and his work, to be heard. These, however, are few and are silenced amidst the adulation that awaits the reader in support of the endeavours of one of humanity's great creators and one who courageously showed the way in overcoming personal adversity.

TMR

BEETHOVEN'S FINANCIAL TRANSACTIONS

Beethoven's negotiations with his music publishers make many references to his compositions. Today they are recognised for what they are – enduring works of art – but referred to in his business correspondence they appear almost as though they were mere everyday commodities – for which he required an appropriate remuneration. Beethoven resented the time he had to devote to the business-side of his affairs. He believed an agency should exist, for fellow artists such as himself, from which a reasonable sum could be paid for the work (composition) submitted, leaving more time for creative enterprises. In the event Beethoven, like Mozart before him, had to deal with publishers largely on his own. Beethoven, though, did benefit in his business dealings from the help he received from his younger brother Kasper Karl (Caspar Carl). From 1800, Carl worked as a clerk in Vienna's Department of Finance in which capacity he found time to correspond with publishers to offer his brother's works for sale and — importantly — to secure the best prices he could. In April 1802 Beethoven wrote to the Leipzig publishers Breitkopf & Härtel: '[You] can rely entirely on my brother who, in general, attends to my affairs.' Whilst Carl promoted Beethoven's interests with determination, he appears to have lacked tact and made enemies. For example, Beethoven's piano pupil Ferdinand Ries — who for a while also helped the composer with his business negotiations — is on record as describing Carl as being 'the biggest skinflint in the world'.

The currencies most referred to in Beethoven's correspondence are as follows:

> Silver gulden and florin: these were interchangeable and had a value of about two contemporary English shillings.
> Ducat: 4 1/2 gulden / florins: valued at about nine shillings.
> Louis d'or: This gold coin was adopted during the Napoleonic wars and the French occupation of Vienna and Austria more widely. It had a value of about two ducats or approximately twenty shillings or one-pound sterling.

Beethoven was never poor — in the romantic sense of 'an artist starving in a garret'. On arriving in Vienna in 1792, he was fortunate to receive financial support from his patron Prince Karl Lichnowsky who conferred on him an annuity of 600 florins — that he maintained for several years. Between the months of February and July of 1796, Beethoven undertook a concert tour taking in Prague, Dresden, Leipzig and Berlin. He was well-received and wrote to his other younger brother Nikolaus Johann: 'My art is winning me friends and what more do I want? ... I shall make a good deal of money.' Later on, in 1809, Napoleon Bonaparte's youngest brother Jérôme Bonaparte offered Beethoven an appointment at his Court with the promise of an income of 4,000 florins. Alarmed at the prospect of losing Beethoven — now the most celebrated composer in Europe — three of Vienna's most notable citizens, namely, the Archduke Rudolph (Beethoven's only composition pupil), Prince Kinsky and Prince Lobkowitz settled on the composer the same sum of 4,000 florins. Inflation, however, brought about by the Napoleonic wars, soon eroded its value; personal misfortune to Lobkowitz and Kinsky also took its toll.

Beethoven undoubtedly had to work hard to secure a reasonable standard of living. Notwithstanding, despite his occasional straitened circumstances, he contributed generously to the needs of others. For example, he allowed his works to be performed without benefit to himself at charitable concerts; in 1815 his philanthropy earned for him the honour of Bürgerrecht — 'freedom of the City'.

Beethoven earned a great deal of money when his music was performed, to considerable acclaim, at several concerts held in association with the Congress of Vienna (1814–15). He did not, though, benefit from it personally; he invested it on behalf of his nephew Karl. More generally, it is one of the misfortunes of Beethoven's life that in money-matters he was somewhat culpably improvident. This is poignantly evident in a letter he wrote on 18 March 1827 to the Philharmonic Society of London — just one week before his death; the Society had made him a gift of £100. He sent the Society 'his most heartfelt thanks for their particular sympathy and support'.

'The solemn spread over five minutes; the dramatic hush and crescendo leading to the recapitualation in the first movement; the astonishing middle episode of the slow movement, and the double alternating repetition of scherzo, and trio; these are the features we recognise as peculiarly Beethovenish in this work.'

Donald Francis Tovey, *Essays in Musical Analysis*, H. Milford, 1935-41, Vol. 1, pp. 34-35.

SELECTED WRITINGS

We open our account of Beethoven's Fourth Symphony in B-flat major, Op. 60 with a selection of writings that convey the regard for this composition as variously expressed by musicologists and musicians. The texts selected derive from various periods and reflect the differing styles of expression and register of language characteristic of their time. They are presented in their chronological order of publication with the intention of revealing, thereby, the evolving estimation felt for this work from the period of its first appearance to closer to the present day.

BEETHOVEN HOUSE, DIGITAL ARCHIVES
The Digital Archives of the Beethoven House in Bonn

consist of facsimile reproductions of music manuscripts (sketches and scores), written documents (notably letters), portraits (Beethoven and his close associates), topographical scenes (Beethoven's many residences), alongside a selection of the composer's possessions and everyday ephemera. Collectively, they provide unique insights into Beethoven's way of working and his relationships with those around him who variously provided him with practical and emotional support and, significantly, assisted him in bringing his music in being.

Of the Symphony under consideration the Digital Archives inform:

> 'The Fourth Symphony Op. 60 has always been outshone by the great heroic symphonies such as the Third, the so-called *Eroica*, the Fifth, the so-called *Destiny* Symphony, and the Sixth, also called the *Pastoral* Symphony. That is, however, not quite fair as a reviewer of the *Allgemeine musikalische Zeitung* [*AmZ*] ('General Musical Newspaper') concluded in 1812 and called the Symphony a clear and straight composition characterised by the ingenuity and energy which was so typical of Beethoven's earlier works. [for the *AmZ's* response to the Fourth Symphony, see elsewhere in our account].
>
> 'The Fourth Symphony was probably played for the first time during one of the private concerts of Prince Lobkowitz. The programme included the first three Beethoven Symphonies as well as a fourth one, still [then] unknown, as the *AmZ* announced on 18 March 1807. One year later, Beethoven dedicated the Symphony to Franz Joachim Reichsgraf von Oppersdorff

(1770–1818) whom he had met on a journey with
Prince Lichnowsky at the Prince's Castle Grätz
close to Troppau.'

Beethoven House, Digital Archives, Library Document,
Sinfonie Nr. 4 (B-Dur), Op. 60.

SIR GEORGE GROVE

The name Grove is familiar to generations of music lovers through association with *Grove's Dictionary of Music and Musicians* of which Grove was the inspiration and source. Sir George Grove, however, did not receive a formal education in music and trained as a structural engineer, being admitted as a graduate of the Institution of Civil Engineers. He worked in this capacity for the first thirty years of his life and it was while he was engaged on the Britannia Bridge that he became known to such luminaries of the age as Robert Stephenson, Isambard Kingdom Brunel, and Sir Charles Barry. Through their influence, Grove made a change of career and was appointed in 1849 to the secretaryship of the Society of Arts – at the period of gestation of the Great Exhibition of 1851. When the exhibition relocated to Sydenham, in the guise of The Crystal Palace, it was as a result of the actions of Grove that the German-born August Manns was appointed, first as bandmaster and later as the conductor of a full-size orchestra. Manns presided over regular concerts for more than forty years, Grove providing numerous programme notes that later formed the basis for his *Dictionary*.

Grove held Beethoven's Fourth Symphony in high regard as is evident from his writing in support of the work:

'Perhaps Beethoven's instinct showed him that it

would be an artistic mistake to follow so very serious a Symphony as the *Eroica* by one equally earnest and profound ... At any rate, the B-flat Symphony is a complete contrast to both its predecessor and successor, and it's as gay and spontaneous as they are serious and lofty. And this, perhaps, is one reason for the fact that No. 4 has never yet had justice done it by the public. As No. 8 lives in the valley between the colossal No. 9 and the almost equally colossal No.7, so No.4 is equally overshadowed by the *Eroica* and the C minor.

'Schumann has spoken of the No. 4 as standing between its companions "like a slender (*schlanke*) Greek maiden between two Norse giants". But humour is hardly the characteristic of a Greek maiden and when we recollect the humour which accompanies the grace and beauty of the Fourth Symphony, and is so obvious to everyone of the movements, it must be admitted, though with great respect, that the comparison losses something of its force.' [The American musicologist Rodney Corkin remarks: 'Schuman's well-known description of the piece as a "slender Greek maiden between to Nordic giants" has done the Fourth Symphony no favours, nor is it a particularly accurate statement.' Rodney Corkin, The Beethoven Reference Site: *Beethoven's Symphonies.* (no date)].

Grove continues:

'At the same time no expression of Schumann, or Berlioz, or any other worshipper of Beethoven, can be too strong for this beautiful work. There is something extraordinarily *entrainant* about it throughout; a more consistent and attractive whole cannot be. In the *Eroica* some have complained of the Funeral March as too long, some of the scherzo as inappropriate, or the finale as trivial; but on the No. 4 no such criticisms are possible; the movements fit to their places like the limbs and features of a lovely statue; and, full of fire and invention as they are, all are subordinated to conciseness, grace and beauty.

'The most obvious characteristic of the work, that which distinguishes it throughout, is its unceasing and irrepressible brightness and gaiety, and the extraordinary finish of the workmanship ... Beethoven must have been inspired by the very genius of happiness when he conceived and worked out the many beautiful themes of this joyous composition, and threw in the spirited and graceful features which so adorn them. The work is animated throughout by a youthful exhilaration more akin to that which pervades Mendelssohn's *Italian* Symphony than anything else we can recall — in the *adagio by* real passion. Such times were rare in Beethoven's life, and we are fortunate in having so perfect an image of one of them preserved for us.'

George Grove, *Beethoven and his Nine Symphonies*. London: Novello, Ewer, 1896, pp. 98—100.

ERNEST MARKHAM LEE

Ernest Markham Lee was an English composer, author, lecturer, pianist and organist whose highly readable *The*

Story of the Symphony (1916) must have endeared itself to many music lovers and helped them to become acquainted with the symphonic repertoire of the period. Lee introduces his discussion of Beethoven's Fourth Symphony by stating:

> 'The gay and delightful Symphony in B-flat, No. 4, Op. 60, is Beethoven in a lighter vein, excepting perhaps the magnificent slow movement which possess all the lofty attributes of dignified symphonic music ... True, it by no means gave satisfaction to its early critics, and no-less a person than the composer of *Der Freischütz* amused himself by penning a humorous and not altogether kind skit upon its originalities and difficulties [see elsewhere]. But even the great influence of Weber and the scoffings of many lesser men could not for long obscure the bright freshness and skilful mastery of the ideas depicted. The Symphony may not for some years have been quite so often played as its more titanic brethren, but in later days it has taken its due place among the immortals, and one from which it is never likely to be removed.'

Ernest Markham Lee, *The Story of the Symphony*. London: Scott Publishing Co., 1916, pp. 59–60.

DONALD FRANCIS TOVEY

The British musicologist, composer, pedagogue and conductor Sir Donald Francis Tovey is perhaps best known for his *Essays in Musical Analysis*. They had their origins as programme notes written by him to accompany the concerts given by the Ried Orchestra, Edinburgh – performed largely under Tovey's direction. The *Essays* were published in six volumes with each volume focusing on a particular category of Beethoven's music. Volumes I and II were devoted to the symphonies; Volume III, the concertos; Volume IV, illustrative music, Volume V, vocal music; and Volume VI, supplementary essays. A seventh volume was published posthumously dealing with chamber music. These writings are still respected today for their musicological erudition that Tovey interspersed with passages of wit and mordant humour. His musical analyses seek 'to facilitate the listener's appreciation of [the music's] artistic content and technical merits'. In Volume One he asserts:

> 'The Fourth Symphony is perhaps the work in which Beethoven first fully reveals his mastery of movement. He had already shown his command of a vastly wider range of musical possibilities than that of Mozart and Haydn. And he had shown no lack of ease and power in the handling of his new resources. But now he shows that these resources can be handled in such a way that Mozart's own freedom of movement reappears as one of the most striking qualities of the whole.'

Donald Francis Tovey. *Essays in Musical Analysis.* London: Oxford University Press, H. Milford, 7 Vols., 1935–41; derived from Vol.1, p. 35.

In his later study *Beethoven* Tovey remarks:

> 'The Fourth Symphony, coming between the *Eroica* and the C minor, is one of those masterpieces which many people insist on despising for being satisfied with its own size. Only a master,

who could produce the *Eroica* Symphony, could have produced this smaller work at all, and, as with the Eighth Symphony, which stands in a similar position between the Seventh and the Ninth, Beethoven felt even more strongly the sense that his powers were extending than when he was producing larger works. As a study in movement, the Fourth Symphony reveals things that we simply have not leisure to notice in larger works.'

Donald Francis Tovey, *Beethoven*. London: Oxford University Press, 1944, p. 66.

DONALD NIVISON FERGUSON

Donald Nivison Ferguson was an American music educator and author who studied music in both America and Europe; he attained the great age of 103. Together with his writings on music he was programme annotator for the Minneapolis Symphony Orchestra. This experience helped to inform his *Masterworks of the Orchestral Repertoire* from which we quote the following:

'To expect Beethoven's next effort in symphonic form to be an extension of such a work as the *Eroica* would be absurd. Indeed, to anticipate the next turn Beethoven's imagination will take after any achievement is always impossible. For there is surely no other composer — and there is perhaps no other artist than Shakespeare — whose imagination covered so wide a range.

'The Fourth Symphony is less commanding than the *Eroica*, but it is not less masterful either in structure or in imagination. No one has attempted to give the work a title, nor could any thinkable one be less than offensive. Yet the world is agreed that this is a species of love music. Schuman described the piece as "a slender Grecian maiden between two Nordic giants", the giants obviously being the *Eroica* and the Fifth. While his metaphor points chiefly toward the incomparable form of the work, it hints also at the glow of passion that shines through the perfect exterior. Though the emotion behind the Symphony is by no means the outspoken and even vaunted passion of the later romanticists, it has its roots in the same region of experience.'

Donald Nivison Ferguson, *Masterworks of the Orchestral Repertoire: A Guide for Listeners.* Minneapolis: University of Minnesota Press, 1954, p. 54.

ROBERT SIMPSON

Robert Simpson was a prolific English composer of eleven symphonies, fifteen string quartets, and four concertos, not to mention a great deal of other music written for various combinations of instruments. During his long service as a BBC producer and broadcaster, he gave talks on his favourite composers including Beethoven, Bruckner, Nielsen and Sibelius, about each one of whom he wrote an informed, scholarly monograph. From Simpson's *Beethoven Symphonies*, we quote the following:

'The paucity of sketches for the Fourth Symphony has given rise to the supposition that it is entirely spontaneous; certainly, the work is so felicitous as to suggest it having been done at a sitting. Yet the Symphony is by no means entirely sunny ... [The] deep mystery and tension of its slow introduction and its probable influence on the dark link between the last two movements of the Fifth. Critical reactions to the first performance of No. 4 found it crude and wayward with detail, lacking "dignified simplicity". Later comment went to the other extreme, culminating in Schuman's famous simile: "like a slender Greek maiden between two Norse giants". Neither view is right, though it is a compliment to the range and subtlety of Beethoven that both are understandable in context. There is no trace of crudity or want of dignity in this wonderfully balanced, richly executed score. But its grace is neither maidenly nor Greek; it is that of a giant who performs relaxed athletic movements with gigantic ease and fluency. There are muscles of steel beneath the silken skin of Beethoven's creature; sometimes they tense and flex with sudden force, though there is rarely more than a hint of irascibility. In the adagio there is deep tenderness, even passion, of a peculiarly masculine kind to which Schuman's image is scarcely apt, and its inner contrast between a pervasively rigid rhythm and the most gloriously free melodic invention Beethoven had yet achieved creates a unique fascination, sublime discomfort of mind and senses.

'Whether or not the Forth was composed in one continuous burst, it abounds in subtleties no less than any other work of Beethoven known to have been more laboriously achieved.'

Robert Simpson, *Beethoven Symphonies*. London: British Broadcasting Corporation, 1970, pp. 24–25.

LOUISE ELVIRA CUYLER

The American musicologist Louise Elvira Cuyler asserts that although in Beethoven's symphonic writing his choice of keys may be considered as being conservative, his subsequent use of them was innovative and adventurous:

> 'Beethoven never exceeded his Classical forebears either in his choice of principal keys for his symphonies or in inter-movemental key-relationships. But within the bounds of virtually every individual movement, he explored daringly remote tonal regions and often the deviant keys into a rational modulatory scheme. By the time of the Fourth Symphony, his excursions to remote keys was spectacular and had infiltrated principal as well as developmental portions of his designs. Beethoven expanded the modulatory process itself, often using a key change as an opportunity to a devious or boldly conceived passage. Elsewhere he replaced the processed modulation with a simple, brusque juxtaposition of keys.'

Louise Elvira Cuyler, *The Symphony*. New York: Harcourt Brace Jovanovich, 1973, p.50.

JOSEPH BRAUNSTEIN

Joseph Braunstein was a Viennese-born American musicologist, teacher and the senior programme annotator for the Chamber Music Society of the Lincoln Center. His programme notes have been described as 'combining scholarly detail and analysis with a sense of atmosphere that conveyed something of a composer's milieu' [*New York Times*]; for example, as a young man Braunstein played violin with the Vienna State Opera Orchestra under the baton of Richard Strauss. Writing of Beethoven's Fourth Symphony he opens his account with the often-quoted words of Robert Schumann:

> 'Robert Schumann described the Fourth Symphony as a "slender Greek maiden between two giants from the North", meaning the *Eroica* and the C minor Symphonies. In these metaphorical terms, Schumann expressed the stylistic difference between these three symphonies. The Third and Fifth are revolutionary creations, while the Fourth appears as an enlarged specimen of the symphonic type developed by Beethoven's predecessors Haydn and Mozart. It is a more lyrical and carefree symphony than the *Eroica* and C minor Symphonies with their bold innovations, contrapuntal complexities, dramatic climaxes and more massive combinations.'

Braunstein remarks on aspects of the work's history and that of its autograph:

> 'The B flat Symphony was very dear to Mendelsohn who included it in the programme that began his activities as conductor of the Gewand-

haus Concerts in Leipzig in 1836. The choice is significant of Mendelsohn's artistic temperament. His brother Paul acquired the precious autograph which later passed to the Royal Library in Berlin. Richard Wagner, on the other hand, while he conducted the B flat Symphony never referred to it in his theoretical writings, although he deals extensively with Beethoven's other symphonies and the problems they posed to the performer and interpreter.' [Richard Wagner's *Prose Works*: 9 volumes edited and translated by William Ashton Ellis. London: Kegan Paul, Trench, Trübner, 1895–98.]

Of the Fourth Symphony's challenges to the performer, and aspects of its orchestration, Braunstein observes:

'The Fourth Symphony is by no means a technically easy piece. Cellists, double bass players and bassoonists of Beethoven's day, and later, cried out in desperation over the requirements [challenges] of their parts in the second and third movements. Beethoven actually wrote a bass passage that was unplayable unless the lowest string was tuned down to achieve an extension of the range so that the required notes could be obtained ... The Symphony is the only one of the nine that employs a single flute. The others employ a pair and some also a piccolo (Nos. 5, 6, and 9).'

Joseph Braunstein, *Musica Æterna, Program* Notes for 1971–1976. New York: *Musica Æterna*, 1978, Vol. 3, pp. 52–53.

MICHAEL BROYLES

Michael Broyles is President of the Society for American Music and a musicologist with research interests in the Classic Era with particular regard to Beethoven. Of the composer's symphonic writing following the *Eroica* Symphony he avers:

> 'In the later symphonies of Beethoven, we find a gradual evolution away from the Classical symphonic ideal. While the outward structure of the symphony was maintained, the style of the heroic decade affected and gradually reshaped the content. In tone and rhetoric some of Beethoven's later symphonies are decidedly unsymphonic. Early Beethoven had attempted to maintain the stylistic tendencies of the sonata genres against the almost constant intrusion of symphonic elements. The opposite occurs in the later Beethoven symphonies — he attempted to continue in the symphonic style, but the style-changes of the years 1804—07 were always there, reshaping and reorienting the works, sometimes in the most fundamental way.
>
> 'The Fourth, Fifth and Sixth Symphonies were all completed in the years 1806—08. Sketches for all three go back to 1803—04, and although they were completed in the order they are numbered, work on each overlapped the others, most of it falling in the 1806—08 period. These symphonies were thus conceived at a time of stylistic change, and in their blending of old and new elements and in their very nature — three radically different symphonic approaches worked out almost simultaneously — they reflect the stylistic turbulence

that existed then, particularly in relation to orchestral music.

'General rhythmic movement and its structural implications remain relatively Classical in the Fourth Symphony. Harmonic activity and its tonal implications do not. Compared to the *Eroica*, Beethoven pulled back in tone, scope and dramatic tension, a decision that allowed him to experiment with some unorthodox procedures. The Fourth Symphony was the first symphony to be completed after the *Eroica*, and its combination of old and new elements reflects the unsettled stylistic period in which it was written.'

Michael Broyles, *Beethoven: The Emergence and Evolution of Beethoven's Heroic Style*. New York: Excelsior Music Publishing Co., 1987, p. 173–74 and p. 186.

WILLIAM DRABKIN

Professor William Drabkin is an English musicologist whose research interests include the study and decipherment of Beethoven's sketchbooks. In his Preface to the Eulenberg edition of the miniature score to the *Eroica* Symphony, he makes the following reference to the composer's Fourth Symphony and its later 'companion' the Eighth Symphony:

'Beethoven's progress as a symphonist did not pursue a single path, or a straight line ... The Fourth Symphony, which was composed quickly in the summer of 1806 and represents something of a return to classical principles (the orchestral forces required for it are the smallest for a Beethoven symphony) may have been released before the Fifth on account of the unfavourable reactions to the *Eroica* after its first performance in 1805. It is more likely that memories of the artistic failure of the first concert featuring the Fifth and Sixth Symphonies prompted the composer to write a pair of musically lighter works, or at least cooler ones, in 1811–12; more than the Fourth Symphony, the Eighth marks a return to eighteenth-century symphonic dimensions.'

William Drabkin, Preface, *Beethoven: Symphony No. 4 Bb major Opus 60* (Study Score), Eulenburg 2011.

ALEC HARMAN, ANTHONY MILNER, AND WILFRID MELLERS

The American musicologist and professor of music Alec Harman, the British composer, teacher and conductor Anthony Milner, and the British musicologist and composer Wilfrid Mellers collaborated in a wide-ranging survey titled *Man and His Music*. In their discussion of Beethoven and his music they place Beethoven as a figure in history and one who made history. The Fourth Symphony was conceived amidst the upheavals in Europe, brought about by the French Revolution, and what the authors have to say, although not directly connected with the Fourth Symphony, has a bearing on the composer and his state of mind at this period:

'No work of art can be "explained" by reference to its historical connotations. Every artist self-evidently "reflects" the values and beliefs of his time ... At the same time any truly creative artist is also making those beliefs. It is true that we cannot fully understand Beethoven without understanding the impulses behind the French Revolution. It is equally true that we cannot fully understand the French Revolution without some insight into Beethoven's music. We can see in his music those elements which are conditioned by his time (for they could not be otherwise) and yet are beyond the topical and local. Beethoven is a point at which the growth of the mind shows itself. He is a part of history: and also of the human spirit-making history.'

Alec Harman, Anthony Milner and Wilfrid Mellers. *Man and His Music: The Story of Musical Experience in the West.* London: Barrie & Jenkins, 1988, pp. 575–6

RICHARD OSBORNE

Richard Osborne has written extensively about music and was a former presenter for BBC Radio 3. He contributed the chapter *Beethoven* to Robert Layton's *Guide to the Symphony* from which he has this to say about the composer's approach to the sequencing of his symphonies and its bearing on the Fourth Symphony:

'After the *Eroica*, Beethoven began work on what we now know as the Fifth Symphony, a fact that rather undermines the idea that he consciously commuted between the powerfully dramatic odd-numbered symphonies and the more lyrical even-numbered ones. That said, the Nine were assembled with a good deal of care (they are, for instance, rooted in eight different key centres) with Beethoven showing characteristic genius in differentiating between works which he worked on more or less simultaneously: the Fourth and Fifth Symphonies and, later on, the Seventh and Eighth. The contrast between the gamesome and lyrical Fourth and the fearsomely dramatic Fifth, which Goethe thought subversive and a threat to civilization as he knew it, is particularly interesting since the two works have a certain amount in common. In the Fourth Symphony, for example, we first meet the idea of Beethoven bringing the third movement Trio round twice, an effect he was also inclined to use in the Fifth ... The drum-led finale of the Fifth Symphony is one of music's most celebrated instrumental inspirations, but no less remarkable in the preparation for the recapitulation of the first movement of the Fourth Symphony where the drum single-handedly reasserts the tonic in B flat.'

Concerning the atmosphere prevailing in the Fourth Symphony, Osborne comments:

'The sense we have at the start of the Fourth Symphony is of a soul lost in darkness was not, however, the real seat of contemporary disaffection with [the] astonishing adagio preface. (The start of Haydn's *The Creation* had no such notoriety.) Rather, it was the extreme slowness of the music harmonically. (Carl Maria von Weber made the point, in a purely negative way, when he exclaimed: "Every quarter of an hour we hear three or four notes. It is exciting!") ... It is said that Beethoven was in love with Countess Therese von Brunsvik whist he was at work on this Symphony, and one can well believe it. A man who can dream up and then so idly forget the kind of melody that flits by at the start of the development is clearly walking on air.'

Richard Osborne, *Beethoven* in: Robert Layton editor. *A Guide to the Symphony.* Oxford: Oxford University Press, 1995, pp. 92–95.

ELIZABETH SCHWARM GLESNER

The music scholar Elizabeth Schwarm Glesner writes of the deceptive humour to be found in the Fourth Symphony:

'The Fourth Symphony is filled with musical jokes, mostly aimed at other musical insiders, though there are also jokes for the rest of us. Beethoven's whimsical mood reveals itself in the Symphony's opening moments. He attaches a slow introduction to the head of an otherwise fast movement. This, in itself, is not unusual. Haydn, for example, did it with great frequency, but the theory always was that the slow introduction would introduce that which follows, hinting clearly at the key to come, rather in the way that an opera overture will quote snippets of the arias and choruses to be heard later in the work. Beethoven, however, has no plan of being so transparent. His key changes meander here and there, and when he finally does arrive at exactly the place that had been hinted at by the opening chord, a harmonically tuned colleague would have reacted with disbelief.

'The Symphony's other three movements also

have their idiosyncrasies. In the lyrical second movement, the strings are awarded an exquisite flowing melody that is constantly interrupted by a recurring "heartbeat" rhythm that sometimes forgets its place in the background and comes surging out into centre stage ... The third movement is ostensibly a minuet. At least that is what Beethoven calls it, but he exaggerates. Here is no graceful courtly dance in powdered wigs. It is too lively, too syncopated, and far too reminiscent of a boisterous folk dance ... By comparison, the fourth movement is fairly straight-forward. It is a brisk and bustling rondo that might have originated at Haydn's desk. Yet the frenzy and fervour that characterizes much of the movement is abruptly detailed in the final page. Sudden tempo changes force the conductor to be on his toes, and a final bassoon solo sounds, more than anything else, like a parting chuckle.'

Elizabeth Schwarm Glesner, Classical Music Pages, *Ludwig van Beethoven, 4 Symphonie*.

THEODOR W. ADORNO

The German philosopher, sociologist and composer Theodor W. Adorno spent many years compiling notes for a projected study of Beethoven. His work remained in this form at the time of his death but was edited and collated by the writer and philosopher Rolf Tiedemann, being published in English translation (Edmund Jephcott) as *Beethoven: The philosophy of music, Fragments and texts* (1998). Adorno worked on his projected Beethoven text through the years 1938–56. Despite this long period of gestation, his work did not progress beyond a great accumulation of diverse texts — 'fragments' — arbitrarily arranged in his files. In his reworking of this material, Tiedemann recast Adorno's texts into 370 numbered sub-texts to which he appended scholarly commentaries. Thereby, he sought 'to organize the material as Adorno himself might have done, had he written the projected book' (*Preface*). From the great body of material, thus co-ordinated by Tiedemann, Adorno discusses the Fourth Symphony in the following terms:

> 'Special attention should be given to certain symphonic passages in the middle [period] Beethoven, for example, in the development of the first movement in the Fourth Symphony and in the *Eroica*, where the music seems to be "suspended", dangling from something to which it is attached. These passages, which are most emphatically distinct from the "floating" passages to be found in Romanticism, will be easily recognisable from the gestures of a conductor who understands them. In such moments he will turn himself into that to which the suspended music is attached, holding it in his raised hands yet without making any intervention.'

Theodor W. Adorno, *Beethoven: The Philosophy of Music, Fragments and Texts*. Cambridge: Polity Press, 1998, pp. 98–99 and pp. 106–07.

MICHAEL P. STEINBERG

The American scholar Michael P. Steinberg is Professor of history, music and German studies at Brown University and was President of the American Academy in Berlin from

March 2016 to August 2018. He has written at length about Beethoven, notably in collaboration with fellow American, the musicologist Scott G, Burnham (*Beethoven and his World*, 2000). Commenting on the Fourth Symphony, Steinberg makes reference to the writings of Robert Schuman, combined with words of caution:

> 'To Robert Schuman, the Fourth Symphony was "a slender Grecian maiden between two Nordic giants", but if we can accept that image at all we must add this maiden is an Atlanta in her springy athleticism. [In classical mythology, Atalanta was a huntress whose name derives from the Greek *atalantos*] It is true that Beethoven's even-numbered symphonies are generally more lyrical, less aggressive than their odd-numbered neighbours. People who plan orchestra programmes also know that, except for the *Pastoral*, the even-numbered ones do less well at the box office. It is dead wrong, though, to play down or to hear past the strength of these pieces, particularly the Fourth and Eighth symphonies, just as it is a form of deafness not to hear the strength in Haydn and Mozart, and to treat their symphonies as charming curtain-raisers.'

Turning once more to Schuman, Steinberg closes his account of the Fourth Symphony with what he describes as 'some good words':

> 'Yes, love [Beethoven], love him well, but never forget that he touched poetic freedom only through long years of study, and revere his never-ceasing moral force. Do not search for the

abnormal in him, but return to the source of his creativeness. Do not illustrate his genius with the Ninth Symphony alone, no matter how great its audacity and scope, never uttered in any tongue. You can do much with his First Symphony, or with the Greek-like slender one in B-flat major!'

Michael P. Steinberg, *The Symphony: A Listener's Guide*, Oxford University Press; reprint edition, 1998, p. 20 and p. 24.

BARRY COOPER

The British musicologist Barry Cooper is internationally recognised for his scholarly studies of the life and work of Beethoven. In addition, Beethovenians have him to thank for his reconstruction of a performing edition of the composer's 10th Symphony — from the many surviving sketches that were left incomplete at the time of his death. Pianists are no less in debt to Cooper for his recently released edition of the Piano Sonatas for The Associated Board of the Royal Schools of Music (ABRSM). In his *Beethoven*, Cooper remarks on the originality to be found in the Fourth Symphony:

'After the enormous size of the *Eroica* it was inevitable that Beethoven's next symphony would be on a smaller scale, but the Fourth is still very substantial and contains many innovations within its traditional four-movement structure ... The slow introduction merges into the main allegro without any clear break, and the actual change of time signature is noted four bars before the arrival of the main theme, then at the repeat of the exposition, what sounds like the end of the slow introduction is incorporated into the lead-back, further blurring the structural outlines. At the recapitulation there is still more ambiguity: after a striking enharmonic change, in which the tympani play a prominent role, the main theme arrives without the four-bar preparation found in the exposition, implying retrospectively that these four bars are not part of the exposition.

'The raised profile given to the tympani in the first movement is continued in the second ... Integrating the tympani into the thematic design — an idea already introduced in the C-minor Piano Concerto — becomes of increasing interest for Beethoven from now on.'

Barry Cooper, *Beethoven: The Master Musicians Series*. Oxford: Oxford University Press, 2000, pp. 158—59.

ALFRED PETER BROWN

Alfred Peter Brown was a Fellow of the American Council Learned Society of Vienna and a Member of the American Musicological Society. In his *The Symphonic Repertoire* he conjectures:

'After the *Eroica*, Beethoven began working on the Fifth Symphony, which in its final affirmation would become an appropriate successor to the Third. After sketching portions of the first two movements, he stopped and began working on the Symphony No. 4. What more appropriate way of diluting any comparison with the *Eroica* than to follow a path-breaking work with one that seems to return to the so-called classicism of Haydn and Mozart. However, Symphony No. 4 was commissioned by Count Oppersdorff, whose estate in Upper Silesia Beethoven visited in 1806. His Second Symphony was performed there, and perhaps Beethoven composed the Fourth more in the style of the Second to accommodate his patron and his ensemble, which would have had virtuoso woodwind players. Such a situation could also have stimulated Beethoven to create a less-romantically inclined composition.

'The Fourth is one of Beethoven's most neglected and underappreciated symphonic essays, partly because we are too much concerned with Beethoven the romantic instead of Beethoven the classicist. The Fourth is more a study in movement than one that emphasizes beautiful and sublime gestures. However, in many ways the Fourth, Sixth, and Eighth Symphonies are more polished and successful efforts than the others. For Beethoven had, as revealed in Symphony No.4, mastered the style of the past and, as the break in his work on the Fifth Symphony might indicate, was struggling in another way to pursue a symphonic language for the future.'

Alfred Peter Brown, *The Symphonic Repertoire*. Vol. 2, *The First Golden Age of the Viennese Symphony: Haydn, Mozart, Beethoven, and Schubert*. Bloomington, Indiana: Indiana University Press, 2002, p. 476 and p. 484.

BEETHOVEN AND VIENNA: GESTATION OF THE B-FLAT MAJOR SYMPHONY

Beethoven composed the B-flat major Symphony in 1806. This was a particularly creative period for him. Between January and March, he revised his Opera *Leonora* with a view to its performance in April and May — incorporating a new Overture (*Leonora* No. 3). The G major Piano Concerto, Op. 58 (1805–06) had recently been completed following which he worked on the String Quartets, Op, 59 (*Razumovsky*), the Violin Concerto Op. 61, and the thirty-two Variations for Piano WoO 16. Having completed the majestic *Eroica* Symphony Beethoven turned his mind to further symphonic achievements. He started work on the Fifth Symphony in C minor, Op. 67 but set this aside to work on the Fourth Symphony. The Composer's biographer Alexander Wheelock Thayer describes these as 'truly a wonderment of masterpieces'.[1] Maynard Solomon suggests, at the period, in question Beethoven 'finds a sense of inner repose'. He explains:

> 'In a deepening trend, which began in 1806 with the Fourth Symphony, the Fourth Piano Concerto, and the Violin Concerto, [Beethoven] now seemed to imbue many of his works with a sense of inner repose that no longer required turbulent responses to grand challenges. A new lyrical strain enters his music, along with a pre-Romantic freedom of harmonic motion and structural design ... This practice results in a sense of calm, spaciousness, and measured nobility of rhetoric ...'.[2]

These are the essential themes of our discussion. However, to place them in context we consider first the circumstances that contributed to shaping Beethoven's life and work at the period when he was turning his mind to the composition of the Fourth Symphony. We consider how he appeared to his contemporaries, in the formal portraits taken of him and through the anecdotes and descriptions left by those who met and worked alongside him. Central to our narrative is Beethoven's awareness of his deteriorating hearing and of the torment he endured at Heiligenstadt. We discuss his new-found resolve and his triumph over what we describe as his 'dark night of the soul'. We trace Beethoven's footsteps back to Vienna and identify various locations where he lived and worked. We broaden the scope of our discussion to consider music-making in Vienna and the concert venues available to Beethoven. In this context, we reflect on the orchestral resources available to him. We make reference to his increasing international reputation with its concomitant invitations to leave Vienna, and the efforts undertaken, by his closest friends and admirers, to secure his presence in Europe's musical capital.

PORTRAITS

A measure of Beethoven's growing fame at this period is indicated by the circumstance of him being persuaded to have his portrait painted by Joseph Mähler — a personal friend of the composer He portrayed Beethoven in an Arcadian setting striking a lyre; in the background is a temple of Apollo. Although this portrait situates Beethoven in a somewhat idealised pastoral setting, the artist is not considered to have sacrificed his appearance in striving for Romantic effect. The was the first of Mähler's four portraits of the composer and was painted sometime in 1804. Beethoven was clearly fond of the painting that remained in his possession until his death.[3]

A few years later, the Berlin artist Isidor Neugass took the composer's likeness. Judging by this portrait, Beethoven was then taking care with his appearance — unlike later in life. Neugass chose to depict Beethoven in a half-length portrait that was fashionable at the time. The closely cropped hair, as depicted in the painting of the composer by Joseph Mähler, is transformed in Neugass's depiction into a stylish *bouffant*. Around his neck is suspended a double lorgnette to assist his reading — Beethoven being somewhat short sighted. There are two versions of the painting: one version originates from the Lichnowsky family and is said to have been made, according to family tradition, by the order of Beethoven's then patron Prince Karl von Lichnowsky; the second version was made for the aristocratic Brunswick family with whom Beethoven was on familiar and affectionate terms.[4]

PERSONAL IMPRESSIONS

The Austrian composer, conductor and pupil of Mozart, Ignaz von Seyfried was on close terms with Beethoven and premiered the original production of his Opera *Leonora-Fidelio* (1805). Seyfried shared lodgings with Beethoven at intervals between 1803 and 1805. Seyfried writes of the period when Beethoven was at work on the composition of his Opera *Fidelio* (revisions of *Leonora*), the Third, Fifth and Sixth Symphonies, and the Fourth Piano Concerto. He remarks: 'At that time Beethoven was bright, always ready for a joke, cheerful, brisk, and full of spirits, witty, and occasionally satirical,' Seyfried was privileged to hear the composer's music as it came from his pen, as he recounts:

> 'He used to play over to me on the piano, as soon as it was finished, every portion of the above-named compositions ... Without giving me time to reflect, he immediately demanded my opinion, which I was able to give freely and frankly, without any fear of offending that false pride from which his nature was entirely free.'

After Seyfried's death his handwritten memoirs were published in an appendix to *Beethoven's Studien im Generalbasse*. These include a brief portrait of Beethoven — styled with a measure of obligatory flattery, as, by then, Beethoven was becoming deified:

> 'Amongst the poets of Germany, Goethe was his favourite; he was fond of Walter Scott. Of the rest of the fine arts, and of the sciences, he possessed, without priding himself upon it, more than a superficial knowledge. In the circle of his intimates he spoke out freely upon politics, and with

such commanding, well-directed and perspicacious views, as one would scarcely have expected from a recluse living only for and in the interests of his Art.'

Of Beethoven's personal relationships, Seyfried writes:

'Rectitude of principle, high morality, propriety of feeling, and pure natural religion were his distinctions. These virtues reigned within himself and he required them at the hands of others. "As good as his word" was his favourite saying, and nothing angered him more than a broken promise. He was always ready, out of warm benevolence, to help others, and that often at the expense of serious sacrifices in his own person. Whoever turned to him voluntarily, and in perfect confidence, might safely reckon upon him for aid. He knew neither avarice nor extravagance, and was but little acquainted with the real value of money, which he used only as a means for procuring the indispensable requirements of life; it was only in the later years that signs of an anxious parsimony became apparent, without, however, interfering with his natural bias for benevolent actions.'

Seyfried was one of the first writers to describe Beethoven's working method:

'Without a little note book, wherein to jot down his ideas upon the instant, he never appeared in the street. If by chance this was referred to in conversation, he used to parody Joan of Arc's words "*nicht ohne meine Fahne darf ich kommen*" ['I dare not come without my Banner'] and with a tenacity quite surprizing did he adhere to this self-imposed law.'

Like other of Beethoven's contemporaries, Seyfried discerned the disorder evident in the composer's domestic affairs:

'[His] household presented an admirable scene of confusion. Books and music were strewn about in all directions — here the remains of a cold breakfast — there sealed or half-empty bottles — yonder upon the desk the rough sketch of a new quartet, and near it the last new poem or romance. On the piano might be seen the half-finished score of a symphony as yet in embryo — on the table a proof-sheet waiting for correction — private and business letters covering the floor — between the windows a respectable stracchino cheese, *ad latus* the fragments of a Verona sausage; yet in spite of this medley, our Composer had the habit, (in manifest contradiction to the fact) of boasting, at every opportunity, of his accuracy and love of order, with all the eloquence of a Cicero. It was only when something that was wanted had to be hunted for, hours, days, and even weeks, and it remained in obstinate seclusion, that he assumed another tone, and the innocent suffered for the faults of another.'[5]

The name Grove is familiar to generations of music lovers through association with *Grove's Dictionary of Music and Musicians* of which Grove was the inspiration and source.

Grove considered Beethoven's emotional entanglements may have had a bearing on the genial manner that he considered permeates the spirit of the Fourth Symphony. But first a few words about Grove himself:

Notwithstanding his position in musicology, (Sir) George Grove did not receive a formal education in music. He trained as a structural engineer, being admitted as a graduate of the Institution of Civil Engineers. He worked in this capacity for the first thirty years of his life and it was while he was engaged on the Britannia Bridge that he became known to such luminaries of the age as Robert Stephenson, Isambard Kingdom Brunel and Sir Charles Barry. Through their influence, Grove made a change of career and was appointed in 1849 to the Secretaryship of the Society of Arts — at the period of gestation of the Great Exhibition of 1851, housed in the so-called Crystal Palace. Orchestral concerts were held here for which Grove provided programme notes that later formed the basis for his *Dictionary* and *Beethoven and his Nine Symphonies* (1896). Writing in the latter, Grove suggested a connection may be found with the Fourth Symphony and Countess Theresa von Brunswick, sister of his intimate friend Count Franz von Brunswick. Beethoven held out hopes of becoming engaged to Theresa but which was not fulfilled. Of these circumstances, Grove remarks:

> 'Though [Beethoven] had been often involved in love affairs, none of them had yet been permanent; certainly, he had never before gone so far as an engagement and when writing [the Fourth Symphony] his heart must have been swelling with his new happiness. Here, then, we have the secret of the first movement ... and an excuse for any height or depth of emotion ... But observe that with all the intensity of his passion,

> Beethoven never relinquishes his hold on his art.
> The lover is as much the musician as he ever was
> and this most impassioned movement is also one
> of the compactest and, at the same time, the most
> highly finished of all his works.'[6]

POST HEILIGENSTADT

Writing of Beethoven in 1806, Barry Cooper remarks:

> 'By the time Beethoven had finished the *Razumovsky* Quartets, he had gained a new self-confidence. Within the four years since the *Heiligenstadt Testament* he had fully mapped out the *new path* [italics added] on which he embarked in 1802, having written new types of composition in all the great genres he evidently considered most important ...'.[7]

With the realisation that his deafness was permanent, Beethoven gave expression to his despondency in the so-called *Heiligenstadt Testament*. This document, in effect a letter to his brothers Carl and Johann, recounts his despair over his worsening condition. Given the poignancy that pervades the document, a parallel is to be found in the lines of John Keats, whose awareness of his impending mortality disposed him to write, 'I have fears that I may cease to be/Before my pen has gleaned my teaming brain'. Significantly, towards the close of his text, Beethoven affirms his resolve to overcome his misfortune in order to complete his artistic destiny. His *Testament* may, in the Aristotelian sense, have helped him to purge his emotions and, through his art, find renewal and restoration.

Beethoven eventually passed through his 'dark night of

the soul', emboldened by his indomitability of spirit and self-belief and with the realization that his 'inner ear' — his precious compositional faculty — was still intact. Saint John of the Cross speaks of 'darkness' representing the hardships and difficulties encountered in life. We take the generic meaning of his words to signify, in Beethoven's case, his triumph over his feelings of depression and the isolation he felt imposed upon him by his encroaching deafness. He returned to Vienna, not with his hearing restored but, to quote Cooper once more, 'with his spirit revived and ready to break new ground in the development of his art'.[8]

We learn of Beethoven's domestic circumstances at this time from a letter he wrote on 14 July 1804 to Ferdinand Ries. From April 1803 Beethoven was provided with an apartment at the Theater an der Wien by Emmanuel Schikaneder, who, from 1801, was the manager of the property. Beethoven's accommodation was modest and he eventually found it unsatisfactory. He explained to his pupil:

> 'If you, dear Ries, know where to find better rooms, I shall be very glad indeed ... I should very much like to have rooms in a large quiet square or on the Bastei.'[9]

The latter is a reference to the Mölkerbastei, an imposing residence located in central Vienna. The property was inherited by Baron Pasqualati, from whom the expression Pasqualati House is derived. Baron Johann von Pasqualati, a close contemporary of Beethoven (1777-1830) was a *Hofagent*, a court official who assisted Beethoven in financial, professional and judicial matters. Moreover, he was a music lover, an accomplished pianist and a founder member of the *Gesellschaft der Musikfreunde*. He was generous to Beethoven and retained his apartment for him during the composer's occasional departures. Beethoven reciprocated this friendship in 1814 by composing the *Elegischer Gesang*, Op. 118 to commemorate the anniversary of the death of Pasqualati's wife. In Beethoven's time Pasqualati house stood on what was then Vienna's city boundary; from his apartment's fourth floor he could look across the leafy surroundings to the *Wienerwald* – Vienna Woods.[10]

ACHIEVEMENT AMIDST INSECURITY

Although the elderly, and much respected, Haydn was still composing, Beethoven had now established himself in Vienna at the forefront of contemporary music — and, for good measure, uncompromising, modern-sounding music. Moreover, he had composed works of significance in all the major compositional genres. By way of illustration, the following is a chronological list of Beethoven's principal works dating from his earliest composition of significance, from his time in Bonn, to the period of composition of the Fourth Symphony in Vienna:

1790–91: Cantata *On death of Joseph II* (WoO.87); 1792–04: 3 Piano Trios (Op.1); 1794–96: Piano Concerto No.2 in B flat (revised 1798) (Op.19), 2 Cello Sonatas (Op.5), 3 Piano Sonatas (Op.2), Piano Sonata in E flat (Op.7); 1797: 3 Piano Sonatas (Op.10), 3 Violin Sonatas (Op.12), 3 String Trios (Op.9); 1798: Piano Concerto No.1 in C (Op.15), Piano Sonata in C minor *Pathétique* (Op.13); 2 Piano Sonatas (Op.14); 1799: Piano Sonata in B flat (Op.22), Septet in E flat (strings & wind) (Op.20), 6 String Quartets (Op.18), Symphony No.1 in C (Op.21); 1800: Ballet *Creatures of Prometheus* (Op.43), Violin

Sonata in A minor (Op.23), Violin Sonata in F *Spring* (Op.24), Piano Sonata in A flat (Op.26), Piano Sonata in E flat (Op.27, No.1), Piano Concerto No.3 in C minor (Op.37); 1801: Piano Sonata in C-sharp minor *Moonlight* (Op.27, No.2), Piano Sonata in D (Op.28); 3 Piano Sonatas (Op.31), String Quintet in C (Op.29); 1802: Romance for Violin and Orchestra (Op.40), Symphony No.2 in D (Op.36); 3 Violin Sonatas (Op.30), Violin Sonata in A *Kreutzer* (Op.47), 15 Variations and Fugue in E flat for piano *Eroica* (Op.35); 1803: Piano Sonata in C *Waldstein* (Op.53), Triple Concerto in C (piano, violin, cello) (Op.56); Symphony No.3 in E flat *Eroica* (Op.55), Oratorio *Christ on the Mount of Olives* (Op.85); 1804: Opera *Fidelio* (revised 1806 and 1814) (Op.72), Piano Sonata in F (Op.54), Piano Sonata in F minor *Appassionata* (Op.57); 1805: Piano Concerto No.4 in G (Op.58), Overture *Leonore No.2* (Op.72a): 1806: 3 String Quartets *Razumovsky* (Op.59), Symphony No.4 in B flat (Op.60), Overture *Leonore No.3* (Op.72a), and Violin Concerto in D (Op.61).

To the foregoing list of compositions — any one of which would have secured the reputation of a lesser composer — may be added a comparable inventory of related works to which Beethoven chose not to assign an *opus* number. Moreover, Beethoven was establishing, what today we would describe as, an international reputation with his music being sought by publishers in Berlin, Paris, London, and Edinburgh. Beethoven was well and truly set upon his self-professed 'new path'.

Notwithstanding his remarkable achievements, Beethoven

was dependent on the sale of his compositions for his livelihood and felt the need to improve his financial position by securing an official appointment within Vienna's musical establishment — as had Mozart twenty years previously. In this context, as the American musicologist H. C. Robbins Landon observes: 'Mozart's death, in dire poverty, was obviously a spectre that haunted Vienna for many years after.'[11]

Doubtless, with such considerations in mind, on 4 December 1807 Beethoven applied for the vacant post of Director at the Royal Imperial Court Theatre. Such a position would, he hoped, help to secure his financial prospects and provide an outlet for his ambitions to be a respected composer for the lyric theatre — a quest he was to pursue for many years as he considered (and rejected) one potential opera libretto after another.

Beethoven's application was no mere whim-of-the-moment impulse. He had previously been employed, from 1803 to 1804, by the Theater an der Wien as its musical director, but, as we have seen, his back-stage residential accommodation was so unsatisfactory as to precipitate his early departure. In his application for the new post of Director, Beethoven describes how he had been obliged 'to struggle with difficulties of all kinds' and how he had not yet been able to establish himself in Vienna in a position that would enable him

> 'to fulfil his desire to live wholly for art, to develop his talents to a still higher degree of perfection ... and to make certain for the future the fortuitous advantages of the present'.

Beethoven gave an undertaking to compose an opera each year which, however, given the exacting artistic demands he made of librettists, he was most unlikely to have been able to fulfil. In addition, he promised to compose 'a divertimento or another work of similar proportions' for all of which he asked for a salary of 2,400 florins — about 240 pounds sterling. The theatre directors gave but cursory consideration to Beethoven's application and promptly rejected it.[12]

Notwithstanding, Beethoven was never reduced to straitened circumstances. Indeed, soon after his arrival in Vienna he enjoyed the support of Prince Karl Lichnowsky who would in time become one of the his most supportive patrons. Evidence of Karl's generosity is that in 1800 he granted an annuity of 600 florins on Beethoven until such time as he could establish his independence and financial security. Lichnowsky maintained his support until at least 1806 — and possibly until 1808. Comments by Beethoven's piano pupil Carl Czerny shed light on Beethoven's feelings at this time and put them into perspective. He writes:

> 'It has often been said abroad that Beethoven was despised and repressed in Vienna. The truth is that even as a young man he received all possible support, attention and encouragement from our great aristocracy which could have been given to a young artist ... It is true that, as an artist, he had to deal with intrigues, but the public were not to blame for that. He was always admired as an unusual character, and his greatness was assumed by everyone who didn't really know him.[13]

JÉRÔME BONAPARTE:
OFFER OF POST OF KAPELLMEISTER

In early November 1808, an opportunity came Beethoven's way — arising, doubtless, as a consequence of a growing awareness of his fame beyond the confines of Vienna. Napoleon's younger brother Jérôme — recently installed as the King of Westphalia — invited Beethoven, through the diplomatic offices of his High Chamberlain, to consider an offer of appointment as his Senior Kapellmeister in Kassel. Despite the somewhat archaic-sounding title, the post held distinct attractions for Beethoven. His duties would not be onerous; he would merely be required to play for Jérôme's personal pleasure and to conduct occasional concerts. Moreover, he was offered a salary of 600 gold ducats (the equivalent of about 4000 gulden/florins or 200 pounds sterling) and an additional 150 ducats for travelling expenses.[14]

The concert pianist turned musicologist Denis Matthews makes the interesting observation that although the title of kapellmeister was becoming somewhat antiquated, in the first decade of the nineteenth century, it may have had a particular resonance for Beethoven. His grandfather had held such an appointment, and this, combined with childhood memories, may, Matthews suggests, have exerted an influence on the composer's subconscious mind.[15]

In the New Year of 1809, Beethoven appears to have made up his mind regarding Jérôme Bonaparte's offer of employment. In a letter to his publisher Breitkopf & Härtel (7 January) he intimates how attractive the position appeared to him regarding the steady income he would receive and the post's other advantages. He complained of the standard of musicians in Vienna, some of whom he accused of hardly being able to read an orchestral score; Beethoven was still resentful of the poor standard of playing they had displayed at his mammoth concert on the previous 22 December 1808. He also believed the composer Antonio Salieri intrigued against him — echoes of 'Mozart and Salieri' — disposing him to exclaim: 'At last, owing to intrigues and cabals and meannesses of all kinds, I am compelled to leave my German fatherland.'[16]

In a postscript to his letter to Breitkopf & Härtel,

Beethoven asked the publisher not to make anything known publicly about his appointment until the final details were confirmed — although he did not object, somewhat conspiratorially, to 'a few hints' about his leaving Vienna being inserted into the *Allgemeine musikalische Zeitung* — the journal published by Breitkopf & Härtel.

BEETHOVEN'S ANNUITY CONTRACT

The 'few hints' of Beethoven's planned departure from Vienna appear to have reached the ears of the Countess Anna Maria Erdödy. She was a competent pianist, an admirer of the composer's music and given to holding frequent musical soirées in her Vienna town house — her family also owned estates in the country. For a time, Beethoven occupied rooms in her apartments, held the Countess in high esteem, and dedicated to her the two Piano Trios Op. 70 and the two Cello Sonatas Op. 102.[17]

By virtue of her social standing, the Countess had the ear of Vienna's nobility, the outcome of which was she made known Beethoven's intended departure to a privileged inner-circle that included the Archduke Rudolph, Prince Ferdinand Kinsky and Count Franz Joseph Lobkowitz. In order to secure Beethoven's continuing presence in Vienna, they resolved to take immediate action and collectively agreed to settle upon him an annuity of 4000 gulden/florins — the equivalent offered to him by Jérôme Bonaparte. Beethoven's new secretary-assistant Baron Franz von Gleichenstein and Countess Erdödy assisted in drawing up an Annuity Contract that was duly ratified on 1 March 1809. Beethoven's patrons were doubly generous; not only did they offer to provide Beethoven with financial support, they did not try to control or monopolise him by placing restrictions on his place of domicile. The terms of their agreement allowed him to reside in Vienna 'or some other town situated in the hereditary lands of His Imperial Majesty'. The Contract also affirmed: '[The] undersigned have made the decision to place Herr Ludwig van Beethoven in a position where the most pressing circumstances shall not cause him embarrassment or impede his powerful genius.' Despite this promised financial support, Beethoven did not secure the title he so much cherished, namely, that of *Imperial Kapellmeister*. The following is an extract from the formal Contract:

> 'The daily proofs that Herr Ludwig van Beethoven gives of his extraordinary talents and genius as a musician and composer awaken the desire that he surpass the greatest expectations that are justified by his past achievements. Since it has been demonstrated, however, that only a person who is as free from care as possible can devote himself to one profession alone and create great works that are exalted and that enable art, the undersigned have made the decision to place Herr Ludwig van Beethoven in a position where the most pressing circumstances shall not cause him embarrassment or impede his powerful genius.'[18]

Beethoven's eminent biographer Alexander Wheelock Thayer remarks that the three signatories to Beethoven's Annuity Contract were doubtless motivated to assist the composer on the grounds: 'What an inexcusable, unpardonable disgrace to Vienna would be the departure of Beethoven under such circumstances!'[19]

Although Beethoven was to remain in Vienna for the rest of his life, the full extent of the reassurance his Annuity Contract offered proved to be relatively short-lived. In 1811, devaluation, resulting from the Napoleonic wars, reduced his 4000 gulden to about 1,600 gulden. Moreover, on 11 September 1811, Count Lobkowitz was obliged to stop his payments for four years because he was declared bankrupt, and on 3 November 1812 Prince Kinsky died suddenly as the result of an accident, compelling Beethoven to legally challenge his heirs to maintain Kinsky's share of the annual payment that he considered was due to him. It was not until around 1815 that his Annuity was restored to something like its original value — about 3,400 gulden.[20]

VIENNA: CONCERT VENUES AND MUSIC-MAKING

We consider the concert venues available to Beethoven and orchestral music-making at the period when the Fourth Symphony was coming into being.

THEATER AN DER WIEN

The theatre owed it origins to the enterprise of the impresario Emmanuel Schikaneder, remembered for his collaboration with Mozart for providing the libretto to his Opera *The Magic Flute*. The theatre opened in June 1801 and was considered to be one of the best equipped theatres of its kind; the music correspondent of the *Allgemeine musikalische Zeitung* declared it to be 'the most comfortable and satisfactory in the whole of Germany'. Beethoven occupied rooms in the theatre, at Schikaneder's invitation, during part of the period he was composing his Opera *Fidelio*.

The theatre was a favourite of Beethoven's and was the venue for the following premieres of his works:

> 5 April 1803: Second Symphony, Third Piano Concerto and the Oratorio *Christ on the Mount of Olives*
> 7 April 1805: Third Symphony, *Eroica*

20 November 1805: First version of Fidelio
23 December 1806: Violin Concerto
22 December 1808: Fifth and Sixth Symphonies,
Choral Fantasy and the Piano Concerto No. 4.[21]

REDOUTENSAAL

Masked balls were held at the Redoutensaal of the Hofburg. It provided a large room with a typical orchestra of some forty players and a smaller room able to accommodate about twenty players. Mozart had written dance music for these functions in the last years of his life and in 1792 Haydn contributed twelve German Dances and Minuets. In 1795 Beethoven, then Haydn's pupil, made his début at the Redoutensaal as a composer of orchestral music with his own dance music.[22]

THEATER AM KÄRNTNERTORTHEATER

The Kärntnertortheater was known as the *Kaiserliches und Königliches Hoftheater zu Wien* (Imperial and Royal Court Theatre of Vienna). Mozart's Piano Concerto K. 503 received its premier there in 1787 as did Beethoven's *Fidelio* in 1814 (in its present-day form) and the Ninth Symphony in 1824. The Kärntnertortheater was a small theatre, even compared with the Burgtheater. It had only three galleries with seats, its upper two floors being provided with benches and space for standing. When full to capacity it may have housed an audience of about a thousand. Musicians at the Kärntnertortheater were paid less than their counterparts at the Burgtheater. String and wind players received a mere 125 florins. To place these figures in context, it has been estimated that during his years in Vienna (1781–91) Mozart's income fluctuated between 800 and 3,800 florins. He lived in relatively spacious apartments that cost him some 460 gulden – broadly interchangeable with the florin.[23]

In 1845, Hector Berlioz wrote enthusiastically to Humbert Ferrand, a friend, fellow musician and writer:

> 'I have not yet told you of the orchestra or chorus of the Kärntnerthor Theatre. Both are first-class; the orchestra especially ... Besides its steadiness, fire, and great mechanical skill, this orchestra has an exquisite sonorousness, owing to the accurate tuning of the instruments with each other and the perfect purity of intonation in the individual instruments ... The intellectual concerts ... form a worthy pendant to our Conservatoire concerts in Paris ... There I heard ... Beethoven's marvellous and matchless [Fourth Symphony] in B flat.'[24]

AUGARTEN

The Augarten was situated on the far side of Vienna's suburb called Leopoldstadt. It featured a landscaped garden, making it a fashionable venue in which concert-goers could promenade in summer. There were usually twelve concerts each season that took place at the early hour of seven o'clock on Saturday mornings — doubtless by way of seeking relief from Vienna's oppressive summer heat. Haydn often attended the Augarten concerts. In its October issue of 1800, the correspondent of the *Allgemeine musikalische Zeitung* wrote:

> '[The orchestra] consisted mostly of amateurs, except for the wind instruments and the double basses. Even ladies of the highest nobility were to be heard. The auditorium was very brilliant, and everything went off with order and with decorum.'

*

Symphonies, overtures, and concertos were often controlled in Vienna entirely by the violinist-leader of the orchestra. Ignaz Schuppanzigh and Franz Clement, as *Concertmeister*, frequently took charge of the orchestra when not playing in opera under the *Kapellmeister* at the keyboard. Contemporaries — such as the Austrian musician Ignaz von Seyfried — described Ignaz Schuppanzigh as being a 'naturally-born and really energetic leader of the orchestra'. He maintained an association with the Augarten for many years before leaving for Russia in 1816. Franz Clement is perhaps best remembered today for his premiering Beethoven's Violin Concerto.'[25]

TONKÜNSTLER-SOCIETÄT

The most important public concerts in Vienna were those of the so-called Tonkünstler-Societät — the 'Society of Musicians' — whose biannual concerts, two at Easter and two at Christmas, raised money for the Society's Widows and Orphans. Beethoven made his first public appearance at the Easter Concert of 1795 when he performed his Piano Concerto in B-flat major, Op. 19. For these concerts, the Society rented Vienna's Burgtheater that could accommodate large orchestras. Haydn had a close association with the Burgtheater with his Oratorios and Beethoven performed at the Burgtheater's Easter concert on 2 April 1798.[26]

LIEBHABER CONCERTE

In 1807 and 1808 a series of twenty concerts were given in Vienna known as the Liebhaber Concerte — 'Music-Lover's Concert'. One of the concerts' principal sponsors was Beethoven's patron Prince Lobkowitz. On 2 February the *Eroica* Symphony was performed together with the composer's Overture to Heinrich von Collin's drama

Coriolan. Beethoven is known to have attended this concert together with his benefactor the Archduke Rudolph. A measure of Beethoven's celebrity is that ten of these concerts included his works. In addition to two performances of the *Eroica* Symphony other works by Beethoven included, Symphonies One and Two, the Piano Concerto No. 1, and the Overture to *The Creatures of Prometheus*.[27]

The Liebhaber-Concerte were sponsored by Johann von Häring, a banker who was recognised for being one of Vienna's foremost amateur violinists; he had the distinction of performing chamber music with Mozart. A measure of his financial and musical standing is that he possessed instruments by Amati, Guarneri, and Stradivarius. Häring made a significant contribution to Viennese musical life and was elected Director (Leader) of the orchestra when the Liebhaber-Concerte commenced. A number of these concerts were also directed by Franz Clement. In the opening concert season 1807–08, Clement directed performances of Beethoven's First, Second, and Fourth Symphonies as well as his First Piano Concerto. From Alexander Thayer we learn:

> 'The audiences were composed exclusively of the nobility of the town and foreigners of note, and among these classes the preference was given to the cognoscenti and amateurs ... [In] twenty meetings, symphonies, overtures, concertos, and vocal pieces were performed zealously and were received with general approval.'[28]

VIENNA UNIVERSITY'S FESTSAAL

A further concert venue was Vienna University's *Festsaal*. This was used by the *Gesellschaft der Musikfreunde* before it had its own hall. Vienna, as Europe's leading musical city, enjoyed a flourishing operatic tradition. Otto Biba, the Austrian musicologist and archive director of the *Gesellschaft der Musikfreunde*, writes:

> 'For the subscription concerts in the winter of 1897–08 in the hall of the University, the following orchestra was employed: 13 first violins, 12 second violins, 7 violas, 6 violoncellists, 4 contrabasses, and a single compliment of winds. Orchestral works by Beethoven, including his first four symphonies, were played ten times in these performances. We must assume, therefore, that the composer approved of an orchestra of this size, with 55 musicians altogether.[29]

Beethoven was additionally fortunate in the promotion of his music insofar as his most wealthy patrons, such as the Princes Lobkowitz and Lichnowsky and Count Razumovsky, maintained high standards of chamber music performance in their own salons. In these venues, touring virtuosi were sought after to showcase their skills. Beethoven himself was obliged to take part on occasions in pianistic contests against such would-be rivals as Joseph Johann Baptist Wölfl (Woelfl) and Daniel Gottlieb Steibelt.

BEETHOVEN'S ORCHESTRA

In his pioneering English-language study *Beethoven*, the American-based, German music critic and musicologist Paul Bekker considers the composer's orchestration:

'Blend of tone was not the root idea of Beethoven's method of orchestral composition. His instrumentation is, in the first place, idealistic rather than practical. The sensuous effects of tone were a secondary consideration with him. He used each colour as a means of symbolic expression. He personified an instrument, and this personal character remained, even when lost in the impression produced by the whole. Beethoven's orchestra is the sum of such individuals, a republic of instruments, and the different "personalities" are displayed and interact in a fashion so marvellous and enchanting (the many working together at the will of one) that the total impression does not absolutely correspond with the requirements of the tone-sense.'

Becker acknowledged Beethoven's debt to his teacher Haydn, but also recognised their very different styles of orchestration:

'Beethoven's model for his individual treatment of instruments was Haydn. Haydn, in contradistinction to Mozart, did not regard the orchestra as a great unit in which the colours of the separate instruments might be prismatically split off. Like Beethoven, he thought of it as an *ensemble* of instruments, as used in chamber music, a collection of entities. He had, however, extraordinary skill, cultivated to perfection, in subordinating the individual instrument at given moments to the whole. Beethoven lacked Haydn's enforced education in such adroitness.

He was more ruthless, and his ruthlessness increased with age.'[30]

There was no such thing as a Beethoven orchestra *per se*. The size and combination of the instruments of a Beethoven's orchestra varied considerably. His orchestration and his orchestra expanded alongside his growing imagination. His typical orchestra consisted of strings with two each of flutes, oboes, clarinets, bassoons, trumpets, horns, and timpani. Over time this combination was modified as follows:

> Symphony No. 1, *Andante* without second flute;
> Symphony No. 2, *Larghetto* without trumpet;
> Symphony No. 3, third horn added;
> Symphony No. 4, one flute;
> Symphony No 5, three trombones (first use of), piccolo, and double bassoon;
> Symphony No. 6, trombones and piccolo — used in the *Storm* — solo cellos in the *Andante;*
> *Battle* Symphony, piccolo, triangle, cymbals, bass drum, three trombones and — 'off stage' — two great drums, two rattles, four trumpets, and military drums;
> Symphony No. 7, a reversion to the 'standard' orchestra;
> Symphony No. 8, second movement without timpani and trumpets, and;
> Symphony No. 9, three trombones, double bassoon, piccolo, triangle, cymbals, bass drum, with four solo voices and chorus.[31]

Despite his German-sounding name, Adam Von Ahnen Carse was an English composer, academic, and music editor who is remembered today for his studies on the history of instruments and the orchestra. Relating to the period in question Carse remarks:

> 'It is always unsound to assume that because a composer — even a "great" composer — wrote a certain note for a certain instrument, this note was necessarily playable on the instruments of the time ... This is especially true of double-bass parts. Beethoven, like Haydn and Mozart, sometimes wrote his orchestral bass part down to low C; but that provides no reason to suppose that a double bass with a low C string was commonly used either in Vienna or elsewhere during the early part of the [nineteenth] century ... Beethoven, like his predecessors and contemporaries, wrote *bass parts*, but not *double bass parts*. They did concern themselves much with either the downward compass or the difficulties of fingering the instrument; they wrote the bass part they wanted, as they would for the cello, and left it to the player to make the best of it, to transpose into the higher octave when it became necessary, and to simplify the quick passages just as they thought fit.'[32]

Carse's reference to the double bass calls to mind Beethoven's meeting with Domenico Dragonetti, the Italian double bass virtuoso *par excellence*; Thayer describes Dragonetti as 'the greatest contrabassist known to history'. By all accounts he was for the double bass what Franz Liszt was to become for the piano. From Thayer we learn Beethoven made Dragonetti's acquaintance in 1799. He relates how the Italian astounded audiences for his technical execution and for his 'deep genuine musical feeling which elevated and ennobled it'. Such was Dragonett's command of the double bass that he could perform the most taxing parts written for the cello. On hearing of this, Beethoven arranged for the two of them to play through the composer's Cello Sonata, Op. No. 5, whereupon:

> 'Beethoven played his part, with his eyes fixed upon his companion, and, in the finale, where the arpeggios occur, was so delighted and excited that, at the close, he sprang up and threw his arms around both players and the instrument.' Thayer adds, ruefully: 'The unlucky contrabassists of orchestras had occasion during the next few years to know that this new revelation of the powers and possibilities of the instrument to Beethoven were not forgotten.'[33]

Thayer's observations had particular meaning with reference to 8 December 1813 when Beethoven's Seventh Symphony received its première in the University's *Festsaal* – with Dragonetti leading the double basses. Those familiar with the composition will be aware that the first-movement coda draws to a close with a famous twenty-bar passage in which a two-bar motif is repeated ten times – during which the double bases almost sound as though they are growling! This proved too much for Carl Maria von Weber who, at the close of the concert, is alleged to have exclaimed: 'Our Beethoven is now ripe for the madhouse!'.

---

[1] Elliot Forbes editor, *Thayer's Life of Beethoven*, 1967, Chapter XIX.
[2] Maynard Solomon, *Beethoven*, 1977, pp. 208–09.
[3] See Beethoven House, Digital Archives, Library Document HCB Bi 1. See also H. C. Robbins Landon, 1970, Plate 5 and accompanying text.
[4] A facsimile reproduction of the Neugass portrait, with accompanying historical

information, can be seen at the Beethoven House, Digital Archives, Library Document B 1093 and Library Document B 1925. See also: H. C. Robbins Landon, 1992, plate 7.

5. Ignaz von Seyfried, *Louis van Beethoven's Studies in Thorough-Bass, Counterpoint and the Art of Scientific Composition*, Leipzig; New-York: Schuberth and Company, 1853, pp. 15–16 and pp. 22–3. See also: Ludwig Nohl, Ignaz von Seyfried, *Beethoven Depicted by his Contemporaries*. London: Reeves, 1880, pp. 49–56.

6. George Grove, *Beethoven and his Nine Symphonies*, 1896, pp. 112–13.

7. Barry Cooper, *Beethoven: The Master Musicians Series*, 2000, p. 162.

8. *Ibid.*

9. Emily Anderson, editor and translator, 1961, Vol. 1, Letter No. 92, p. 111.

10. For a comprehensive survey and discussion of the many houses Beethoven occupied at various periods, see: *Beethoven's Residences*, in Hans Conrad Fischer and Erich Kock, *Ludwig van Beethoven: A Study in Text and Pictures*, 1972. pp. 113–120.

11. H. C. Robbins Landon, Beethoven: *His Life, Work and World*, 1992, p. 153.

12. For a full translation of Beethoven's application, see: Elliot Forbes, editor, *Thayer's Life of Beethoven*, 1967, pp. 426–7. Beethoven clearly spent considerable time composing his application that runs to several manuscript pages. A Facsimile copy of a portion of the application can be seen at the Beethoven House, Digital Archives, Library Document H. C. Bodmer Collection, HCB BBr 111.

13. As quoted in: Hans Conrad Fischer and Erich Kock, *Ludwig van Beethoven: A Study in Text and Pictures*, 1972, p. 32.

14. Elliot Forbes, editor, *Thayer's Life of Beethoven*, 1967, p. 442.

15. Denis Matthews, *Beethoven, Master Musicians*, 1985.

16. Emily Anderson, editor and translator, 1961, Vol. 1, Letter No. 192, pp. 211–12.

17. For a fuller account of Countess Anna Maria Erdödy, see: Peter Clive, 2001, pp. 101–2.

18. The wording of the Contract is reproduced in full in: Theodore Albrecht, editor and translator, 1996, Vol. 1, Document No. 134, pp. 205–6.

19. Elliot Forbes, editor, *Thayer's Life of Beethoven*, 1967, pp. 453–9.

20. Hans Conrad Fischer and Erich Kock, *Ludwig van Beethoven: A Study in Text and Pictures*, 1972, pp. 27–9.

21. For reference to the Theater an der Wien in the wider contex of music making in Vienna, in the early nineteenth century, see Otto Biba, *Concert life in Beethoven's Vienna* in: Robert Winter editor, *Beethoven, Performers, and Critics*, 1977. Detroit: Wayne State University Press, 1980, pp. 77–93.

22. H. C. Robbins Landon, *Beethoven, A Documentary Study*, 1977, pp. 33–34.

23. Quoted, with adaptations, from Mary Sue Morrow, *Concert life in Haydn's Vienna: Aspects of a Developing Musical and Social Institution*, 1989, pp. 71–81, and pp. 113–15. Morrow's account of Vienna's principal theatres includes seating plans and contemporary engravings of both their exteriors and interiors.

24. Hugh Macdonald editor, *Berlioz: Selected Letters*, 1995.

[25] For a comprehensive study of concert life in Beethoven's Vienna see: Anne-Louise Coldicott, *Beethoven's Musical Environment* in: Barry Cooper, *The Beethoven Compendium: A Guide to Beethoven's Life and Music,* 1991, pp. 87–91. For a survey of the orchestral resources available to Beethoven see: Adam von Ahnen Carse, *The Orchestra from Beethoven to Berlioz: A History of the Orchestra in the First Half of the 19th Century, and of the Development of Orchestral Baton-Conducting,* 1948, p. 306.

[26] H. C. Robbins Landon, *Beethoven, A Documentary Study,* 1977, pp. 33–34.

[27] For contextual information see: Theodore Albrecht editor and translator, 1996, Vol. 1, Letter No. 128, pp. 197–99.

[28] Elliot Forbes editor, *Thayer's Life of Beethoven,* 1967 p. 428.

[29] Otto Biba, *Concert life in Beethoven's Vienna* in: Robert Winter editor, *Beethoven, Performers, and Critics: The International Beethoven Congress, Detroit, 1977.* Detroit: Wayne State University Press, 1980.

[30] Paul Bekker, *Beethoven,* 1925, pp. 156–57.

[31] Adapted from: Paul Mies, *Beethoven's Orchestral Works* in: *The Age of Beethoven, The New Oxford History of Music,* Vol. VIII, Gerald Abraham editor, 1988, pp. 122–23.

[32] Adam von Ahnen Carse, *The Orchestra from Beethoven to Berlioz: A History of the Orchestra in the First Half of the 19th Century, and of the Development of Orchestral Baton-Conducting,* 1948, pp. 306–7.

[33] Elliot Forbes editor, *Thayer's Life of Beethoven,* 1967 p. 208.

CREATION ORIGINS

Having considered Beethoven in the context of his social and musical connections with Vienna, we now direct our discussion to the creation origins of the Fourth Symphony in B-flat major, Op. 60.

We repeat 1806 was a creative period for Beethoven. In addition to the composition of the Symphony in B-flat major, Op. 60, he worked on the Piano Concerto in G major, Op. 58, the three String Quartets, Op. 59 (*Razumovsky*), the Violin Concerto in D major, Op. 61, and his Opera *Leonora* (*Fidelio*), Op. 72. For the latter he composed the Overture *Leonora* No. 3, Op. 72b — one of the work's *four* overtures. After completing the *Eroica* Symphony, Beethoven did not commence work directly on the Fourth Symphony. Instead, he began work on what would become the celebrated Symphony No. 5 in C minor, Op.

67. However, he set this aside for various reasons. Thayer suggested, with the work comparatively advanced, Beethoven felt disposed to take his next symphony 'in a different direction'— one having a more relaxed mood and character.[1] He elucidates:

> 'The Symphony in B-flat major Op. 60 was the great work of this summer season [1806]. Sketches prove that its successor, the Fifth in C minor, had been commenced, and was laid aside to give place to this. Nothing more is known of the composition except what is imparted by the author's inscription on the manuscript: "Sinfonia 4ta, 1806, L. v. Bthvn.".'[2]

A further reason why Beethoven set aside the C minor Symphony was his providential encounter with Count Franz Joachim Wenzel Oppersdorff — the Fourth Symphony's dedicatee.

Beethoven's encounter with Count Oppersdorff came about through the composer's connection with his then patron Prince Karl Lichnowsky. We have remarked Lichnowsky was Beethoven's foremost supporter of Beethoven, following his arrival in Vienna, who provided him with financial support. In 1806 Beethoven accompanied the Prince with his entourage to his summer retreat, a country estate at Grätz near Troppau, Silesia. Confirmation of this is evident from a letter Beethoven wrote on 3 September to the publisher Breitkopf and Härtel explaining, he had 'a good deal of business in hand' and of his 'short trip to Grätz where I am now staying'. Later in his letter he revealed 'the business in hand', remarking:

> 'I can ... send you immediately *three Violin*

> Quartets [Op. 59, *Razumovsky*], *a new Pianoforte Concerto* [Op. 58], a new Symphony [considered to be a reference to the Fourth Symphony, Op. 60], the score of my Opera [*Leonora*], and my Oratorio [*Christus am Ölberge*].'

The italics regarding the quartets and the concerto are Beethoven's.

Customarily Beethoven would have rented summer lodgings in the countryside, but in 1806 accepted Lichnowsky's invitation — in effect for a short vacation — to find respite from his tribulations — both musical and personal. His Opera had not gone well in Vienna and in May his younger brother Kaspar Karl married a young woman by the name of Johanna Ries — of whom Beethoven did not approve; she bore their only child, Karl, later in September — circumstances that virtually terminated Kaspar Karl's role as his brother's secretary-assistant.

Concerning Lichnowsky, he had been both a friend and pupil of Mozart and was an accomplished pianist. He shared his love of music with Count Oppersdorff whose neighbouring estate was situated in Upper Silesia near Oberglogau — only about a day's journey from Lichnowsky's estate. Such was the Count's enthusiasm for music, he maintained a well-appointed orchestra in his household. Thayer records:

> '[Oppersdorff] was an enthusiastic music-lover and maintained an orchestra which he was so anxious to have complete that he demanded that all who were in his service could play a musical instrument. Through ties, partly of friendship, partly of kinship, the Oppersdorff family had

various connections with many of Austria's noble families, such as Lobkowitz and Lichnowsky.'[3]

During Beethoven's sojourn in Silesia, Count Oppersdorff, had his orchestra perform the composer's Second Symphony. As a consequence, Beethoven became on friendly terms with the Count; in subsequent correspondence he honoured him with the salutation 'my beloved friend'. We have described the meeting between Beethoven and Oppersdorff as being 'providential'. This was the case insofar as the Count commissioned a further symphony from Beethoven (the Fourth) – with the prospect of a second one to follow (the Fifth).[4] Musicologist Elizabeth Schwarm Glesner observes:

> '[The] Count enjoyed [the Second Symphony] so much that he immediately commissioned a new symphony, offering the composer a grand sum for the work's dedication. At that time, Beethoven was at work on what would eventually be the Fifth Symphony, a work he had started in earlier, darker days. [We recall Beethoven's anguish over his loss of hearing and the torment over his unrequited love]. Now, calmer and more contented, he set that traumatic score aside and began a cheerier symphony for the Count, one more in the mood of the Second Symphony that the Count found so pleasing.'[5]

The Count was indeed prepared to pay Beethoven handsomely; he received payments of some 850 florins from Oppersdorff, mostly paid in advance.[6] However, notwithstanding his expectation of having his name associated with *two* Beethoven symphonies, in the event he had to be content with the dedication of just *one* – the Fourth Symphony. Following the custom of the day Oppersdorff was to retain the score of the B-flat major Symphony for a period, in this case of six months, for his personal use. At the close of this period Beethoven was then at liberty to sell the work to a publisher.

Commenting on Beethoven's creative impulse that gave inception to the Fourth Symphony, the musicologist Peter Hauschild makes the following observations:

> '[Beethoven] promised [Count Oppersdorff] his B-flat major Symphony. The work came to be viewed in earlier Beethoven literature as a "commission". Though this still concurs with the musical practice in the 18th century, it gives rise to a certain unspoken disparagement when associated with a work by Beethoven. His labour on this project was also seen as one of the lengthy interruptions of his work on the Fifth Symphony, which he had commenced two years previously but did not complete until 1808 ... The Fourth Symphony was created before this, as a product of the composer's free artistic will and out of an inner need, like his other symphonies.'[7]

As already inferred, Beethoven may have set aside work on the Fifth Symphony for the reason that, on receiving Oppersdorff's commission, he may have considered the C minor Symphony's revolutionary fervour and its *sturm und drang* character would be too expressive for the Count, disposed, as he apparently was, to the calmer manner of the Second Symphony. As we shall in due course see, Count Oppersdorff had to be content with the dedication of the B-flat major Symphony whilst the dedication of the C minor

Symphony was conferred, jointly, upon Count Andrey Razumovsky and Prince Joseph von Lobkowitz.

It will be recalled (see above), Beethoven wrote to Breitkopf and Härtel on 3 September offering the publisher 'a new symphony' — taken to be a reference to the B-flat major — and suggesting the work was already through-composed. It should be borne in mind, though, that on occasions Beethoven was not averse to offering works for publication that were still incomplete — or not even started! Assuming the Fourth Symphony was completed in the autumn of 1806, Beethoven must have composed the work expeditiously. His usual method of composing was to jot down ideas as they occurred to him on his walks in the country. In the case of the Fourth Symphony, however, no preparatory sketches of this kind have survived 'to enlighten us on the gradual emergence of the ideas and their elaboration'.[8]

Barry Cooper cites a miscellaneous collection of loose leaves, known as 'Landsberg 12', concerning which he remarks:

> 'It contains 38 leaves of various shapes and sizes, including material from the Second, Fourth, Fifth, Sixth, and Ninth Symphonies ... [A] few of the leaves originated in genuine sketchbooks but most were probably separate initially.'[9]

Musicologist Terry Barfoot proposes:

> '[The] absence of surviving sketches for the Symphony No. 4 would suggest, like the music itself, that it was a spontaneous outpouring. Yet the work is by no means entirely sunny in disposition, since it also contains passages of considerable intensity.'[10]

On 18 November, Beethoven wrote once more to Breitkopf and Härtel with a view to securing a contract with him for the publication of the compositions he had offered in his earlier letter of 3 September. Concerning the Fourth Symphony he writes, circumspectly:

> 'I cannot yet give you the Symphony I promised you, because a *distinguished gentleman* [italics added] has taken it from me. But I still retain freedom to publish it after six months.'

The 'distinguished gentleman' is clearly a reference to Count Oppersdorff. With the expectation that Breitkopf and Härtel would eventually publish the Fourth Symphony, Beethoven concluded his letter:

> 'Perhaps it will possible for me to have the Symphony engraved *sooner* [Beethoven's italics] than I have been able to hope for the present. If so, you may have it at an early date — But do reply soon — so that I may not hold you up.'[11]

Despite these entreaties — and Beethoven flattering Breitkopf and Härtel 'I always much prefer your firm to all other firms and shall continue to do so' — nothing came of these negotiations.[12]

Although the sketches for the B-flat major Symphony have not come down to us, the autograph score has survived. It is the first of the composer's symphony-autographs so to do and is dated 1806. Musicologist Jonathan del Mar has made a study of the manuscript from which we learn:

> 'Today the autograph remains unbound. The cover of the slip-case in which it is contained

bears the name of its former owner, Heinrich Beer, before it passed to the Mendelssohn family. [The autograph] essentially shows Op. 60 in its final form. Beethoven is known to have made some later emendations, such as the addition of tempo (metronome) indications [see later].'

Del Mar adds: 'Beethoven took particular care in the writing out of the wind parts alternating *Solo* and *Tutti* indications in dark-brown ink.'[13]

These latter observations are consistent with remarks Sir George Grove made following his study of the autographs of the Beethoven symphonies at the close of the nineteenth century:

> 'One of the remarkable features of Beethoven's autograph scores is the minute exactness with which the marks of expression (*f, p, sfp, crescendo, etc.*) and other dynamic indications are put in; and the way in which they are repeated in the manuscript up and down the page, so that there may be no misunderstanding of his precise intention as to every instrument in hand ... [they] show how determined he was to leave nothing to chance.'[14]

The autograph score was once owned by Messrs. Mendelssohn-Bartholdy from whom it passed in 1908 to the Music Division of the Prussian State Library, Berlin. The Mendelssohns' was one of the richest of all private nineteenth-century collections of Beethoven manuscripts. That of the Fourth Symphony was presented to the Berlin Royal Library by Ernst von Mendelssohn-Bartholdy. It had been left to him by his father, Paul Mendelssohn-Bartholdy, brother of the composer. The collection was previously owned by the Berlin collector Heinrich Beer and included the autographs of the Fifth, and Seventh Symphonies.[15]

Although Count Oppersdorff had paid Beethoven for the exclusive rights to the Fourth Symphony for an initial period of six months — following the composer-patron relationship of the day — it remains a matter of speculation whether Oppersdorff's own orchestra ever first performed the work at Oberglogau.[16] The accepted opinion is the B-flat major Symphony received its premier in March 1807 at a private concert that took place in the Vienna residence of Prince Franz Joseph Lobkowitz. This was one of two subscription concerts arranged for Beethoven by Prince Lobkowitz that also featured the Fourth Piano Concerto in G minor. We can assume the audience on these occasions must have been highly exclusive, being both of a private nature and taking place within a princely household.[17]

The first public performance of the Fourth Symphony had to wait until April 1808 when it was played at a concert in Vienna's Burgtheater. As for Prince Lobkowitz, he was now Beethoven's foremost patron, following a violent quarrel between Beethoven and Prince Lichnowsky. This had come about following Beethoven's refusal to play for some visiting, and apparently rather arrogant, French officers. An altercation between Beethoven and Prince Lichnowsky was evidently prevented only by Count Oppersdorff's timely intervention. Later, when returned to Vienna, Beethoven, still not mollified, is known to have dashed to pieces a small marble bust of the Prince that he kept by his writing desk.[18]

Given that Count Oppersdorff had paid Beethoven handsomely for the prior use of the Fourth Symphony — only to learn of it being premiered (as believed) at Prince Lobkowitz's — it is more than likely he may have felt slighted and may even have harboured some disaffection towards the composer — see later.

As with so many of Beethoven's compositions, publication of the Fourth Symphony came about only after protracted negotiations with various music publishers. It is to these we now direct our narrative.

We recall once more Beethoven's letter of 3 September 1806 to the Leipzig-based music publisher Breitkopf and Härtel. At this time the head of the publishing firm was Gottfried Christoph Härtel — Bernhard Breitkopf, his founding partner, having died some years previously. Beethoven assured Härtel he was interested in securing an understanding with his firm with a view to promoting the sale of his compositions in Germany. However, he reserved the right to sell single works to publishers in other countries notably, France (Paris), England (London), and Scotland (Edinburgh). Meanwhile, he offered Härtel the Fourth Symphony, doubtless anticipating the time when he would be free to sell the work to him after having been released from his obligations to Count Oppersdorff to whom, as remarked, he had offered its exclusive use for a period of six months. In a postscript, on the back of the envelope, he informed Härtel of his summer-time address at Prince Lichnowsky's in Troppau, Silesia.[19]

On 13 September, Härtel responded to Beethoven's letter asking what prices he wanted for his works. He suggested the two parties should enter into a three-year contract, thereby ensuring his firm would secure exclusive rights for the publication of the composer's new works in Germany. Härtel was aware that Beethoven was receiving offers from other publishing houses to bring out his works. Beethoven had also intimated he was considering leaving Vienna and would thereby be free to publish his works in Paris or London.[20]

Illustrative of the forgoing is that on 1 November, Beethoven wrote to the Scottish music publisher George Thomson, based in Edinburgh, in response to Thomson's request to have the composer harmonize various Scottish airs — as Haydn had done so for him previously. Thomson, though, was concerned Beethoven's song-settings might be too challenging for 'the young ladies' for whom they were intended. Beethoven responded — the letter was written in French and was only signed by Beethoven:

> 'I will take care to make the compositions easy and pleasing, as far as I can and as far as is consistent with that elevation and originality of style which favourably characterises my works and from which I shall never stoop.'

Later in his letter Beethoven offered Thomson the prospect of receiving other compositions:

> 'I can promise you ... three trios for violin, viola and violincello, and three quintets for two violins, two violas and violincello ... three quartets and finally two sonatas for pianoforte with accompaniment for two violins and flute, and one quintet.[21]

Although Thomson did not take up all of Beethoven's suggestions, he did eventually publish over a hundred Scottish folksongs to Beethoven's accompaniments. With reference to this list of compositions, Thayer remarks: 'It affords a striking example of Beethoven's habit of working on several compositions at the same time.'[22]

Beethoven did not respond to Härtel's letter of 13 September until 18 November. He exonerated himself for his tardiness explaining how his sojourn with Prince

Lichnowsky had disrupted his normal routine. He asserted he was willing to enter into Härtel's suggested three-year contract but only on condition that he was also at liberty to sell his works 'to England or Scotland, or France'. In any future negotiations with Härtel, Beethoven urged him 'to rely entirely on *my word of honour*' [Beethoven's italics]. He proposed instead of setting up a contract, as Hartel was requesting, adding he 'would quote [Härtel] the fee for each work — and a fee as low as possible'. With regard to the works in hand he states: 'For the time being I am offering you three Quartets [*Razumovsky*, Op.59] and a Pianoforte Concerto [No.4, Op. 58].'

Regarding the Fourth Symphony he explained:

> 'I cannot yet give you the Symphony I promised you [on 3 September] because a distinguished gentleman has taken it from me. But I still retain the freedom to publish it after six months.'

Beethoven is clearly referring here to his continuing obligations to Count Franz von Oppersdorff. As to the fees he wanted for his compositions, he requested 600 gulden for the three Quartets and a further 300 for the Concerto. The silver gulden and Viennese florin were interchangeable and had a value of about two contemporary English shillings. Beethoven did not state the price he wanted for the Fourth Symphony.[23] This, however, is apparent from the record of the composer's subsequent financial transactions. Thayer records that Count Oppersdorff paid Beethoven 500 florins for the Fourth Symphony.[24] This was a considerable sum amounting to the equivalent of fifty pounds sterling in contemporary English money-values.

Our consideration of Beethoven's negotiations with publishers takes us into the following year 1807. It was then that Beethoven became personally acquainted with Muzio Clementi when he was on a business trip to Vienna. Clementi was perhaps the ultimate all-round, musical polymath being variously a composer, virtuoso pianist, pedagogue, conductor, music publisher, editor, and piano manufacturer. Clementi transacted his business affairs from London and, receiving word of Beethoven's reputation, was anxious to publish some of his works there.

On 22 April 1807 Clementi wrote to his business partner William Frederick Collard based in London: 'By a little management and without committing myself, I have at last made a complete conquest of that *haughty beauty* [Clementi's italics] Beethoven.' Clementi explained how he had persuaded the composer to have his works published in England (London) and how his publishing house would take care of him. Beethoven obligingly gave an undertaking to prepare a list of his available publications. Clementi told Collard he had agreed with Beethoven to take in manuscript: the three String Quartets Op. 59; Symphony No. 4, Op. 60; the Overture *Coriolan*, Op. 62; the Concerto for Pianoforte No. 4. Op. 58; and the Violin Concerto, Op. 61. Clementi described the Violin Concerto as being 'very beautiful' and which, at his request, Beethoven had offered to adapt for the pianoforte — what would in effect become Piano Concerto, Op. 61a. For all these works Beethoven was to receive the handsome sum of two hundred pounds sterling.[25]

On the same day, Clementi wrote to Breitkopf and Härtell informing the publisher of the personal friendship he had established with Beethoven and of the Contract he had agreed with the composer. He explained, it ceded to him the proprietary rights to publish in England the Piano Concerto No. 4, Op. 58, the three *Razumovsky* String Quartets, Op. 59, the Symphony No. 4, Op. 60, the Violin Concerto, and the Overture *Coriolan*, Op. 62.[26]

The Quartets were subsequently published by Clementi in 1809—10 together with the Violin Concerto — also, as adapted by Beethoven, as a Piano Concerto. The Contract between Clementi and Beethoven, written in French, was signed by the signatories to both parties and dated 20 April 1807.[27] The Fourth Symphony, Overture and Piano Concerto were duly despatched to England by courier but it seems they never reached Clementi's publishing house and were never published by him — despite the handsome price he had paid for this set of compositions. The military conflict in Europe may have disrupted the already tenuous postal services. If Clementi did in fact receive the works in question, a disastrous fire that consumed his London premises may offer an alternative explanation for his failure to fulfil all his publication intentions. This may also explain why Beethoven had to wait until the spring of 1810 to receive his payment.[28]

On 26 April Beethoven wrote to the Bonn music publisher Nikolaus Simrock offering him the publications he had for sale:

'I intend to sell the following six new works to a firm of publishers in France [Ignaz Pleyel who had a publishing firm in Paris], to one in England [Muzio Clementi] and to one in Vienna [Bureau des Arts et d'Industrie].'

The six works in question were: Piano Concerto No. 4 (Op. 58), the three Razumovsky String Quartets (Op. 59), Symphony No. 4 (Op. 60), Violin Concerto (Op. 61), Overture to *Coriolan* (Op. 62) — to the text of Collin's tragedy — and the transcription of the Violin Concerto for piano. For this remarkable list of compositions, Beethoven requested the payment of 1200 gulden— about 120 pounds sterling. He requested payment in in Augsburg currency. This was a more stable currency than the paper money of the period; although Beethoven was not very good at arithmetic he was shrewd in his pecuniary dealings with publishers.[29]

On 26 April Beethoven wrote a further letter to the Paris publisher Camille Pleyel who was the elder son of Ignaz Pleyel. Both father and son had frequented Vienna on business trips when Beethoven made their acquaintance. Beethoven offered Camille the same list of publications for sale that he had suggested to Nikolaus Simrock.[30] In the event, however, Camille did not take up Beethoven's offer.[31]

Although doubtless disappointed by Pleyel's negative response to his publication proposal, Beethoven was clearly pleased with his business dealings with Clementi. This is evident from a letter he wrote on 11 May to Count Franz von Brunswick. He was an excellent cellist and his wife an accomplished pianist. Beethoven dedicated his celebrated *Appassionata* Piano Sonata, Op. 57 to Franz. In his letter, Beethoven enthused to the Count:

> 'This is just to tell you that I have come to a very good arrangement with Clementi — I am to get 200 pounds sterling and, what is more, I shall be able to sell the same works in Germany and France — and, in addition, he has given me further orders — so that by this means I may hope even in my early years to achieve the dignity of a true artist.'[32]

Franz was the brother of Josephine and Therese to whom Beethoven jointly dedicated his Piano Duet Variations on *Ich denke dein,* WoO 74 when they were his piano pupils in the years 1799–1804. Moreover, he was in love at various times with both sisters and the two of them have, as a consequence, been considered as candidates for the composer's *Immortal Beloved* — Josephine in particular. Schindler describes Franz von Brunswick as: 'One of the most enlightened connoisseurs of Beethoven's music who could truly call himself Beethoven's pupil.'[33]

Beethoven must also have been disappointed by the response he duly received from Nikolaus Simrock. He wrote to Beethoven on 31 May, initially expressing his interest in publishing the works the composer had offered him for sale. What he subsequently has to say, however, is interesting in that it sheds light on the challenges to the music-publishing business at this time in Europe — in addition to the problems of piracy. Simrock complained of the effect the French occupation was having: '[At] no time ... has the music business been as very slow as it is now, and keeps getting slower daily.' He could not meet Beethoven's demands explaining, with reference to the French currency that was then in circulation: 'All that I can do in my lean situation is to scrape together 1,600 livres.'[34]

On 16 June Beethoven wrote to Baron Ignaz von Gleichenstein about his business dealings with the various publishers to which we have made reference. Gleichenstein was an official in Vienna's War Department and a close friend of the composer, to whom he rendered many practical services. Beethoven described Gleichenstein as being 'attracted to everything that was beautiful and good' and showed his appreciation of the support he received from him by conferring on him the dedication of his Cello Sonata, Op. 69. In his letter, Beethoven sought Gleichenstein's advice regarding his approaching the publisher known in German as the Kunst- und Industrie-Comptoir and in French as the Bureau des arts et d'Industrie.

Beethoven had established a working-relationship with this firm as early as 1802 when they had published his arrangement, for string quartet, of the Piano Sonata, Op. 14 — the only occasion Beethoven ever made such an arrangement. From 1808, the 'Bureau' did in fact became Beethoven's principal publisher and eventually brought out some forty first-editions of the composer's works. One of the partner's in the firm was Joseph Sonnleithner, a Director of the Theater an der Wien and remembered today for supplying Beethoven with the libretto to his Opera *Fidelio*.[35]

On 23 June Beethoven wrote to the Bureau des arts et d'Industrie whose affairs were managed by the firm's senior partner Joseph Schreyvogel; through his position he played a prominent part in Vienna's cultural life. Beethoven informed Schreyvogel: 'My friend, Herr von Gleichenstein has a proposal to make to you about me. If you were to accept it you would greatly oblige me.' The 'proposal' was to publish the collection of works he had previously offered to Breitkopf and Härtel, Muzio Clementi, Camille Pleyel, and Nikolaus Simrock. Beethoven was in poor health at the time and was doubtless relying on Gleichenstein to help him with his business affairs.[36] It appears Gleichenstein's approach to the 'Bureau', on the composer's behalf, was successful since Beethoven wrote to him later in the month remarking: 'I sent the Symphony [Op. 60] to the Industriekomtor [sic]. No doubt they have received it.'[37]

In the same letter as the foregoing, Beethoven asked a favour of Gleichenstein: 'Will you be so kind as to deliver this to the copyist tomorrow — It refers, as you see, to the Symphony'. This can be taken to be a reference to the Fourth Symphony and further implies Beethoven was making progress with having the work prepared for publication. Some days later Beethoven followed this with a further letter — more exactly a note (undated) — urging Gleichenstein to secure a better price for the works he was offering for sale:

> 'I think that you should insist on being paid at least 60 gulden more than the fifteen hundred (assumed to be the sum the Kunst- und Industrie-Comptoir were offering), or, provided you consider it compatible with my integrity, the sum of sixteen hundred.'[38]

In 1808, Count Oppersdorff was still not in possession of the symphony he had commissioned. Doubtless with this in mind, Beethoven wrote to him sometime in March (the letter is undated): '*My beloved friend*' — Beethoven's italics and the salutation he reserved for those whom he regarded as 'fellow brothers in art' (another of Beethoven's typical expressions of endearment). '*Your Symphony* has been ready for a long time and ... I am sending it to you by the next post.' Turning to business matters he continues:

> 'You should add 50 gulden, for the copies I have made for you [which] have cost that amount at least — But if you don't want the Symphony let me know this well before next post-day. If you do take it, however, then cheer me up as soon as possible with the 300 gulden which you still owe me.'

Of some significance is that Beethoven then makes jocular reference to the scoring of the composition:

> 'The *last movement of the Symphony* has three trombones and a piccolo — and, although it is true there are not three kettledrums, yet this combi-

> nation of instruments will make more noise and, what is more, a pleasing noise than six kettle-drums.'

The mention of trombones indicates Beethoven is referring to the scoring of the Fifth Symphony – that he apparently still had in mind to sell to Oppersdorff.[39]

Meanwhile, Beethoven was resuming his correspondence with Breitkopf and Härtel to whom he wrote on 8 June. He revealed he had sold 'seven major works' to the Industrie Comptoir of Vienna adding, 'nearly all of which can be obtained in engraved form – and in general that firm is glad to have any of my works'. The 'great works' in question were Opp. 55–61, which, of course, include the Fourth Symphony. Notwithstanding, Beethoven entreated:

> 'Yet, as I have already told you several times (see above), I would prefer your firm to all others; and if only you would deal with me with less hesitation, I am convinced that you and I would make a profit.'

As an encouragement to Härtel, he offered for sale: the Fifth and Sixth Symphonies, Opp. 67 and 68; the Cello Sonata, Op. 69; and the Mass in C minor, Op. 86. Beethoven asked 900 gulden 'for the whole lot'.[40]

Beethoven appears to have found Härtel to be no-less resolute than himself in his business negotiations since he was obliged to write to him once more. Later in July (another undated letter) he offered to reduce the prices he was asking for his compositions. He now requested 700 gulden remarking: 'I am ... receiving less – but that is really my limit.' He made it a condition of sale, though, that Härtel would accept the C minor Mass; the publisher harboured doubts about this complaining 'there is no demand for church works'. To this Beethoven responded defiantly: 'I pay attention not only to what is profitable but also to what brings honour and glory.'[41]

In the meantime, Beethoven appears to have had a change of heart and to be less demanding. Eager to see his Mass in print he wrote once more to Härtel on 16 July:

> 'I am willing to release you entirely from everything connected with the Mass — so, I am making you a present of it. Even the cost of having it copied you need not defray ... I am absolutely convinced that once you have performed it at your winter concerts in Leipzig, you will certainly want to provide it with a German text and publish it. Whatever its fate may be, it now belongs to you.'

Dr. Christian Schreiber, a distinguished theologian subsequently provided a German translation of the Latin text.

Having given the Mass free to Härtel, he now requested 600 gulden for the publication of the Symphonies Opp. 67 and 68 and the Cello Sonata, Op. 69, but with the addition of the two Piano Trios, Op. 70 — that Beethoven describes as being 'now rather scarce'.[42] The two parties (antagonists) eventually reached a compromise and in 1809 Härtel duly published the Symphonies, Cello Sonata and Piano Trios in April, May and August respectively, and the Mass in 1812.

Having sold the publication rights of the Fifth and Sixth Symphonies to Messrs Breitkopf and Härtel, Beethoven must have felt obliged to explain himself to Count Oppersdorff who was still waiting for the symphony he had commissioned in 1806. On 1 November he wrote to the Count:

> 'You will probably have formed an unfavourable

> impression of me. But necessity drove me to hand over to someone else [Breitkopf and Härtel] the Symphony which I promised you, and another one as well.'

Beethoven sought to placate Oppersdorff saying: 'Rest assured, however, that you will soon receive the Symphony which is especially intended for you' [the Fourth Symphony, Op. 60].[43]

Thereby, Count Franz Joachim Wenzel Oppersdorff finally received Beethoven's Fourth Symphony in B-flat major, Op. 60 together with its dedication. Reflecting on the many twists and turns in the creation origins of the composition, and Beethoven's protracted negotiations with publishers, Peter Clive observes:

> 'Thus, if Oppersdorff had expected an entirely new work, he must have been disappointed. The fact that there is no record of any further contact between him and Beethoven, after November 1808, has been interpreted as an indication that he was probably displeased with Beethoven's comportment in the matter.'[44]

Having traced the creation origins of the Fourth Symphony, we consider the significance that the key of a composition had for Beethoven and for the performance of his works to be played at their 'correct' tempo.

Concerning the adoption of a key for a particular composition, Anton Schindler, Beethoven's amanuensis during his later years, relates how Beethoven was interested in the writings of the contemporary mystical poet and musician Christian Schubart.[45] He characterised the musical keys with feelings and ascribed to them a certain 'psyche'.[46]

To the key of B-flat Major, Schubart assigned the attributes of 'cheerful love, clear conscience, hope, [and] aspiration for a better world'. Many would argue these are some, at least, of the characteristics to be found in the genial manner of the Fourth Symphony. Besides the Fourth Symphony, Beethoven chose the key of B flat for several other significant works throughout his life including: String Quartet Op. 18, No. 6; Piano Sonata Op. 22; Piano Trio, 97 (*The Archduke*); Piano Sonata Op. 106; and String Quartet Op. 130. To these compositions may be added: the *Allegretto Scherzando* of the Eighth Symphony, Op. 93; the *Credo* of the Mass in D, Op. 123; and the *Adagio* of the Ninth Symphony, Op. 125 – all 'life affirming' works.[47]

With the advent of Johann Nepomuk Maelzel's metronome (1816–17), Beethoven seized upon its potential as a means of securing reliable tempi for the performance of his works. A report in the *Wiener Vaterländische Blätter* ('Vienna Patriotic Periodical') stated:

> 'Herr Beethoven looks upon this invention as a welcome means with which to secure the performance of his brilliant compositions in all places in the tempos conceived by him, which to his regret have so often been misunderstood.'[48]

On 17 December 1817, the *Allgemeine musikalische Zeitung* published a list of 'the tempos for every movement of the symphonies of Herr L. v. Beethoven as determined by the composer using Maelzel's metronome'. Beethoven also had a pamphlet printed by the publisher Sigmund Anton Steiner that gave his suggested metronome markings for the string quartets he had composed to date, namely, Opp. 18, 59, 74 and 95 and also included markings for his first eight symphonies.[49] Steiner had met Beethoven sometime in 1803. His publishing house specialised in printing sheet music and lithography and his premises became an informal meeting place for Beethoven and his friends.[50]

Beethoven's enthusiasm for the metronome is conveyed in a letter he wrote sometime in November 1817 to Ignaz Franz von Mosel; Mosel, a composer, violinist and writer on music, arranged and conducted the first concert given by the Gesellschaft der Musikfreunde. In his letter, Beethoven enthused:

> 'I am heartily delighted to know that you hold the same views as I do about our tempo indications which originated in the barbarous ages of music. For, to take one example, what can be more absurd than *Allegro*, which really signifies *merry*, and how very far removed we often are from the idea of that tempo. So much so that the piece itself means the *very opposite of the indications* ... As for me, I have long been thinking of abandoning those absurd descriptive terms, *Allegro, Andante, Adagio, Presto*, and Maelzel's metronome affords us the best opportunity of doing so. I now give you *my word* that I shall *never again* use them in any of my new compositions.'[51]

With regard to contemporary performance-practice, Beethoven's metronome markings are today considered by some authorities to be too fast. It has been suggested the reason for this is that Beethoven, in his later years, was confined by deafness to an inner world of *imagined* sound and ascribed quicker markings to his music than he would have if he had the benefit of experiencing his music *in performance*. However, the English conductor Sir Roger Norrington — respected for his historically-informed performances of Baroque and Classical music — cautions against dismissing Beethoven's tempo indications too readily:

> 'Beethoven inherited a whole series of traditional speeds, including an *Allegro* which was not very fast and an *Andante* which was by no means slow. He [was] most insistent on the importance of using a metronome (partly, no doubt, because his deafness prevented him from directing performances). In virtually every case his metronome marks tally with an eighteenth-century understanding of tempo indications.'[52]

The first edition of the Fourth Symphony was published in Vienna in 1808 by the Bureau des Arts et d'Industrie. Consistent with the procedures of the period, the work was not published in full score but in parts. 1808 was an auspicious one for Beethoven since, alongside the B-flat major Symphony, it saw the publication of the other major works of the composer to which we have made occasional reference, namely: Piano Concerto in G major, Op. 58; *Razumovsky* String Quartets, Op. 59; Violin Concerto in D major, Op. 61; Piano Concerto in D major, Op. 61a (arrangement of the Violin Concerto); and Overture *Coriolan*, Op. 62.

Two sets of original manuscript parts for orchestra, for the Fourth Symphony, are extant bearing annotations by Beethoven. These were used for early performances in and beyond Vienna. Today these are preserved in the Archive of the Lobkowitz family at Roudnice and in the Archive of the Gesellschaft der Musikfreunde. The original set of orchestral parts continued to be used for performance into the 1840s and 1850s, although containing many insertions and alterations regarding dynamics and articulation and even changes in note values — as requested by various conductors.[53] The Title Page of the Bureau des Arts et d'Industrie first edition reads:

'IVme
SINFONIE
á 2 Violons, Alto, Flûte, 2 Hautbois, 2 Clarinets
2 Cors, 2 Basfsons, Trompettes, Timballes
Violoncello et Bafs
Composée et Dédieé
À Monsieur Le Comte Oppersdorff
Par
LOUIS van BEETHOVEN
Oeuvre 60
À Vienne et Pesch au Bureau des Arts et d'Industrie
[Plate] 596'[54]

In conclusion, we consider the publication of the full score of the B-flat major Symphony.

The American musicologist Frederick Freedman has undertaken a study of the early publication of the full-score editions of the symphonies of Haydn, Mozart, and Beethoven by the London-based publishers Cianchettini and Sperati. From his researches we learn the following.

Francesco Cianchettini and P. Sperati established a publishing house and music shop in London in 1805 where they became known as 'Importers of Classical Music'; none other than the Prince of Wales was their Patron. In May 1807, they announced their intention to publish '*A Compleat Collection of Haydn, Mozart, and Beethoven's Symphonies*'. Haydn was then still alive and was recognized as the greatest living composer. The symphonies of Mozart were beginning to be published posthumously. As for Beethoven, as Freedman remarks:

> '[Then] only thirty-seven years old, [he] was looked upon by most critics as an eccentric composer who antagonized performers and listeners alike by his lengthy, difficult, and "dissonant" music.'

With this in mind, the inclusion of Beethoven by Cianchettini and Sperati in their publication venture is all the more enterprising.

As remarked, at the period in question, and for many years later, it was the custom to issue symphonic works in separate orchestral parts. The London partners' proposal is all the more remarkable since, as they announced in their prospectus, they planned to publish the symphonies, by subscription, *in full score*. The enterprise started well and included eighteen symphonies by Haydn (1807 and 1809), four by Mozart — including K. 550 and K. 551 (1808), and Beethoven's symphonies One, Two, and Three (1809). Regrettably, with only sixty-two subscribers Cianchettini's and Sperati's pioneering venture founded and consequently the planned publication of a full-score edition of the Fourth Symphony did not materialize.

Their achievements, however, did not pass unrecognised. The correspondent to *The Harmonicon*, the leading London music journal of the day observed:

> 'That, under such circumstances, Mr. Cianchettini should have withdrawn without completing his design, no longer excites us to wonder; we are only surprised that he proceeded so far, and brought out his work in so neat and correct a manner.'

*

Freedman himself concludes with words of caution and endorsement:

> '[It] should be observed that Cianchettini and Sperati merely reissued material that was already available, and while their editions claimed neither approval nor authenticity ... they performed, nevertheless, a useful service in being the first to make some of these great works available to the British public — and the world at large — in full score. This alone should ensure them an honourable place among the music publishers of their time'.[55]

On 13 May 1822, Nikolaus Simrock in Bonn wrote to Beethoven urging him to make progress with the completion of the *Missa Solemnis* for which he had paid 100 Louis d'or. In the course of his letter, Simrock adds: 'For the present I have undertaken to publish your six Symphonies [i.e. Nos. 1–6] in full score.' He gives the reason:

> '[I] wanted to dedicate to my worthy old friend a worthy monument, and I hope you will be satisfied with the edition, since I have done my utmost for it.'[56]

The scores of the First and Second Symphonies appeared in the spring of 1822, that of the *Eroica* a few months later, and that of the Fourth Symphony in 1823. In the event, notwithstanding his expressed intentions, Simrock never published the scores of the Fifth and Sixth Symphonies. They were published later by Breitkopf & Härtel in 1826.

George Grove made a study of Simrock's score of the Fourth Symphony and described it in the following terms:

'The score is 8vo — crown octave 6 inches x 9 inches (15 cm x 23 cm) of 195 pages, uniform with those of Nos. 1, 2, and 3.'

Grove gives the following description of the Title Page:

'4me Grande Simphonie en Si flat (B dur) composé et dédiée à Monsr. Le Comte d' Oppersdorff par Louis van Beethoven. Op. 60. Partition. Prix 16 Fr. Bonn et Cologne chez N. Simrock. 2078.'

Grove adds:

'The care with which Beethoven marks his *nuances* and other indications for the players is nowhere more conspicuous than here. Dots, dashes, and rests are anxiously discriminated, and it almost makes one's head ache to think of the labour that is concealed in these gay and lively pages. In fact, the details of all kinds in these immortal works are prodigious. In that respect they are like Hogarth's pictures in which every time you look you see some witty or pertinent point which you had not noticed before.'

Grove is here referring to the *original* score. He observed that a later score by Breitkopf and Härtel ignores some of these minute differences, to which he remonstrates: 'They are the composer's own insertions and he marked nothing of the kind without full intention and should be shown.'[57]

In 1862 the full score of the Fourth Symphony was published as part of the *Gesamtausgabe* — complete edition — by Breitkopf & Härtel, Leipzig in 1862. The opportunity was taken to correct various textual errors to produce, in

see: Beethoven House, Digital Archives, Library Document, HCB Br 68. See also, Emily Anderson editor and translator, 1961, Vol. 1, Letter No. 134. Pp. 152–153.
[20] Neither Emily Anderson nor Theodore Albrecht makes reference to the letter of 13 September 1806. It is cited, however, by William Altmann in, *Preface* to Score of Fourth Symphony. Dover Publications, 1976 (reprint).
[21] Emily Anderson editor and translator, 1961, Vol. 1, Letter No. 136, pp. 154–56.
[22] Elliot Forbes editor, *Thayer's Life of Beethoven*, 1967 pp. 405–06.
[23] Emily Anderson editor and translator, 1961, Letter, No. 137, pp. 156–58.
[24] Beethoven acknowledged receipt of payment for the Fourth Symphony on 3 February 1807. See: Elliot Forbes editor, *Thayer's Life of Beethoven*, 1967 p. 402.
[25] Theodore Albrecht editor and translator, 1996, Vol. 1, Letter No. 119, pp. 186–88. For an audio version of this letter, together with the German text, see: Beethoven House, Digital Archives, Document Sammlung H. C. Bodmer, HCB BBr 84.
[26] *Ibid*, 1996, Vol. 1, Letter No. 118, p. 185.
[27] Emily Anderson editor and translator, 1961, Vol. 3, Document 3, pp. 1419–20.
[28] Alan Tyson, *The Authentic English Editions of Beethoven*, 1963, pp. 51–52.
[29] Emily Anderson, editor and translator, 1961 Vol. 1, Letter No. 141, pp. 166–67. See also: Beethoven House, Digital Archives, Library Document, H. C. Bodmer, HCB Br 222.
[30] Emily Anderson, editor and translator, 1961 Vol. 1, Letter No. 140, pp. 165–66.
[31] Camille Pleyel's letter to Beethoven has not survived but see: Beethoven House, Digital Archives, Library Document, NE 161 –audio and text letter– and for a contemporary portrait of Ignaz Pleyel see Document B 2131.
[32] Emily Anderson editor and translator, 1961, Vol. 1, Letter No. 143, pp. 168–69.
[33] Anton Felix Schindler, *Beethoven as I Knew Him*, edited by Donald W. MacArdle and translated by Constance S. Jolly from the German edition of 1860, 1966, p. 305.
[34] Theodore Albrecht editor and translator, 1996, Vol. 1, Letter No. 121, pp. 189–90. As suggested by Alan Tyson, 1963, pp. 51–52.
[35] Emily Anderson editor and translator, 1961, Vol. 1, Letter No. 145, pp. 170–71.
[36] *Ibid*, Letter No. 147, p. 172.
[37] *Ibid*, Letter No. 148, pp. 172–73.
[38] *Ibid*, Letter No. 149, p. 173.
[39] *Ibid*, Letter No. 166, pp. 187–88.
[40] *Ibid*, Letter No. 167, pp. 188–89.
[41] *Ibid*, Letter No. 168, pp. 190–91.
[42] *Ibid*, Letter No. 169, pp. 191–92.
[43] *Ibid*, Letter No. 173, pp. 199–93.
[44] Peter Clive, 2001, pp. 252–53.
[45] Anton Felix Schindler, *Beethoven as I Knew Him*, edited by Donald W. MacArdle and translated by Constance S. Jolly from the German edition of 1860, 1966, pp. 366–7.
[46] Christian Schubart outlined his views in: *Ideen zu einer Aesthetik der Tonkunst*, 1806. Schubart considered A-flat minor implied 'difficult struggle'

Jonathan Del Mar's words 'a serious critical edition which served the musical world well for the past 130 years'. This was in due course followed by various others of which particular mention may be made of the full scores by the following: by C. F. Peters Leipzig (1902); miniature score published by Ernst Eulenberg, Leipzig with a preface by the German scholar Wilhelm Altmann. (1920); in the same year an edition by Breitkopf & Härtel; and a miniature score published in the Philharmonia series, Vienna (1923).[58]

[1] As discussed by Joseph Braunstein, *Musica Aeterna, Program* Notes for 1971–1976. New York: *Musica Aeterna*, 1978, Vol. 3, pp. 52–53.
[2] Elliot Forbes editor, *Thayer's Life of Beethoven*, 1967 p. 410.
[3] *Ibid*, p. 402.
[4] H. C. Robbins Landon, *Beethoven: His Life, Work and World*, 1992, p. 138 and Barry Cooper, *The Beethoven Compendium: A Guide to Beethoven's Life and Music*, p. 50.
[5] Music scholar, Elizabeth Schwarm Glesner, Classical Music Pages, *Ludwig van Beethoven, 4 Symphonie.*
[6] Peter Clive, *Beethoven and His World*, 2001, pp. 252–53.
[7] Peter Hauschild, *Ludwig van Beethoven, Symphonie Nr.4.* Breitkopf & Härtel. *Preface to Miniature Score*.1996.
[8] Joseph Braunstein, *Musica Aeterna, Program* Notes for 1971–1976. New York: *Musica Aeterna*, 1978, Vol. 3, pp. 52–53.
[9] Barry Cooper, *Beethoven and the Creative Process*, 1990, p. 83.
[10] Terry Barfoot, *Symphony No.4 in B-flat major, Op. 60: Notes to the BBC Radio Three Beethoven Experience,* Tuesday 7 and Wednesday 8 June 2005, www.bbc.co.uk/radio3/Beethoven
[11] Emily Anderson editor and translator, 1961, Vol. 1, Letter No. 137, pp. 156–58.
[12] See: Elliot Forbes editor, *Thayer's Life of Beethoven*, 1967 p. 402.
[13] Quoted, with adaptations, from: Jonathan Del Mar, Ludwig van *Beethoven, Symphony No. 4 in B-flat major, Op. 60, Critical Commentary* [to the Autograph score]. Bärenreiter Kassel, BA 9004 (undated).
[14] George Grove, *Beethoven and his Nine Symphonies*, 1896, p.111.
[15] William Altmann, *Preface to the Score of Fourth Symphony*. Dover Publications, 1976 and Douglas Porter Johnson editor, *The Beethoven Sketchbooks: History, Reconstruction, Inventory*, 1985, p. 37.
[16] See, for example, Peter Hauschild, *Ludwig van Beethoven, Symphonie Nr.4.* Breitkopf & Härtel. *Preface to Miniature Score*.1996.
[17] See, for example, Joseph Braunstein, *Musica Aeterna, Program* Notes for 1971–1976. New York: *Musica Aeterna*, 1978, Vol. 3, pp. 52–53.
[18] Peter Clive, *Beethoven and his World*, 2002, pp. 203–04.
[19] For a facsimile reproduction of the letter, together with an audio interpretation,

and B minor suggested 'patience' and 'calm – awaiting one's fate'! In comparison, C major was for him the key with the connotation 'completely pure'.

47 As considered by George Grove in, *Beethoven and his Nine Symphonies*, 1896.
48 Elliot Forbes editor, *Thayer's Life of Beethoven*, 1967 p. 544.
49 Anne-Louise Coldicott, *Performance Practice in Beethoven's Day* in: Barry Cooper, 1991, pp. 280–09.
50 For a facsimile reproduction of an engraving of Sigmund Anton Steiner, combined with contextual information, see: Beethoven House, Digital Archives, Library Document, B. 184.
51 Emily Anderson editor and translator, 1961, Vol. 2, Letter No. 845, p. 727. See also: Carlos Chávez, *Musical Thought*, 1961. From 1958–59 Chávez was the Charles Eliot Norton professor at Harvard University and in his Fifth Lecture he quoted Beethoven's letter to Ignaz Franz von Mosel with contextual commentary.
52 Roger Norrington, Liner notes to *Beethoven, Symphonies 1 & 6*, The London Classical Players, EMI CDC 7497462, 1988.
53 With acknowledgment to: Jonathan Del Mar, *Ludwig van Beethoven, Symphony No. 4 in B-flat major, Op. 60, Critical Commentary*. Bärenreiter Kassel, BA 9004 (undated). See also: Wayne M. Senner, Robin Wallace and William Meredith editors, *The Critical Reception of Beethoven's Compositions by his German Contemporaries*, 1999, Vol.1, p. 59.
54 For a facsimile reproduction of the Title Page to the Fourth Symphony, in the edition published by the Bureau des Arts et d'Industrie (catalogue No. 596), see: Beethoven House, Digital Archives, Library Document, HCB C Op. 60.
55 Frederick Freedman, *First, Second and Third Symphonies by Ludwig van Beethoven*, Detroit reprints in music, 1975.
56 Theodore Albrecht editor and translator, 1996, Vol. 2, Letter No. 285, pp. 203–04. See also: Elliot Forbes editor, *Thayer's Life of Beethoven*, 1967 p. 817.
57 George Grove, *Beethoven and his Nine Symphonies*, 1896, p. 96 and pp 110–11.
58 With acknowledgement to Jonathan Del Mar, Ludwig van *Beethoven, Symphony No. 4 in B-flat major, Op. 60, Critical Commentary*. Bärenreiter Kassel, BA 9004 (undated).

RECEPTION HISTORY

Beethoven enjoyed the benefit of having early performances of his orchestral music performed before receptive musicians and music connoisseurs. These took place at informal gatherings in the great salons of his patrons Prince Lichnowsky and Prince Lobkowitz. Over time, with public performances of the symphonies taking place in Vienna and further afar in Leipzig and Berlin, reviews of the composer's music were published in such journals as the *Allgemeine musikalische Zeitung* and the sister Journal the *Berliner Allgemeine musikalische Zeitung*.

With the benefit of repeated hearings, Beethoven's orchestral music became more favourably assimilated and understood. For example, in 1818 the English musician Cipriani Potter visited Vienna, became acquainted with Beethoven, and wrote of his meeting with the composer and of the reception of his music: '[It] is now listened to with an attention and delight that his real friends and admirers could scarcely have anticipated.' Potter's testimony was later published in 1861 as *Recollections of Beethoven, with Remarks on his Style*, in issue 226 of the London *Musical Times*. And in 1821, fellow Englishman John Russell (not to be confused with the diplomat Lord John Russell) recorded his impressions of music-making on the continent in his *A Tour of Germany and some of the Provinces* in which he records: 'Beethoven is the most celebrated of living composer's in Vienna, and in certain departments, the foremost of his day.'[1]

In our discussion of the reception history of Beethoven's Fourth Symphony in B-flat major, Op. 60, we first consider the response to the music following its performance in concerts held during Beethoven's lifetime. We then proceed to cite its reception through the medium of transcriptions for the piano and small instrumental ensembles. Our survey then considers reception in the nineteenth century, including early reception in France (Paris) and England, notably through the concerts promoted by the fledgling Philharmonic Society of London. We conclude by making reference to later nineteen-century reception and that expressed nearer to own time.

RECEPTION IN BEETHOVEN'S LIFETIME
FIRST PERFORMANCES

1807

The first performance of the Fourth Symphony took place in the palace of Prince Lobkowitz in Vienna in March 1807 — the precise date is unknown. This performance was given using a set of orchestral parts that is preserved today in the

Archiv der Gesellschaft der Musikfreunde. Another set of orchestral parts is also preserved in the archives of the descendants of Prince Lobkowitz at their country estate at Roudnice — where it is believed the Fourth Symphony was performed shortly after its composition.[2] Beethoven's biographer Alexander Wheelock Thayer cites the reception the composition received as reported in the April 1807 issue of the contemporary *Journal des Luxus und der Modern*:

> 'Richness of ideas, bold originality and fullness of power, which are the particular merits of Beethoven's muse were very much in evidence to everyone at these concerts; yet many found fault with lack of a noble simplicity and the all too fruitful accumulation of ideas which on account of their number were not always adequately worked out and blended, thereby creating the effect more often of rough diamonds.'[3]

The Fourth Symphony was performed later on 15 November at a benefit concert. Anton Felix Schindler, writing of this later in his study of the composer *Beethoven as I Knew Him* (1860), gave a more fulsome account of the Symphony's early reception:

> 'The composer had the pleasure of seeing the immediate success of his new Symphony. Its impact was stronger than any of the others, stronger even than that of the First Symphony in C major, which had made its début eight years earlier. The Viennese critics hailed the new work without reserve or qualification, an honour that

had been granted to almost no other instrumental composition by Beethoven.'4

Reflecting on the warmth of reception of the Fourth Symphony by the Viennese' critics, present-day authorities consider they may have been favourably disposed to accept it because of many of the work's Haydnesque characteristics, not least the adoption of the key of B-flat major that Haydn had made familiar to the public in his own Symphony No. 98 (1792) and Symphony No. 102 (1794).

A series of concerts was established in Vienna in 1807–08, known variously as the *Musikalische Institut, Liebhaber-Concerte, Freunde der Tonkunst, or the Gesellschaft der Musikfreunden* – in effect 'Music-Lover's Concert'. These were promoted by Johann von Häring, a banker who was recognised for being one of Vienna's foremost amateur violinists; he had the distinction of performing chamber music with Mozart. A measure of his standing is that he possessed instruments by Amati, Guarneri, and Stradivarius. Häring made a significant contribution to Viennese musical life and was elected Director (Leader) of the orchestra when the *Liebhaber-Concerte* commenced. A number of these concerts were also directed by the celebrated violinist Franz Clement, known to Beethovenians for premiering his Violin Concerto.

In the opening concert season 1807–08, Clement directed performances of Beethoven's First, Second, and Fourth Symphonies as well as his First Piano Concerto.[5] From Thayer we learn:

> 'The audiences were composed exclusively of the nobility of the town and foreigners of note, and among these classes the preference was given to the cognoscenti and amateurs ... [In] twenty

meetings, symphonies, overtures, concertos, and vocal pieces were performed zealously and were received with general approval.[6]

The twenty concerts took place in Vienna between 12 November 1807 and 27 March 1808. The first concert was given in the Mehlgrube — a venue where balls and concerts featured in the social calendar and where Mozart had once performed. Other concerts were held in the *Festsaal* of the University. Audiences were by subscription or invitation and could number over 1,300. Ten of the twenty concerts included works by Beethoven: Symphonies No. 1 (twice), No. 2 (twice), No. 3 (twice), and No.4. Other works of Beethoven's that received performances were his Piano Concerto No.1 and the Overtures to *The Creatures* of *Prometheus* and Collin's *Coriolan* (twice). Schindler recalls

> 'Beethoven ... became associated with this Society of devoted music lovers. At a December meeting of the group he himself conducted the *Eroica* Symphony and the première of the *Coriolan* Overture. At a later gathering he conducted the B-flat major Symphony, which was greeted this time with far louder applause than when it was first given.'[7]

In 1807, the twenty-one years old Carl Maria von Weber heard a play-through of the Fourth Symphony and did not find it to his liking. George Grove recalls Weber's response to the music:

> 'I have just come from the rehearsal of a symphony [the B-flat major] by one of our newest composers [Beethoven]; and though ... I have a

tolerably strong constitution, I could only just hold out, and five minutes more would have shattered my frame and burst the sinews of my life ... The first violincello (bathed in perspiration) says that for his part he is too tired to speak, and can recollect nothing like the warming he has had since he played in Cherubini's last operas. The second violincello is of the opinion that the Symphony is a musical monstrosity, revolting alike to the nature of the instruments and the expression of thought, and with no intention whatever but that of mere show-off.'

Weber continued:

'First a slow movement full of short disjointed ideas, at the rate of three or four notes per quarter of an hour; then a mysterious roll of the drum and passage of the violas, seasoned with the proper quantity of pauses and *ritardandos*; and to end all a furious *finale*, in which the only requisite is that there should be no ideas for the hearer to make out, but plenty of transitions from one key to another — on to the new note at once! never mind modulating! — above all things, throw rules to the winds, for they only hamper a genius.'[8]

In his later years, Weber modified his headstrong opinions of Beethoven's music and became an admirer, for example, of *Fidelio* that he championed with enthusiasm.

1808

The *Allgemeine musikalische Zeitung* (*General music newspaper — AmZ*) was a German language periodical that commenced publication in 1798 under the direction of its owner and founder Gottfried Christoph Härtel. Its publisher was Breitkopf & Härtel of Leipzig with whom Beethoven had many negotiations. The periodical reviewed musical events taking place in the German-speaking nations and in other countries. As such, it was amongst the first to bring to the attention of the musically minded public an awareness of Beethoven's compositions and of their originality — that the periodical's contributors frequently found to be all too disturbing. In 1800 the *AmZ* published a review ostensibly in celebration of Joseph Haydn, to whom it accorded 'the first place' with regard to his symphonies and quartets, 'wherein no one has yet surpassed him'. Beethoven, a still relatively unknown composer, is not, however, overlooked; the reviewer comments how he may even usurp the venerable master 'if he calms his wild imaginings'. In due course the *Allgemeine musikalische Zeitung* received news of Beethoven's compositions with increasing respect.

In the *AmZ* issue for 27 January 1808, titled 'News from Vienna', the journal's music correspondent was mostly captivated to report on a concert held to celebrate the marriage of Francis I to his third wife Maria Ludovica. A performance of Gluck's Opera *Armida* [that he considered to be rather 'too modern-sounding'] had been given on 9 January to an invited audience that consisted of the Emperor and his new wife together with their household. We are told:

> '[The] boxes [were] filled with the diplomatic corps, the entire parterre full of ladies in their finery, upon whom many millions of diamonds seemed to sparkle ... all this made a unique, truly uplifting occasion.'

In addition to remarking on this event in the royal, social

calendar, the music correspondent also commented on a performance of Beethoven's Fourth Symphony that had taken place on 27 December 1807 at one of the *Liebhaber* concerts – it had also been performed at an earlier benefit concert on 15 November. Of the December performance the correspondent observed:

'The subject of modern music leads me naturally to Beethoven's newest Symphony in B flat, which was repeated at our local amateur [*Liebhaber*] concert under the direction of the composer. In the theatre it did not succeed greatly, but here it received a great deal of what seems to me to be well-deserved applause. The *Allegro* is very beautiful, fiery, and rich in harmony, and the minuet and trio also have a distinct, original character. In the *Adagio* one might sometimes wish that the melody were not so much divided up between the various instruments ...'.[9]

1811

On 23 January the *AmZ* published an article titled 'News from Leipzig'. This related to the annual concert for the benefit of elderly musicians and their widows and opened with Beethoven's Symphony No. 4 – in an edition published by the Industrie-Comptoir. The *AmZ's* music correspondent reported:

'This as yet apparently little known, spirited work (B-flat major, E-flat major, B-flat major) contains a solemn, magnificent introduction, a fiery, brilliant, powerful *Allegro*, an *Andante* that is well crafted and charming throughout, a very original, wonderfully attractive scherzando, and

> a strangely put-together, but effective, finale. On the whole, the work is cheerful, understandable, and engaging, and closer to the composer's justly beloved Symphonies Nos. 1 and 2 than to Nos. 5 and 6. In the overall inspiration we may place it closer to No. 2; the curious individual turns of phrase, by which Beethoven has recently frightened many performers and angered many listeners, and which hinder rather than further the effects, are not used excessively. The Symphony, which is anything but easy to perform, was played extremely well and was applauded unanimously.'[10]

The concert ended with a performance of Beethoven's concert aria *Ah! perfidio*. Composed in 1795 or 1796 it was very popular in Beethoven's lifetime. Regarding Beethoven's support of charitable enterprises, as mentioned in the *AmZ* review, over time Beethoven became a staunch supporter of benefit concerts for Vienna's Widows and Orphans that was later recognised by him being conferred the honour of the freedom of the city.

1812

On 3 June the following year the *AmZ's* the music correspondent informed readers of the musical productions heard during the Winter Season in Mannheim:

> 'The first evening [of the season] opened with the Symphony in B-flat major of the musical *Jean Paul*, Beethoven, which had not yet been heard here *publicly* — a work upon which the composer has bestowed all the originality and energy shown by the earlier productions of his muse, without

> marring its clarity with bizarreries, such as disfigure many of his works, excellent examples being the *Pastoral* Symphony and the *Eroica* — a work that in genius, fire, and effect can be compared only to the C minor Symphony and in clarity only to the first in C major, but that in difficulty of execution can be compared to none.'[11]

From the foregoing it is evident that even in such a musically active city as Leipzig, some five years had elapsed before the Fourth Symphony received its first performance since it had first been heard in the salon of Prince Lobkowitz. Of perhaps greater interest is that the *AmZ's* music correspondent likened Beethoven to the contemporary German writer Jean Paul. This was the pen name of Johann Paul Richter that he styled in homage to the French writer Jean-Paul Rousseau. Richter's writings were immensely popular at the time with their *Beethovenian* overtones of early Romanticism.

1813

On 6 January 1813 a concert took place in Vienna's Grosse Redoutensaal. It was directed by the French violinist Pierre Rode with whom Beethoven was on friendly terms; it was to him Beethoven dedicated his last Violin Sonata Op. 96. At the concert in question, Rode programmed the first movement of the Fourth Symphony — by now several years old. When Beethoven heard of the concert he was, though, none too pleased, as is evident in a letter he wrote in early January to the Countess Maria Fuchs — one of the many women of noble birth with whom he was then acquainted. He complained to her:

> 'Give Rode my best [wishes], only tell him that I

> must reproach him that he has not asked me for something new or still unknown from among my compositions.'

To put these words into context, we recall that at this period Beethoven was at work on the Seventh and Eighth Symphonies and had, musically-speaking, moved on from his Op. 60.[12]

Later in May, Joseph von Varena requested Beethoven to send him the scores of some compositions that he required in fulfilment of charity concerts that he was organizing in Graz. These were to benefit *The Society of Ursulines* to whom Beethoven referred as 'The Reverend Ladies'. Varena was a highly placed lawyer, a resident of Graz, and an active member of the Steiremärkischer Musikverein. Beethoven had made Varena's acquaintance in 1812, whilst visiting the spa at Teplitz, and thereafter remained on friendly terms with him. On 27 May, Beethoven responded to Varena's request informing him of his intention to send him three choruses and a bass aria with chorus, from his stage music to the *Ruinen von Athen*, as a well as a march and *two symphonies*.[13] According to Thayer, the latter were the Fourth and Fifth Symphonies.[14] As a result of Varena's endeavours, Graz audiences came to know various works of Beethoven that they might not otherwise have had an opportunity to hear at this time.

On 11 August the music correspondent of the *AmZ* reported on concerts that had taken place in Milan; these included performance of six symphonies that had not been heard there before. Three of these were Mozart's, namely K. 543, K. 551 (*The Jupiter*) and K. 504 (*The Prague*). The latter were apparently given preference over Haydn's symphonies. The music critic then remarked:

'Attention was now focused on Beethoven. The one in B-flat major was performed ... It did not please at all. The ... one in C minor was revered and it was compared to the First Symphony by this master, in C major. Finally, the *Pastoral* ... pleased only now and then, and people said: "Si vede il gran genio, ma c'è poco canto" – 'There is great genius here, but little song'.

The correspondent elaborated:

'[People] in Italy wish to pass judgement upon Beethoven's music immediately upon first hearing it (and you can easily imagine *how*). His C minor Symphony only pleased uncommonly after repeated hearings; probably the same thing will happen with the *Pastoral* and the Symphony in B flat.'[15]

1816

On 30 October 1816 a short notice appeared in the *AmZ* under the heading 'News from Kassel'. What the music critic has to say illustrates how, ten years after its composition, the Fourth Symphony was still proving to be a challenge, notwithstanding its relatively restrained manner, by Beethoven's standards:

'That this composer follows an individual path in his works can be seen again from this work; just how far this path is a correct one, and not a deviation, may be decided by others. To *me* the great master seems here, as in several of his recent works, now and then excessively bizarre, and thus, even for knowledgeable friends of art, easily incomprehensible and forbidding.'[16]

1819 – 1821

The Vienna concert season of 1819–20 was significant for the introduction of a new series of concerts promoted under the title of *Concerts Spirituels*. These were styled on a concert series, of the same name, that had been founded in Paris some years earlier. The aim of both series was to offer public concerts whose programmes combined sacred choral and instrumental music. The Vienna concerts owed their inception to Franz Xaver Gebauer, an organist-composer, choirmaster, music director of the city's Augustinian Church, and a committee member of the *Gesellschaft der Musikfreunde*. A notice in the *Allgemeine musikalische Zeitung* announced:

> 'On 1 October 1819, a new concert series was started, soon to be known as the *Concerts Spirituels* ... Herr Gebauer makes the proposal to form a special society of a moderate number to bring to performance only symphonies and choruses excluding all virtuoso music [pure display music] and bravura singing.'

The 'moderate number' refers to the performers who were all amateurs and who played largely from sight. In the eighteen concerts of the first season, 1819–20, Beethoven's first four symphonies were performed together with the *Pastoral* Symphony.

The second season (1820–21) consisted of ten concerts which included the Symphonies in C minor, Op. 67, A major, Op. 92, and F major, Op. 93. In 1821–22 the *Eroica* appeared once more with Symphonies One, Two and Six and in 1825 it received a further performance alongside Symphonies Five and Six.[17]

1822

In 1822 the Fourth Symphony was evidently continuing to disturb the music critic of the *AmZ*. On 12 June he reported on the music that had been performed earlier on 28 May at the Lower Rhine Music Festival. The second concert of the Festival had incorporated a performance of the Fourth Symphony that the music correspondent described as being 'familiar to you'. For him, though, it contained 'more bombast than substance'. He considered the performance to have been 'capably managed' — a tribute, albeit a modest one, to the skill of the musicians. The critic appears to have been more impressed by a rendering of the Overture to Mozart's *The Magic Flute*, that also featured on the programme, disposing him to remark '[It] gripped and transported me'.[18]

1825

In 1825 the violinist Karl Holz was assisting Beethoven as his secretary-factotum — he had temporarily supplanted Anton Schindler in this capacity. In January, the violinist Ignaz Schuppanzigh was commencing a series of subscription concerts with his newly formed String Quartet. He was first violin and the other members were Karl Holz, second violin; Franz Weiss, viola; and Joseph Linke cello. Although by profession an official in Vienna's Finance Office, Holz, was an accomplished violinist and conductor — he occasionally directed the *Concerts Spirituels*. From these circumstances we learn of a further performance of the Fourth Symphony. On 2 April, Holz called on Beethoven in order to consult him about the tempi of the Fourth Symphony. Holz was doubtless aware of Beethoven's wish to have his symphonies performed at their correct tempi. This resolve had been strengthened, a few years earlier, with the introduction of Maelzel's metronome — of which Beethoven had become a pioneering advocate. Holz was preparing to conduct the Fourth Symphony at one of the concerts of the Gesellschaft der Musikfreunde. It took place two days later in Vienna's Redoutensaal.[19]

The *Berliner Allgemeine musikalische Zeitung* (*BAmZ*) was a journal founded in 1824 by the music theorist Adolf Bernhard Marx in collaboration with the Berlin music publisher Adolph Martin Schlesinger. Marx created the journal out of what was originally a supplement to *Der Freymüthige*, entitled *Zeitung für Theater, Musik und bildende Künste*. The publication of a new music periodical in Berlin occurred at a time when the city, not then noted for its musical life, was on the verge of becoming a cosmopolitan centre. The new journal enjoyed an unexpectedly high degree of popularity owing, in large part, to Marx's editorial style. In contrast to the Leipzig *Allgemeine musikalische Zeitung*, the *BAmZ* focused on detailed analyses of works as opposed to merely reporting on individual musical events.

In its issue of 25 May 1825, the *BAmZ* published an article by the poet and respected music critic Ludwig Rellstab — known to Schubertians for contributing the texts to the first seven songs of the composer's *Schwanengesang*. The article in question was titled, 'Travel Reports by Rellstab — Vienna'. Rellstab enthused about the Fourth Symphony:

> 'If I were called upon to give an opinion on this long-familiar work, I would undertake to point out that practically no other work of Beethoven's shows so effective control of the overall form as in this Symphony. The individual movements are so beautifully juxtaposed, everything develops so

naturally, as only the most accomplished master would be able to bring about, for: "Only from perfected powers can grace step forth".'[20]

1826

Heinrich Carl Breidenstein was a native of Beethoven's home town Bonn where he was Professor of musicology at the University. His pioneering lectures covered the history, theory, aesthetics, and psychology of music. He was active in the town's musical life as an organizer and conductor of concerts and founded an orchestra and choral society that gave performances of Beethoven's works. It was Breidenstein who first suggested that a memorial to Beethoven should be erected in Bonn that was subsequently unveiled, with much ceremony, in 1845.

On 17 December 1826, Breidenstein wrote in enthusiastic terms in support of Beethoven in the journal *Bonner Wochensblatt* which, as its name implies, had a circulation in the neighborhood of Beethoven's home town. He opens his account:

> 'It falls within my purpose to gradually acquaint the local music-loving public with the outstanding recent symphonies, and specifically with those of Beethoven. Everyone recognizes the extraordinary nature of Beethoven's achievement in this area, and he is rightly considered to be the founder of a new (that is, the newest) epoch in instrumental music, inasmuch as he uses the materials of his art in a manner that was not yet fully granted to his great forerunners Haydn and Mozart — although this by no means compromises their originality.'

Breidenstein next draws on the writings of Ernst Theodore Hoffmann — one of the most prominent proponents of Beethoven's instrumental music in the early nineteenth century. He did much to further the recognition of Beethoven's accomplishments and to place his music within the context of literary Romanticism. Breidenstein quotes Hoffmann who placed Beethoven alongside Haydn and Mozart:

> ' "[Haydn's] symphonies lead us into a vast green meadow, now into a joyous, colourful crowd of fortunate people ... Into the depths of the spirit kingdom we are led by Mozart. Fear surrounds us, but in the absence of torment, it is more a foreboding of the infinite — In this way, Beethoven's instrumental music also opens up to us the kingdom of the gigantic and unsurmountable. Glowing beams shoot through the kingdom's deep night, and we become aware of gigantic shadows that surge up and down, enclosing us more and more narrowly and annihilating everything within us, leaving only that interminable longing, in which every pleasure that had quickly arisen with sounds of rejoicing sinks away and founders." '

Breidenstein next affirms: 'What Hofmann says here about Beethoven's instrumental music in general is entirely appropriate to the B-flat major Symphony'.

He elucidates:

> 'The introduction to the first movement begins with fearfully drawn-out minor sonorities followed by staccato ones, and flows with growing

brilliance into the onward *Allegro*. The theme of the *Adagio* is as simple as it is original. Two tones (E flat descending to B flat), which are repeated like the strokes of two unlike hammers, run through the entire movement and are united with the sweeter melodies, taken up first by this, then by that, then by all the instruments. The principal motive in the minuet actually falls into two-four time, but is here forced into three-four, producing a unique, one might say comically indignant, effect. In the Trio the wind instruments begin a rich but earnest melody, which seems to be mocked by the violins and other string instruments, inasmuch as they interrupt it with isolated, playful motives, which completely decline participation and, by means of a joyous *unisono*, contend for victory. The re-entry of the minuet both ends and renews the struggle. The full splendour of the combined effect is then developed in the finale.'[21]

TRANSCRIPTIONS

Donald Francis Tovey was an advocate of the realization of orchestral music through the genre of piano reductions and, thereby, its further enjoyment. What he has to say provides a fitting introduction to this part of our discussion of the Fourth Symphony, bearing on the manner in which it was presented to the public, in the form of transcriptions, in the years following its composition:

> 'People who can play pianoforte duets should not despise the humble four-hand arrangements of symphonies. The non-musician needs every

variety of stimulus to his imagination that he can get, and the stimulus of taking an active part in music is of all stimulation the least liable to become narcotic.'[22]

Beethoven himself was reluctant to make transcriptions of his own works and, when he did sanction such adaptations of his music, he placed them in the hands of his most trustworthy piano pupils, namely, Carl Czerny and Ferdinand Ries. Noteworthy transcriptions of his own-making include: the String-Quartet arrangement of the Piano Sonata in E major, Op. 14, No. 1; a partial piano transcription of the Seventh Symphony; and, most significant of all, his four-hand piano-arrangement of the *Grosse Fuge*.

What vexed Beethoven, in particular, was the publication of *unauthorised* transcriptions of his works — that he usually condemned for their lack of facility. On 20 October 1802, he had a notice placed in the *Wiener Zeitung* complaining of the publication of two String Quintet arrangements derived from his First Symphony. These had been published by Breitkopf & Härtel without his knowledge. He protested:

'The making of transcriptions is on the whole a thing against which nowadays (in our prolific age of transcriptions) a composer would merely struggle in vain.'[23]

The following year, on, 22 October 1803, Beethoven learned of a proposal that occasioned him to have a further notice displayed in the *Wiener Zeitung* stating:

'WARNING: Herr Karl Zulehner, an engraver at Mainz, has announced an edition of my

> complete works for the pianoforte and stringed instruments. I consider it my duty to inform all friends of mine that I have nothing whatever to do with this edition ... Furthermore, I must point out that such an edition of my works, undertaken illegally, can never be complete, inasmuch as several new ones are already to appear in Paris; and these Herr Zulehner, who is a French national, my not reprint.'[24]

Despite Beethoven's publicly-expressed words of caution, piano and chamber transcriptions of his Fourth Symphony appeared from various composer-arrangers and publishers during his lifetime. In this part of our text We identify the more noteworthy of these.

An early transcription for piano of the Fourth Symphony came from the hand of Freidrich Stein. In the context of Beethoven, the virtuoso pianist, Stein deserves a few words of introduction. His father, Johann Andreas Stein, was one of the most gifted and inventive piano and organ builders in the second half of the 18th century. Stein's workshop delivered excellent instruments, characterised by various new developments and techniques such as the 'Viennese action' — characterised by its lightness of touch. Three of Stein's children, namely, Nannette, Matthäus Andreas, and Friedrich, relocated to Vienna where they became friends of Beethoven. Nanette and her husband Andreas Streicher founded one of the most successful piano factories in Vienna. Friedrich, an accomplished pianist, transcribed piano adaptations of Beethoven's Fourth Symphony and the Overture *Coriolan*. Since Friedrich died in 1809 he must have composed these soon after the first performances of the Fourth Symphony and the Overture in 1807.[25]

Friedrich Stein had intentions to make further transcriptions of Beethoven's Fifth and Sixth Symphonies. This is evident from a letter Beethoven wrote on 4 March 1809 to the publisher Breitkopf and Härtel. He asked Härtel if he was interested in such an undertaking and what he would be prepared to pay.[26] Härtel's reply is not known but he appears not to have been interested in the proposition; Stein's arrangement, for two pianos, of the Fourth Symphony was subsequently published in 1809 by the Kunst- und Industrie-Comptoir.

In 1813 another Freidrich, the German musician Friedrich Mockwitz (1773–1849), published a transcription of the Fourth Symphony for piano four-hands. He had made similar arrangements of the symphonies of Haydn and Mozart as well as transcriptions of their overtures and string quartets. On 30 March 1804, the *AmZ* published a review of Mockwitz's transcription that had been recently published by Breitkopf & Härtel of Leipzig. The music correspondent opened with a brief panegyric in support of the Fourth Symphony:

> 'This wonderful work, rich in imagination and full of life, in which, almost as in Beethoven's Sixth Symphony, what serves and what constitutes music are placed close to each other in their extent, bent together, and as much as possible blended – has here been arranged for two keyboard players with insight and diligence, without being made difficult to perform.'

Notwithstanding his enthusiasm, the *AmZ's* music critic realized transcriptions have their limitations:

> 'In those places where the effect is based primarily

upon the charm of particular instruments, [a transcription] can scarcely go further than to produce a pleasant recollection for those to whom the original is not unknown. The same is true of those pieces where the very full ornamented but gentle accompaniment of the string instruments is added to very simple, sustained notes of the wind instruments. Apart from these places, the work makes even in this form a distinctive effect and invigorates irresistibly.'

The critic revealed the growing awareness of Beethoven's symphonies amongst the musically-minded public:

'[Beethoven's] symphonies have now been so widely disseminated that the reviewer scarcely needs to add that this Number 4 is the one in B-flat major whose original appeared four or five years ago.'[27]

In 1815 Beethoven wrote to his former piano pupil Ferdinand Ries, then established as a successful composer in London, requesting his assistance. It appears Beethoven was aware that transcriptions had been made, in England, of his first six symphonies and he requested copies of these to be sent to him for the use of one of his '*most trusted and dearest friends in Vienna*' — Beethoven's italics. He does not identify the friend in question but provided Ries with the following details:

'Nos. 1, 2, 3.
Grand Symphonies composed by L. van Beethoven
Arranged by Mr. Masy.

'Nos. 4. 5. 6.
Grand Symphonies performed at the Philharmonic Society
Composed by L.van Beethoven, arranged for 2 Violins, 2 Tenors,
1 Flute, 2 Violincellos and Basso by W. Watts
London.'[28]

Other transcriptions of the Fourth Symphony include the following instrumental arrangements:

> String quintet (2 violins, 2 violas, cello), anonymous composer, Kunst- und Industrie-Comptoir, 1809
> Septet (2 violins, 2 violas, flute, cello, double bass or 2 cellos), by W. Watts. L. Lavenu, 1810
> 2 pianos, thought to be by Anton Diabelli, Kunst- und Industrie-Comptoir, 1819
> 2 pianos eight hands, by August Horn, Breitkopf und Härtel (date unknown)
> 2 pianos eight-hands, by Theodor Kirchner, Peters (date unknown), and
> for piano four-hands, by W. Watts, Simrock, 1823.

In 1830 the celebrated composer-pianist Johann Nepomuk Hummel made a quartet-arrangement of the Fourth Symphony for flute, violin, cello, and piano. This was published by Schott of Mainz, Germany's second oldest music publisher after Breitkopf & Härtel that had been founded by Bernhard Schott in the year of Beethoven's birth, 1770. On 23 April 1830, the Journal *Iris* carried a review of Hummel's transcription whose opening remarks pay tribute to the fame of Beethoven's Fourth Symphony as it was perceived in 1830:

'About Beethoven's Fourth Symphony, which is perhaps the most admirable of all his works, we may well be excused from commenting further ... [The] arrangement having been made by so experienced and gifted a musician as Hummel, can hardly have failed to turn out well.'

The music critic justified the making of transcriptions:

'Not everyone has the opportunity to hear the greatest orchestral creations in their original integrity; thus, arrangements of this sort, which make them accessible to smaller groups of players, should be taken gratefully by all fair-minded persons. Performances on the pianoforte alone is not easy, indeed, if one makes strict demands of oneself, it is very difficult. Such a splendid work, however, may indeed require some effort, and one will gladly make the sacrifice in diligence in order not to lose as little as possible of the effect.'[29]

For much of Beethoven's life Carl Czerny, his extraordinarily gifted piano pupil, served the composer in a number of ways. For example, he premiered the composer's First Piano Concerto in 1806 and in February 1812, when still only twenty-one, he premiered the taxing *Emperor* Piano Concerto. After Beethoven's death, in 1827, Czerny made arrangements for piano duet of all nine Beethoven symphonies that were published between 1827 and 1829 by Heinrich Albert Probst.

In time, Czerny's piano transcriptions were eclipsed by the more grandiose transcriptions of Franz Liszt. He made piano transcriptions of all Beethoven's nine symphonies that preoccupied him over a period of almost thirty years. The pianos available to Liszt had a more extended octave-range and greater sonority than those of Czerny's day. Such instruments — precursors of the modern-day concert grand — doubtless served to embolden Liszt in his keyboard figuration.

By 1837, Liszt had completed transcriptions of the Fifth, Sixth, and Seventh Symphonies. In 1839, Heinrich Adam heard Liszt play his arrangements of the last three movements of the *Pastoral* Symphony. Although not a musician himself — he was a painter of landscapes and architectural subjects — he wrote in the *Allgemeine Theaterzeitung*:

> 'Only an artist like Liszt, who, in addition to a limitless veneration of Beethoven, possess the rare gift of understanding the great German composer; only such an artist was able, and could venture, to undertake so hazardous an undertaking'.[30]

In 1843, Liszt arranged the third movement of the *Eroica* Symphony that was later published in 1850. It was not until 1863 that Beethoven's publisher, Breitkopf & Härtel, suggested to Liszt that he should transcribe the complete set of Beethoven symphonies. He applied himself to the task with the diligence of a disciple following in the steps of his master. He noted down the names of the orchestral instruments, for the pianist to imitate, and added pedal marks and fingerings for the benefit of amateurs and sight-readers. The full set of transcriptions was finally published in 1865, bearing a dedication to Hans von Bülow — himself a pianist possessed of formidable powers. Musicologist Alan Walker is of the opinion Liszt's Beethoven-symphony transcriptions 'are arguably the greatest work of transcription ever completed in the history of music'.[31]

BEETHOVEN — THE GEWANDHAUS — FELIX MENDELSOHN

Writing of the year 1804, and the assimilation of Beethoven's orchestral music, Thayer remarks:

> 'The First Symphony had hardly left Hoffmeister's press when it was added to the repertory of the Gewandhaus Concerts at Leipzig, and during the three following years was repeatedly performed at Berlin, Breslau, Brunswick, Dresden, Frankfurt-am-Main, and Munich.'

This success, alongside that of other of the composer's works, disposed Thayer to further enthuse:

> 'Beethoven, then, although almost unknown personally beyond the limits of a few Austrian cities — unaided by apostles to preach his gospel, owing nothing to journalist or pamphleteer ... had, in the short space of eight years, by the simple force of his genius as manifested in his published works, placed himself at the head of all writers for the pianoforte, and in public estimation had risen to the level of the two greatest of orchestral composers. The unknown student that entered Vienna in 1792, was now, in 1804, a recognised member of the great triumvirate, Haydn, Mozart and Beethoven.'[32]

The Gewandhaus Orchestra became a staunch supporter of Beethoven's orchestral music. It performed. Beethoven's First Symphony in 1801 with that of his Second Symphony following in 1804 and the *Eroica* in 1807. In 1809, the *Pastoral* Symphony was heard and in the same year the C minor Symphony was given from manuscript parts. The Gewandhaus Orchestra featured the *Choral* Symphony in its 1826 concert season. Ten years later, the standing of the Gewandhaus Orchestra was raised by the appointment of Felix Mendelsohn as the Orchestra's Music Director – *Gewandhauskapellmeister* – an appointment he held until his untimely death in 1847. Mendelsohn looked on his appointment as Director of the Gewandhuas Orchestra as a great opportunity. On 6 November 1835 he wrote to his family describing his new post:

> '[Not] being a government appointment, subordinate to any official authority, but a free association formed for the purpose of promoting good music, and desirous of engaging a director able to use the best means towards the realisation of that purpose.'[33]

Mendelsohn established his authority as a conductor but exercised it lightly. He strove to achieve the strict tempo of a movement and was ready to acknowledge the skills of the players. Significantly, he paid closer attention to the details of the score than pervious conductors of the orchestra. In his study of conductors and the orchestral tradition, Percy Young writes:

> 'Mendelsohn, one of the most personable young men ever to stand on a rostrum, and blessed with a talent for public relations, established the real authority of the orchestral conductor, whose pre-eminence dates from 4 October 1835, when Mendelsohn undertook his first concert with the Gewandhaus.'[34]

The programme opened with Mendelsohn's own *Calm Sea and a Prosperous Voyage* and concluded with Beethoven's Fourth Symphony.

BEETHOVEN'S RECEPTION IN FRANCE

The early reception of Beethoven's music, in France – and to his symphonies in particular – was ambivalent. His critics considered it to be 'bizarre' and incomprehensible. However, his devotees, albeit mostly young musicians, considered his works to be no less than representing 'the standard of judgement for, and gateway to, all future developments in music'.

We detect something of the early aloofness towards Beethoven's music from the circumstances of the composer and music publisher Heinrich Simrock – brother of the more famous music publisher, in Bonn, Nikolaus Simrock. Heinrich sold music in Paris from 1802 but was not, apparently, very successful in finding purchasers for Beethoven's compositions among even the more musically-minded during the early 1800s.

The Italian violinist Giuseppe Cambini lived in Paris for a period and from there he contributed articles to the *Allgemeine musikalische Zeitung* and the *Tablettes de Polymnie*. Writing in the latter, in 1811, he remarked on the impression made on him after hearing Beethoven's first two symphonies:

> 'The composer Beethoven, often bizarre and baroque, sometimes sparkles with extraordinary beauties. Now he takes the majestic flight of the eagle, then he creeps along grotesque paths. After penetrating the soul with a sweet melancholy, he soon tears it by a mass of barbaric chords. He

> seems to harbour doves and crocodiles at the same time.'³⁵

Beethoven's symphonies, as remarked, found favour In Paris with young musicians — not surprisingly, being open-minded and unburdened with the weight of tradition. Students at the Conservatoire commenced a series of concerts — *Concerts Français* — that were modestly called *Exercises Publics*. Notwithstanding their amateur status, they were assisted by the forward-looking François-Antoine Habeneck. From 1804 he served as their *lauréat*, initially as their violinist-leader and from 1806 as their conductor. Such was the precision of the students' playing that the correspondent writing in a contemporary issue of *The Quarterly Music Magazine* enthused: '*The Exercises* of [the Conservatoire's] pupils are the most brilliant concerts in Paris.'³⁶

It is a measure of Habeneck's standing that he joined the orchestra of the Opéra-Comique in 1804 and shortly after moved to the Opéra where he succeed Rudolphe Kreuzer — of *Kreuzer* Violin Sonata fame — as principal violin. From 1821 to 1824 he was Director of the Opéra. Habeneck's most lasting achievements, though, were the introduction of Beethoven's music to France and the founding of the *Société des Concerts du Conservatoire*. Of this, Adam von Ahnen Carse writes:

> 'Habeneck, judging that the time was not yet ripe for disclosing the beauties which lay in the works of the great Viennese masters, was in no hurry to force them on an unwilling public, and waited patiently for the moment when he could embark on the plan which he had so much at heart.'³⁷

In 1818 Habeneck was put in charge of the *Concert Spirituel* at the Opéra and later, in 1821, he performed Beethoven's Second Symphony. Habeneck was aware, however, of the audience's objection to its *Larghetto*, obliging him to replace it with the *Allegretto* of the then popular Seventh Symphony. In his recollections Hector Berlioz, an ardent admirer of Beethoven, recalled that the enterprise – which today would be condemned as being nothing less than an atrocity – was so successful that the entire Symphony had to be repeated, in this form, and, moreover, met with great applause. Berlioz further recalls 'after this concert, Beethoven's [French] admirers began to outnumber his detractors'.[38]

By 1828, Habeneck had at his disposal some 86 instrumental players alongside a choir of some 79 voices. Their programmes became known as the *Société des Concerts*. Six regular concerts were given in each music season, occasionally supplemented by two or three others. A typical programme included a symphony, an overture, a concerto, and one or two choral items. Between 1828 and 1837, Beethoven's symphonies were performed on no fewer than 68 occasions, compared with 7 Haydn symphonies and 5 of Mozart. During the period 1838 and 1847, Beethoven's symphonies once more dominated the orchestral repertoire with 90 performances against 23 of Haydn and 15 of Mozart.

Beethoven's music in France found another champion in François Castil-Blaze. Although at heart a composer, he was known more widely to the public as a musicologist, music critic, and music editor – he published various editions of Beethoven's works. From 1820 his articles appeared in *Musical Chronicles* and the *Journal des débats*; these were mostly in the form of reviews of concerts. From 1827 his articles began to appear in the *Revue musicale* in which he enthused:

> 'The Symphonies of Beethoven present a union of all musical potentialities, the severe harmony blends without effort with the charms of melody. The phrases of song, conceived together with the sentiment of varied harmonies which receive those phrases, accept without repugnance all the embellishments that a wise hand puts upon them.'

In 1830 Castil-Blaze wrote about a performance of the Fourth Symphony:

> 'Its last movement was distinguished by beautiful craftsmanship and elaboration, by surprises, by unexpected entries and effects that would appear bizarre if Beethoven had not embellished them through the whole magic of his art, the whole fire of his genius.'[39]

By 1828, Beethoven's music had made a lasting impression on the youthful Hector Berlioz. This was despite the difference between the musical language that he himself was fashioning and that of his hero — his own *Symphonie Fantastique* was but only two years distant. Berlioz particularly admired Beethoven's slow movements — notably that of the Seventh Symphony — and disposed him to liken Beethoven to 'an eagle soaring aloft'. Writing to his father on 20 December 1828, he exclaimed: 'This is no longer music but a new art.'[40]

Berlioz's contribution to the promotion of Beethoven came initially not through performances of his music but through his critical writings. For example, in 1829, he published a short biography of Beethoven in the *Critique Musicale*. After his return from Italy in 1832 — Berlioz had been awarded the *Grand prix de Rome* – he commenced a series of studies prompted by concert performances at the Conservatoire; these were published in a number of journals especially the *Journal des débats* and the *Revue et gazette musicale de Paris.*'

Throughout, Berlioz regarded himself as one of Beethoven's champions in France, in opposition to the more reticent members of the old school who remained hostile to the composer's new-sounding music. He relates, for example, his attempt to win over his own teacher Jean-François Le Sueur, following a performance of the Fifth Symphony at the Conservatoire. To his regret, though initially shaken by the experience, Lesueur remained aloof.

The German writer and historian Friedrich von Raumer travelled extensively in Europe, including visits to England. He thereby had opportunities to hear concerts given in Paris and London. Writing of these in the April 1836 issue of *The Musical World*, he states:

> 'If I may venture ... to compare London with Paris, the result, on the whole, is this. The mass of instruments may be equal; but the effect is better in the *Salle* at Paris, and the French performers on the stringed and wind instruments seem to me more thoroughly artists than the English. In London, you hear distinctly that the music is produced by many; whereas, in Paris, it appears as if the whole were the work of one mind and one hand.'[41]

Friedrich von Raumer's observations lead us to further considerations of the reception of Beethoven's music beyond continental Europe.

BEETHOVEN'S RECEPTION IN ENGLAND

Among the earliest records of the Fourth Symphony appearing in England is that which relates to the enterprise of the amateur musicologist John Sterland. He is known to have copied-out the work in full score that he dated 13 June 1807. His score bears the Title Page: 'Sinfonia by Beethoven written in Score by [John] Sterland, Op. 60. London 13 June 1807 Performed at the Harmonic Society.'

Sterland did not state the date of the Harmonic Society's performance but it is thought it must have taken place shortly after he wrote out the score. If this is the case, it antedates by 13 years or more the Philharmonic Society's first known performance that took place in 1821 – to be discussed shortly. The Harmonic Society concerts were held in a number of London's taverns in the early years of the nineteenth century and earned praise 'for having promoted and kept alive the love of and practice of the higher order of instrumental music in London'. Sterland, in due course, presented his score of the Fourth Symphony to the newly-founded Philharmonic Society.[42]

The Harmonicon was an influential monthly music journal that was published in London from 1823 to 1833. It was edited for a period by William Ayrton (1777-1858.). In his role as concert impresario, he is remembered today by Mozartians for introducing London audiences, in 1817, to the first performance of *Don Giovanni*. Ayrton was by nature something of a polymath being elected to Fellowships of both the Royal Society and the Society of Antiquaries as well as being a founder-member of the Royal Institution. His wide-ranging attainments were reflected in his writings for *The Harmonicon* that included such diverse topics as music reviews, news of contemporary musicians and composers, and articles on music theory including studies of the physics of sound.

On 21 February 1825, Beethoven's Fourth Symphony was performed together with Haydn's Military Symphony, under the direction of Sir George Smart. This disposed the music critic of *The Harmonicon* to compare the two works and their composers:

> 'The two symphonies performed in this concert are less well-known than most of the other orchestral compositions of the same authors. That by Beethoven has few traits that strike generally, and at once, but possesses much to please the true connoisseur, and betrays none of those eccentricities that are often at variance with established rules. The other [Haydn's], which is the eleventh of those composed for Salomon's Concerts, is much more airy and popular in its style.'[43]

Johann Peter Salomon was a founder member of the Philharmonic Society and, as an accomplished violinist, led its first concert on 8 March 1813. Moreover, it was as a consequence of Salomon's enterprise that London audiences had become acquainted with Haydn's last symphonies that he had commissioned from Haydn in 1791 and 1795. Although Salomon lived and worked in London for most of his life, he was a native of Bonn where the youthful Beethoven had made his acquaintance. He died in London in 1815. Learning of this, Beethoven remarked in a business letter to Ferdinand Ries – then living and working in London: 'I am greatly saddened at the death of Salomon, for he was a noble-minded man whom I remember well from my Childhood.'[44]

Mention has been made of the Philharmonic Society of London. The early reception of Beethoven's orchestral music in England is closely associated with the foundation years of The Philharmonic Society.

The Society was founded in London in 1813. Its stated aims were

> 'to promote the performance, in the most perfect manner possible, of the best and most approved instrumental music [and] to encourage an appreciation by the public in the art of music'.

The founding Directors were enterprising insofar as they resolved to promote 'that species of music which called forth the efforts and displayed the genius of the greatest masters'. These included contemporary composers such as Beethoven, Cherubini, and Carl Maria von Weber. Beethoven's pupil Ferdinand Ries was elected a Director of the Society and was active in the promotion of his former teacher's symphonies. Perhaps Ries's most significant contribution, in this context, was the role he played in 1822 in encouraging the Philharmonic Society to commission Beethoven's *Choral* Symphony.

The following is a record of the number of occasions the Philharmonic Society performed Beethoven's symphonies from the period of its inception to the close of the nineteenth century:

Symphony No. 1, (19); Symphony No. 2, (39); Symphony No. 3, (52); Symphony No. 4, (54); Symphony No. 5; (77); Symphony No. 6; (69); Symphony No. 7, (65); Symphony No. 8, (47); and Symphony No. 9, (73).

The Society gave its first concert in the Argyll Rooms, Regent Street, London on Monday 8 March 1813. The impresario Johann Salomon was the Leader and Muzio Clementi directed at the piano. A Beethoven symphony was performed but was not identified in the records. At the second concert, on Monday 15 March, another Beethoven symphony was performed, also not identified. At the fourth concert, on 3 May, the British-African violinist George Polgreen Bridgetower took part in a performance of a Beethoven string quartet; Bridgetower is remembered today as the intended dedicatee of the *Kreutzer* Violin Sonata. In this opening season of concerts, J. B. Cramer and Charles Neate — the latter an associate of Beethoven and a founder-member of the Society — performed at the pianoforte. On 21 June another Beethoven symphony was performed.

In his Centenary survey of The Philharmonic Society of London (1813–1912), Myles Birket Foster states:

> 'It is difficult in these days of musical plenty [1912], when there is a superfluity of orchestral organisations, and a still greater number of good players in want of orchestral positions, to realise that in the year 1813 there was no permanent orchestral society in London open to the public ... there was no band fit to play really good orchestral works, by which is meant those symphonies, overtures, etc., ... In this state of starvation, The Philharmonic Society was founded to provide a pabulum.'[45]

Until March 1816, the programmes for the Philharmonic Society made reference to a symphony by Beethoven simply with the designation 'Symphony' — with no further information. It is assumed these citations refer to the first four symphonies. From April of that year his symphonies are more specifically identified. So, for example, the concert for

15 April 1816 includes the Fifth Symphony in C minor which, moreover, was the first performance of this work in England.

The Fourth Symphony was advertised, as such, for the first time in the 1821 concert season when it was performed on 12 March., This concert was particularly memorable since it also included the first performance, in England, of Mozart's Piano Concerto in D. The soloists was Cipriani Potter — himself a founder-member of the Philharmonic Society.

In 1817 the composer-pianist Cipriani Potter had made Beethoven's acquaintance in the hope of receiving composition lessons but Beethoven declined — his only composition pupil was the Archduke Rudolph. On 29 April 1836, Potter recalled his meeting with Beethoven in an article for *The Musical Times* under the title *Recollections of Beethoven*. In this he sought to dispel the then popular view of the composer as being 'a morose and ill-tempered man'. He insisted: 'This opinion is perfectly erroneous.' Potter acknowledged Beethoven could be irritable, passionate, and sometimes of a melancholy mind but all of which affectations he believed arose from his deafness. Regarding Beethoven the composer, Potter stated:

> 'The most prominent feature in Beethoven's music is the *originality* of his ideas even in his mode of treating a subject and the conduct throughout of a composition. No author is so free from the charge of *mannerism* as Beethoven.'[46]

With Beethoven's growing fame, and the deepening understanding of his music, Potter's article was republished in *The Musical Times* on 1 December 1861 — the year of the London Great Exhibition. This may not be entirely coincidental, since several of Beethoven's works were subsequently performed at its venue in the Crystal Palace.

The Fourth Symphony had to wait until 19 May 1823 for its second-named performance. By this time, it was the custom to feature some six or seven symphonies by Beethoven in the Society's concert programmes. The Fourth Symphony was given the following year and again in 1825. In the history of Philharmonic Society, 1825 was, however, more memorable for including the first performance of Beethoven's so-called *Choral* Symphony. On the Title Page of the score Beethoven had written: 'Geschrieben für die Philharmonische Gesellschaft in London'. The actual performance of the *Choral* Symphony took place on 21 March under the direction of Sir George Smart.[47]

The Fourth Symphony proved to be a popular work with audiences at the Chrystal Palace. George Grove, writing in his *Beethoven and his Nine Symphonies* (1896), records the work was performed no fewer than thirty-three times over the period 1855 to 1899.[48]

LATER NINETEENTH-CENTURY RECEPTION

On 22 June 1828, the music correspondent of the *Beiblatt der Kölnischen Zeitung* reported on a series of concerts, one of which featured Beethoven's Fourth Symphony. The occasion disposed him to enthuse:

> 'The Symphony ... demonstrated in an unsurpassable performance that nothing more magnificent has been written of this kind, nor might ever be written again. The orchestra was truly enchanted, and loud applause rewarded the performers, who showed us instrumental music in its true greatness and magnificence.'[49]

Later in the summer of 1828 the Journal *Cäcilia* published a review of the Rhine Music Festival that had taken place in Cologne. *Cäcilia* was published by the Mainz publisher Schott's and Sons who had given their Journal its title in honour of *Cecilia*, the patroness of musicians. The Director of the 1828 Festival was none other than Ferdinand Ries, now returned to his native homeland. Once more Beethoven's music found an appreciative critic: 'There are no words to describe the deep, powerful spirit of this work from his *earlier* and most beautiful period.'

Regarding the interpretation of the music, however, the critic was more guarded:

> 'The performance was adequate to the work. Some details were superbly performed, while others fell below expectation. Particularly the *Adagio* and the menuetto and trio have their great difficulties. Least praiseworthy of all were the tempos, which at times were two fast and even inconsistent. Excessively fast tempos often obscure the most beautiful effects. The portrait becomes unclear, obscured by mist, even blotted entirely.'[50]

Perhaps Ries, as Beethoven's former pupil, thought he should respect his teacher by loyally adhering, in his interpretation of the Symphony, to his suggested metronome tempo-indications that the critic clearly considered to be too fast — a view sometimes expressed today even by adherents of so-called 'authentic performance'.

Adolf Bernhard Marx made significant contributions to music criticism in his role as editor of the influential periodical *Allgemeine musikalische Zeitung*. He was an admirer of Beethoven's music and paid homage to him in his *Ludwig van Beethoven: Leben und Schaffen*, Berlin, 1859. On 20 March 1830, Marx wrote a review of the Fourth Symphony in the *AmZ's* sister Journal the *Berliner Allgemeine Musikalische Zeitung*. He opened his discourse with rhetorical questions and enlarged on what Beethoven and his music meant to him:

> 'What did Beethoven want? What could he give? Simply a composition of great and noble design? So, our aestheticians would advise him — those aestheticians, old and new, who see music only as a play of forms, who expect only the most generalized evocation of unspecified feelings, since it is incapable of "expressing the concrete". Beethoven had a different point of view. As an artist, he could do nothing with lifeless abstractions; to create life, life from out of his own life, was his calling, as it is for all artists. The artist knows what his art is capable of; he before all others; he alone.'[51]

Marx compared Beethoven, the symphonist, with other composers:

> 'The Beethoven symphony was but a repeated testimony to the fulfilment of the highest duty of the artist. It is one of the works of the immortal tone-poet and belongs in the same sphere with Mozart's, Spohr's, and other symphonies ...'.

At the time Marx was writing, Louis Spohr (1784—1859) was considered to be 'one of the central figures of the early Romantic period in music, equally celebrated for his operas and his instrumental works'.

Marx continued:

> 'Everyone can sense that whatever drew the poet into his work filled him completely; with love he dedicated himself completely to it; and this *true love* shows him in every moment what is proper, protects him from every foreign admixture, from every caprice. His flattering words calm and inspire us just when the time is right; his most powerful storms of sound shake us, albeit to a joyous trembling; he uplifts us even with the sense of his terror and our own weakness, whereas the arbitrary strokes of other works offend us with a sense of blindly raging power.'[52]

When the youthful Felix Mendelssohn was resident in Paris, he had occasion to write on 14 February 1832 to his former music teacher Carl Friedrich Zelter. His remarks provide insights into the state of musical performance in Paris at that time and of the reception of Beethoven's symphonies:

> '[It] is the Paris Conservatoire that gives the concerts; but more than that, it is the most perfect performance to be heard anywhere ... The general arrangements, too, are very appropriate and sensible ... Moreover, the hall is a little one, so that for one thing the music makes twice the effect and we hear every detail twice as clearly and for another thing the audience is small, very select, and yet seems a large gathering.'

Beethoven's orchestral music was clearly finding favour, as Mendelsohn remarked:

'The musicians themselves delight in Beethoven's great symphonies; they have made themselves thoroughly familiar with them, and are happy to have mastered the difficulties. Some of them, including Habeneck himself, undoubtedly have a perfectly genuine love of Beethoven; but as for the others, who are the loudest in their enthusiasm, I do not believe a word they say about it; for they make this an excuse for decrying the other masters — declaring Haydn was merely a fashionable composer, Mozart an ordinary sort of fellow; and such narrow-minded enthusiasm cannot be sincere. If they really felt what Beethoven meant, they would also realize what Haydn was, and feel small; but not a bit of it, they go briskly ahead with their criticism. Beethoven is uncommonly popular with the concert public, as well, because they believe that only the connoisseur can appreciate him; but only a small minority really enjoy him, and I cannot abide the disdainful attitude towards Haydn and Mozart; it infuriates me.'[53]

When Felix Mendelsohn was appointed as the conductor of the Gewandhaus Orchestra in Leipzig he set about enriching the town's musical life by developing the skills of the orchestra. On a visit to Leipzig in 1840, the German conductor and composer Ferdinand Hiller remarked on the improvements Mendelsohn — his close friend — had achieved:

'[Mendelsohn's] talent as a conductor was especially favourable to the performance of orchestral works. Vigorous leaders had managed, before his time, by the help of their fiddling, to put plenty of spirit and precision into them but no one had ever imagined so deep a conception or such artistic finish in the performance of the great symphonies.'

Mendelsohn's first concert with the Gewandhaus Orchestra took place on 4 October 1835 and was attended by the composer's biographer Wilhelm Lampadius (*Felix Mendelsohn Bartholdy: ein Gesammtbild, eines Lebens und Wirkens*, Leipzig, 1886). Of Mendelsohn's interpretation, Lampadius recalled: 'Beethoven's B-flat major Symphony was given with a precision till then unknown in Leipzig'. He continued:

'Mendelsohn had carefully studied the piece, and directed it in person – an arrangement new to us, but of eminent propriety. There had been no lack of excellence in former days, when the concert-master and the first violin had the direction of Beethoven's symphonies, yet of that nice shading, that exact adaptation of each perfect harmony of all instruments, attained under Mendelsohn's direction, there had been no conception. The performance of the B-flat Symphony – that ethereal soulful music – was one of the master-effects gained by Mendelsohn as a director. Every rendering threw new light upon it, so that the listeners were compelled to say, "So perfectly performed we never heard before".'[54]

In 1838 the Scottish-born music critic and musicologist

George Hogarth published a *Musical History, Biography, and Criticism* that contributed to establishing Beethoven's reputation with English — and particularly London — audiences. He gave prominence to Beethoven of whom he enthused:

> 'As a musician, Beethoven must be classed along with Handel, Haydn, and Mozart. He alone is to be compared to them in the magnitude of his works, and their influence on the state of the art.'

Beethoven's orchestral compositions earned Hogarth's particular endorsement:

> 'In his music there is the same gigantic grandeur of conception, the same breadth and simplicity of design ... In Beethoven's harmonies the masses of sound are equally large, ponderous, and imposing as those of Handel, while they have a deep and gloomy character particular to itself. As they swell in our ears and grow darker and darker, they are like the lowering storm-cloud on which we gaze till we are startled by the flash, and appalled by the thunder which bursts from the bosom. Such effects he has especially produced in his wonderful symphonies. They belong to the tone of his mind, and are without parallel in the whole range of music ...'.

Hogarth expatiates:

> 'The music of Beethoven is stamped with the peculiarities of the man. When slow and tranquil in its movement, it has not the placid composure

of Haydn, or the sustained tenderness of Mozart; but it is grave, and full of deep and melancholy thought. When rapid, it is not brisk or lively but agitated and changeful – full of "sweet and bitter fancies" [quoting Shakespeare: *As you like it*] – of storm and sunshine – of bursts of passion sinking into the subdued accents of grief, or relieved by transient gleams of hope or joy. There are movements, indeed, to which he gives the designation of *scherzo*, or playful; but this playfulness is as unlike as possible to the constitutional jocularity to which Haydn loved to give vent in the *finales* of his symphonies and quartets ... They contain, however, many of Beethoven's most original and beautiful conceptions; and are strikingly illustrative of the character of his mind.'[55]

Cosima Wagner was the illegitimate daughter of the Hungarian pianist and composer Franz Liszt and his mistress Marie d'Agoult. Her second marriage to Richard Wagner was an act of sustained veneration for the man and his music. Much of this is preserved in the 2,500 pages of her Diary. In her Diary of 17 September 1873, Cosima recorded remarks made by Wagner about Beethoven:

'At lunch he talks about Beethoven's Fourth Symphony. [Wagner remarked]: "One could not understand the striking difference between it and the *Eroica* if one did not see that it contains the seeds of that unworried mood (containment of emotion) which first emerged in the *Eroica* and the quartets and rose to a godlike humour – runner-up to the Eighth!".'[56]

George Bernard Shaw's fame as a playwright and polemicist has eclipsed his reputation for being a discerning music critic. Eugene Gates, of the Faculty of the Royal Conservatory of Music, Toronto, writes:

> '[Shaw] was ... the most brilliant British music critic to emerge in the late-nineteenth century. His vision of the ideal critic was not a passive reporter of musical events, but rather a vital and initiating force within the music community.' (*Journal of Aesthetic Education*, Vol. 35, No. 3, 2001.)

Shaw was committed to the principle of making music criticism both intelligible and entertaining. To this end he invented the persona of *Corno di Bassetto* (in music, the basset horn) to serve as his spokesperson. Shaw's collected writings on music fill no fewer than three sturdy volumes. On 22 August 1877, Shaw attended an all-Beethoven concert at London's Covent Garden at which the Fourth Symphony was performed by 'the Philharmonic band'. Shaw was not impressed, as he remarked later in the 29 August issue of *The Hornet* – a London newspaper with a reputation for promoting acerbic criticism. *The Hornet*, for example, once portrayed Charles Darwin as an elderly orang outang! Of the Fourth Symphony, and its performance, Shaw wrote disparagingly:

> 'The Symphony was that in B flat, No. 4 and in its execution was in nowise remarkable. In deference to popular impatience, symphonies are played at Covent Garden without repeats, and, considering the conditions of performance, we think this is a wise arrangement.'[57]

We encounter Shaw once more, this time writing in the capacity of music critic for *The Scots Observer* – sometime in 1890. Shaw was apparently no more impressed by the standard of orchestral performance than he had been in 1877:

> 'In all Beethoven's symphonies there is one movement, and only one, that the Philharmonic band can play, and that is the *finale* of the Fourth, which consists almost entirely of semi-quavers. Yet this vapid and useless orchestra needs but a good conductor – a conductor who at rehearsal would do something more than race it through.'

Shaw was himself a capable pianist and played piano-reductions of Beethoven symphonies with his sister. This disposed him to quote Richard Wagner:

> '"[The] real reason of the success of Beethoven's music is that people study it not in concert rooms but at their own pianos; and the irresistible power is thus fully learnt – though in a roundabout way." '[58]

RECEPTION NEARER TO OUR OWN TIME

In 1914 The British musicologist Donald Francis Tovey was appointed to the Ried Chair of Music at the University of Edinburgh. The title derived from its founder General John Ried who was an army officer and musician. Tovey played an active part in the establishment of the Ried Orchestra for which he supplied scholarly concert programmes that subsequently formed the basis for his influential Essays in Musical Analysis. To celebrate the twenty-fifth concert of the Reid Orchestra, on 4 March 1920, Tovey published a souvenir pamphlet titled, The needs of an Orchestra. In this he remarked on the challenges the performance of Beethoven's Fourth Symphony posed, particularly for a newly established orchestra:

> 'Not until we had some practice in things of which inexperienced players and listeners can see the difficulty, could we expect to have a clear idea of the kind of tone production and rhythmic accuracy that is necessary for playing simple things broadly, naturally, and persuasively. I confess to have been much amused at finding that one of the programmes, in which we played Mozart's E flat Symphony and Beethoven's Fourth Symphony, was considered in some quarters a marked success on the ground that for once we had selected things well within our powers. Mozart is always a very dangerous composer for brilliant modern performers to attempt at sight. As for Beethoven's Fourth Symphony, that serene expression of health and happiness is one of the most nerve-racking things a young orchestra could possibly tackle, and I kept it back for three years before I ventured to produce it.[59]

Writing more specifically about the Fourth Symphony, and about the nature of musical prejudice, Tovey states:

> 'As in later years, Beethoven followed his gigantic Seventh Symphony by the terse and unshadowed comedy of his Eighth, so he followed his *Eroica* Symphony (the longest of all his [symphonic] works except the Ninth) by a symphony of the

proportions and scope of which are, except for three powerful passages, almost within the range of Mozart and Haydn. Yet the exceptional passages are in no way "out of the picture"; and the contemporary critics who accused Beethoven's Fourth Symphony of every fault a symphony could have, would have had more difficulty than we in picking them out. The solemn spread over five minutes; the dramatic hush and crescendo leading to the recapitulation in the first movement; the astonishing middle episode of the slow movement, and the double alternating repetition of scherzo, and trio; these are the features we recognise as peculiarly Beethovenish in this work. To contemporaries, they were mere additional eccentricities in a work in which the whole style, being Beethoven's, was [considered] notoriously extravagant; and the chances are that if the work had been produced under the name of Mozart or Haydn, the outstanding features would not have been noticed at all, and the work would have been sleepily accepted as a masterpiece at once.'[60]

The English writer and music critic Sir Neville Cardus was widely read for his contributions to *The Manchester Guardian*; he counted several distinguished musicians amongst his personal friends. Cardus's approach to music criticism has been described as 'romantic and instinctive'. Yehudi Menuhin once remarked: 'He reminds us that there is an understanding of the heart as well as of the mind ... in Neville Cardus, the artist has an ally.' We encounter Cardus in 1934 on the occasion when Sir Thomas Beecham gave a concert in Manchester's Free Trade Hall – to mark his becoming President of the Hallé Society:

'[We] were given a performance of the Fourth Symphony of Beethoven which caused the work to sound the loveliest and most spontaneous in existence. It was good to have Beethoven put before us in a way in genial and approachable vein. But how remarkable is the introduction — to a symphony so light-hearted! The processes of musical imagination are so free they can go beyond the logic of the prosaic universe; the shaded solemnity of the Fourth Symphony's opening does not contradict the jolliness to come, yet there is no logic of the reason that can say why the symphony should begin with a moment so vast and mysterious. Sir Thomas conducted the introduction with a magnificent feeling for intensity and expansion; then, he gave us a transition to the *allegro vivace* which was a masterpiece of instantaneous rhythmical release, subtle shading, headlong, but perfectly controlled.'[61]

The Austrian conductor, composer and pianist Felix Weingartner is today primarily remembered for his interpretations of Beethoven's symphonies — he was the first conductor to make commercial recordings of all nine symphonies. As a young boy, Weingartner recalls his first awakening interest in Beethoven that was to set the course of his future destiny as a major interpreter of the composer's works. He attended a concert given by the Styrian Musical Association that included a performance of Beethoven's Fourth Symphony. Of this experience, Weingartner relates:

'The very first notes of the introduction fired me with enthusiasm; I listened breathlessly and was startled when the mood of mystery was suddenly dispelled by *fortissimo* tones. In my opinion nothing else that evening, not even the rest of the Symphony, could compare with that introduction. Once again, I declared my intention of becoming a musician ... The deep impression which Beethoven's Fourth Symphony, particularly the introductory movement, had made on me at the concert, induced my music-master to go through all the symphonies with me beginning with the First, in the form of duets which he played with me.'[62]

Writing in his widely popular *The Concertgoer's Companion* (1984), Anthony Hopkins comments:

'[The] Fourth [Symphony] has always tended to be overshadowed by its two mighty neighbours. Nevertheless, the Fourth has magical qualities, and is perhaps the best orchestrated of the nine. The opening in particular is unforgettable for the liberty of its sound. During the slow introduction the music seems to be feeling its way towards a destination only dimly perceived. At last, after long deferment, a series of brief ascending scale-fragments, crisp and sharp as the crack of a whip, leads us into the main theme *Allegro*.'[63]

In 1985 the music scholar and author Rossana Dalmonte interviewed the Italian composer Luciano Berio, noted for his pioneering work in electronic music. Their conversation turned to the reason why musically-minded people are drawn to talking about certain kinds of music. Berio suggested:

> 'They don't necessarily have to be works that we identify with, but ones we draw close to and observe – in other words love – because they seem more richly impregnated with history than do other works because we find ourselves more freely able to invest them with what is perhaps the unrealized best of ourselves, and with a more open expression of our musical unconsciousness.'

Beriot qualified his generalisations:

> 'Nobody thought of asking Beethoven what music was. But nowadays they do ... But to imagine Beethoven explaining his Fourth Symphony, for the benefit of court dignitaries, is grotesque, indeed quite repulsive.'[64]

The French composer, organist and ornithologist Olivier Messiaen is known for his exploration of sound-worlds and sonorities inspired by bird song. Aware of this, in 1992 fellow Frenchmen, the composer and music critic Claude Samuel, discussed with him a theatrical production with a religious theme centred on Saint Francis. The stage production was by the theatre director of the Paris Opera Sandro Sequi. This entailed various bird sounds and, significantly, the depiction of an angel. Samuel raised the moment in the production when a gerygone and kestrel announce the entrance of the angel. This prompted Messiaen to respond:

> 'Unconsciously, Sandro Sequi thus brought back two memories for me: that of Berlioz referring in his *Memoirs* to Beethoven's Fourth Symphony – Berlioz spoke highly of the slow movement,

which he said reminded him of "an angel looking at the world" — and that of two paintings by Ciurlionis that specifically depict an angel high atop a footbridge from which it looks upon an enormous rotating globe, representing our planet or the movement of the universe.'

Messiaen concluded the conversational exchange with words of Saint Francis that also make a fitting conclusion to this part of our discussion of the reception of Beethoven's Fourth Symphony in B-flat major, Op. 60:

' "God dazzles us by an excess of truth; music transports us to God by an absence of truth." '[65]

---

[1] For accounts of Potter's and Russell's recollections of Beethoven, see: Oscar George Theodore Sonneck, *Beethoven: Impressions of Contemporaries*, Oxford University Press, 1927, p. 101 and p. 108; Peter Clive, 2001, pp. 269–70 and pp. 298–99; and Anne-Louise Coldicott, *Reception* in: Barry Cooper, *The Beethoven Compendium: A Guide to Beethoven's Life and Music*, 1991, p. 294.

[2] Jonathan Del Mar, Ludwig van *Beethoven, Symphony No. 4 in B-flat major, Op. 60, Critical Commentary*. Bärenreiter Kassel, BA 9004 (undated).

[3] Elliot Forbes editor, *Thayer's life of Beethoven*, 1967 pp. 416–17. George Grove also discusses the reception of the Fourth Symphony, see: *Beethoven and his Nine Symphonies*, 1896, pp. 126– 27.

[4] Anton Felix Schindler, *Beethoven as I Knew Him* edited by Donald W. MacArdle and translated by Constance S. Jolly from the German edition of 1860, 1966, pp. 136–37.

[5] Peter Clive, 2001, p. 73 and pp. 149–50.

[6] Elliot Forbes editor, *Thayer's Life of Beethoven*, 1967 p. 428.

[7] Anton Felix Schindler, *Beethoven as I Knew Him* edited by Donald W. MacArdle and translated by Constance S. Jolly from the German edition of 1860, 1966, p. 138.

[8] George Grove, *Beethoven and his Nine Symphonies*, 1896, pp. 101–02.

[9] Wayne M. Senner, Robin Wallace and William Meredith editors, *The Critical Reception of Beethoven's Compositions by his German Contemporaries*, 1999, Vol.1, pp. 54–55.

[10] *Ibid*, pp. 55–56.

[11] *Ibid*, pp. 56–57.

[12] For the context and discussion of the circumstances, see: Theodore Albrecht, 1996, Vol. 2, Letter No. 169, pp. 2–3, note 4.

[13] Emily Anderson editor and translator, 1961, Vol. 1, Letter No. 424, pp. 418–19.

LATER RECEPTION: MUSICOLOGY

We draw our discussion of Beethoven's Fourth Symphony in B-flat major to a close in the form of a documentary-style collection of texts. These are derived from the writings of musicologists and performing artists bearing on the musicology inherent within the composer's Symphony, Op. 60. They are presented in the chronological sequence of their publication. Thereby, they convey the evolving estimation felt for this composition from the period of its first appearance to nearer to our present time.

The authorities, from whom quotations are derived, are identified with brief, prefatory texts. These are intended to assist the reader place what the authorities have to say within the wider context of their musicological understanding, and appreciation, of Beethoven's music. Those authorities who have been introduced already, in our opening section *Selected Writings*, are designated with an asterisk — *.

HEINRICH FRIEDRICH RELLSTAB

Heinrich Friedrich Rellstab was a capable pianist but is remembered primarily as a poet and music critic. Such was the influence of his writings about music it is said he had 'an effective monopoly on music criticism'. Schubertians owe a lasting debt to Rellstab for providing him with the texts to the first seven songs of his posthumously-titled S*chwanengesang*. It was also Rellstab who conferred on Beethoven's Piano Sonata Op. 27, *quasi una fantasia*, the epithet *Moonlight*. Writing of Beethoven's Fourth Symphony, in the 25 May 1825 issue of the *Berliner Allgemeine musikalische Zeitung*, Rellstab declared — in the evocative style of the period:

> 'Like an oppressive storm [the adagio] slowly and suddenly draws near, obscures the peaks of the mountains, hides the sun, and threatens with light thunder ... From time to time the wind instruments give added emphasis, as though a gentle, steadier sigh were urging itself between the uneasy drawings of breath ... Out of this bold splendour the irresistibly forward-rushing *allegro* [vivace] rises up and carries us triumphantly forward in a full, surging stream.
>
> 'Not only this but the movements in themselves are so superbly crafted that each is formed perfectly within itself ... The cheerful, yet frightfully daring minuet stands in opposition to its trio like man and wife. The minuet is agitated like the wild impetuosity of manly anger ... The trio, on

> the other hand, insinuates itself with gentle pleading and seeks to soothe the breast …'.
>
> 'I do not know how to describe how the joyfully mischievous and yet so lovely and graceful last movement of this Symphony affects me. It is a continually bubbling, living spring, which rushes gracefully past, sometimes in happy, teasing leaps and sometimes in a wavelike dance, always clear and always deep. Indeed, it is so deep that the sun and sky are mirrored in it, and we see through the clear water into the fullness of the universe, which only a great, noble soul can feel and so return. Full of the deepest, most heartfelt veneration I give thanks to the master, who through great genius created something so wonderful.'

As recorded in: Wayne M. Senner, Robin Wallace and William Meredith editors, *The Critical Reception of Beethoven's Compositions by his German Contemporaries*. Lincoln: University of Nebraska Press, in association with the American Beethoven Society and the Ira F. Brilliant Center for Beethoven Studies, San José State University, 1999, Vol.1, pp. 61–63.

HECTOR BERLIOZ*

Hector Berlioz published his thoughts on orchestral music and its instrumentation in his *Grand Traité d'Instruments et d'Orchestra* of 1843–44. Of Beethoven's Fourth Symphony he comments:

> 'Here, Beethoven abandons ode and elegy and returns to the style of his Second Symphony, less

solemn and elevated but perhaps no less difficult. The score is essentially lively, brisk, and cheerful, or else imbued with a heavenly sweetness. Save perhaps for the contemplative adagio introduction, the first movement is full of joy. The staccato motif that opens the *allegro* is merely a frame on which the composer hangs other melodies more worthy of the name so that what seemed initially to be the main theme turns into an accessory idea ... [After] a rather energetic *tutti*, the fist violins break the first theme into fragments with which they have a playful *pianissimo* conversation with the second violins; this ends in sustained dominant-seventh chords of the key of B natural ... After two such appearances, the tympani fall silent to let the strings gently murmur other fragments of the theme and arrive via a new enharmonic modulation at a B-flat, six-four chord. The tympani, entering again on B flat — now a true tonic instead of a leading tone, as it was the first time — continue the tremolo for about twenty measures ... [The] other instruments come into play, tossing incomplete bits of phrases into their progression above the continual growl of the timpani, reaching a climax on a general *forte* as a majestic B-flat triad is sounded by the full orchestra. This marvellous crescendo is one of the most musical inventions that I know. It scarcely has a rival besides the crescendo that ends the famous *scherzo* of the C minor Symphony ... That, in the [Fourth Symphony], starts *mezzo-forte*, dies away for a moment in a *pianissimo* that drifts under harmonies of vague, infinite colouring, then reappears with chords of a more settled tonality and explodes only when the cloud, veiling this modulation, has been wholly dissipated. It reminds one of a river whose peaceful waters vanish suddenly, only to emerge from their subterranean bed as a furious foaming cascade.

'As for the *Adagio*, it defies analysis. Its forms are pure, its melody so angelic and so irresistibly tender, that the consummate art of the structure is entirely concealed. From the first few measures, one is gripped by feelings that finally become painful in their intensity. Only in one of the giants of poetry is there anything to compare with this sublime page by the giant of music. Indeed, nothing resembles more closely the impression produced by this adagio than one's experience of reading in the *Divine Comedy* ... This movement seems like a sigh by the Archangel Michael when, overcome by an attack of melancholy, he stood on the threshold of the empyrean contemplating the cosmos.

'The scherzo consists almost of rhythmic phrases in duple time that are made to fit the movement's measures in triple ... The melody of the trio, given to the winds, is of a delicious freshness. Its tempo is slower than that of the rest of the scherzo, and its elegant simplicity is enhanced by contrast with the little phrases that the violins toss off like so many teasing sallies.

'The finale — gay and sprightly — returns to conventional rhythmic forms; it is a ceaseless chatter of sparkling notes, interrupted by some wild, rasping chords, angry outbursts like those .... elsewhere in the composer's work.'

Hector Berlioz, *Grand Traité d'Instruments et d'Orchestra*, Paris, 1843–45, as quoted in: Elizabeth Csicserry-Ronay, translator and editor. *Hector Berlioz: The Art of Music and other Essays: (A Travers Chants)*. Bloomington: Indiana University Press, 1994, pp.17–18. For a more accessible version of this text, see: Michael Austin, The Hector Berlioz website: *A Critical Study of the Symphonies of Beethoven* from *A Travers Chants*.

CLARA SCHUMANN

In her lifetime Clara Schuman was recognised for being one of the most accomplished pianists of her day. She received early instruction from her father who encouraged her to memorize the works she intended to perform in public — something of an innovation for the period. Clara came to public attention during the Vienna concert season 1837–38, when, still only eighteen, she gave a series of recitals that included such challenging pieces as Beethoven's *Appassionata* Sonata. Her marriage to her composer-husband Robert has, perhaps, unjustly, eclipsed Clara's own standing as a composer. On their wedding day Robert gave Clara a diary that now serves musicologists as a form of autobiography of their shared interests and accomplishments in music. (see, for example, Berthold Litzmann editor, Clara Schumann: *An Artist's Life, based on Material found in Diaries and Letters*. London: Macmillan; Leipzig: Breitkopf & Härtel, 2 Vols., 1913.

In 1862 Clara Schumann received an invitation to perform at the Paris Conservatoire. This was a considerable honour — and a measure of her musical standing — since ordinarily admission to perform at the Conservatoire was only after applying to do so in writing. One the works she performed was Beethoven's Piano Concerto in E-flat major

— *The Emperor*. On 21 March, Clara wrote to Johannes Brahms, her close friend and confident, of her experience of one of the Conservatoire's concerts:

> 'I heard a concert at the Conservatoire the other day; from the point of view of technique it was the most perfect I ever heard, but — cold. Everything is calculated for effect, and often the whole composition is sacrificed for that without compunction. They often play a magnificent theme without any light and shade or warmth, and then suddenly they bring out some one point in such a way that the whole audience is electrified. But nowhere else does one hear such *pp* and *ff*, such *crescendo* and *diminuendo*, for instance in Beethoven's B-flat major Symphony, the transition back to the subject in the first movement makes one quite cold down the back. I have never before heard the last movement taken so fast — but what perfection! They always take the quick movements too rapidly, at one moment comes a passage in which the violins have an opportunity for display, and the next a *presto* scale for the bassoon, and one thinks of the composer's meaning, if only each can shine by himself as a virtuoso.' [See the related remarks below on over-fast tempi by Richard Strauss]

Berthold Litzmann editor, *Letters of Clara Schumann and Johannes Brahms, 1853–1896*. New York, Vienna House.1971, Vol. 2, pp. 294–95.

SIR GEORGE GROVE*

In his *Beethoven and his Nine Symphonies* of 1896, Sir George Grove writes:

'The Fourth Symphony like the First, Second, and Seventh of the nine, opens with an introduction, adagio, to the first movement proper, *allegro vivace*, an introduction as distinct in every respect from its companions as if it were the work of another mind. It commences with a low B-flat *pizzicato* and *pianissimo* in the strings, which, as it were, lets loose a long holding note above and below in the wind, between which the strings move slowly in [a] mysterious phrase, in the minor key ... The introduction is thirty bars long, and as its close is approached the tone brightens, and the *Allegro* — the first movement proper ... bursts forth brilliantly in B-flat major ... This portion of the work is of the most bright and cheerful character throughout — the principal subject in staccato notes — but how different from the staccato notes of the introduction! — alternating with a smooth passage for the wind, and ending with a burst on the final chord.

'In the First Symphony ... Beethoven has taken the drum [tympany] out of obscurity in which it previously existed, as one of the merely noisy members of the band, and given it individuality. In the C minor Piano Concerto and in the Violin Concerto the drum is again brought into notice, but in the present working-out and in the next movement Beethoven goes further in the same direction, and gives his favourite a still more prominent role ... The drum begins a long roll on the keynote (B flat) which lasts twenty-six bars, the first eighteen of them being very soft, and the remaining eight increasing to *fortissimo*; and as the climax to this the original theme is returned to ... It is interesting to compare it with the corresponding portion in any one of Haydn's symphonies, and see how enormously music had gained, not in invention, wit, or spirit, but in variety of structure, colour, and expression, during the years preceding 1806.

'The second movement, adagio, is not only an example of the celestial beauty which Beethoven (the deaf Beethoven) could imagine and realise in sounds, but is also full of the characteristics of the great master. Here we rise from good humour and pleasure to passion, and such a height of passion as even Beethoven's fiery nature has perhaps never reached elsewhere ... The movement opens with a figure containing three groups of notes in the violins which serve as a pattern for the accompaniment of a great portion of the movement, and are also a motto or refrain, a sort of catch-word, which is introduced now and then by itself with great humour and telling effect — now in the bassoon, now in the basses, now in the drum ... We venture to call it the "drum figure". In its capacity of accompaniment to the heavenly melody of the principal subject, it is most lulling and soothing; when employed by itself it is full of humour.

'The workmanship throughout is masterly in combinations of instruments, and in imitative passages, and every embellishment possible; while at the same time the effect of the whole is pure and broad, and free from the faintest trace of *masquinerie* or virtuosity. "Believe me, my dear friend", says Berlioz ... "Believe me, the being who wrote such a marvel of inspiration as this movement was not a man. Such must be the song of the Archangel Michael as he contemplates the world's uprising to the threshold of the empyrean".'

'[In the third movement] we return to the key of B flat, and to the term "Minuet", which has vanished from the symphonies since No.1 ... The Minuet of the Fourth Symphony is, however, still further removed from the old accepted minuet-pattern than that of the First Symphony ... This movement shares with the corresponding portion of the Seventh Symphony the peculiarity that the Trio is twice given and the Minuet repeated each time ... In the present case the repetitions of both Minuet and Trio are given each time identically, the only addition being the three bars at the very end, in which, as Schuman says, "the horns have just one more question to put".'

'[Lively], vigorous, and piquant as are the first and third movements, they are in these qualities, surpassed by the Finale, which is the very soul of spirit and irrepressible vigour. Here, Beethoven reduces the syncopations and modifications of rhythm which are so prominent in the first and third movements, and employs a rapid, busy, and most melodious figure in the violins, which is irresistible in its gay and brilliant effect, while the movement as a whole is perfectly distinct from that of the first allegro. It is as much a *perpetuum mobile* as any piece ever written with that title ...

The working out is not less lively or humorous than that of the first movement ... [Though] full of drollery, Beethoven is constantly showing throughout how easy it is for him to take delight into a far higher atmosphere than mere fun. The movement places him before us in his very best humour: not the rough, almost course play, which reigns in the mischievous unbuttoned [*aufgeknopft*], rougher passages of the finales to the Seventh and Eighth Symphonies; but a genial, cordial pleasantry, the fruit of a thoroughly good heart and genuine inspiration. What can be gayer music than the following coda ... or what more touching than the passage in which he says goodbye in a tone of lingering affection as unmistakable as if he had couched it in words.

'So ends this delightful movement, and in parting from it, it is well to remember that it is the last gay *finale* that will be vouchsafed to us ... The finale of No. 5 is triumphant, of No. 6 religious, those of 7 and 8 romantic and rough; but the careless delight of this beautiful movement we shall encounter no more.'

George Grove, *Beethoven and his Nine Symphonies*. London: Novello, Ewer, 1896, pp. 106–25.

ERNEST MARKHAM LEE*

Ernest Markham Lee's, *The Story of the Symphony* (1916), introduced a generation of music lovers to Beethoven's symphonies and their place within the genre of orchestral music. Of the Fourth Symphony he remarked:

'The *Adagio* which preludes the work is of noble dignity, and forms a suitable commencement to a movement of large proportions. Starting with a solemn unison for strings, we soon hear disconnected quavers, a presage of the idea to be developed in the *Allegro*. The detached quavers and the unison idea serve amply for material, and with a gradually quickening "rush up" of the violins we are soon launched upon the merry and joyous allegro, with its gaily tripping subject ... One other idea — a syncopated one for the strings — completes the material of this movement, and after the usual repeat we enter upon the development. The ending of this section is of remarkable beauty, the drum being used as a harmonic factor; and the hushed chords lead by skilful change from the key of B to that of B flat. The "rush up" to the main subject is even more exhilarating than the first, and the same mood prevails in the regular recapitulation which follows, the short coda bringing all to a merry conclusion.

'A gentler and deeper note is touched in the *Adagio* — a long love-song of tender expression and of intense feeling. In the very first bar we have a rhythmic idea started by the second violins which is of prime importance, and is allotted to every instrument of the orchestra during the course of the movement, not even excepting the drums ... The movement contains a wealth of loveliness which permeates every bar, and the utilisation of matter is remarkable for its resourcefulness as well as for its extreme beauty.

'The *Minuet*, so called, has far more the characteristics of a scherzo than it had in the

14. Elliot Forbes editor, *Thayer's Life of Beethoven*, 1967 pp. 557–58.
15. Wayne M. Senner, Robin Wallace and William Meredith editors, *The Critical Reception of Beethoven's Compositions by his German Contemporaries*, 1999, Vol.1, pp. 58–59.
16. *Ibid*, pp. 59–60.
17. Elliot Forbes editor, *Thayer's Life of Beethoven*, 1967, pp[. 770–72 and David Wyn Jones, *The Symphony in Beethoven's Vienna*, 2006, p. 188.
18. Wayne M. Senner, Robin Wallace and William Meredith editors, *The Critical Reception of Beethoven's Compositions by his German contemporaries*, 1999, Vol.1, p. 60.
19. Elliot Forbes editor, *Thayer's Life of Beethoven*, 1967 p. 942.
20. Wayne M. Senner, Robin Wallace and William Meredith editors, *The Critical Reception of Beethoven's Compositions by his German Contemporaries*, 1999, Vol.1, p. 61. The words cited in double quotation marks are adapted from *Corinthians 2*.
21. Derived, in part, from the foregoing, pp. 64–65.
22. Donald Francis Tovey, *Beethoven*, 1944, pp. 15–16.
23. Emily Anderson editor and translator, 1961, Vol. 3, Appendix II, p. 1434.
24. *Ibid*, p. 1435.
25. For a portrait of Nannette Streicher, together with a brief history of her connection with Beethoven, see: Beethoven House, Digital Archives, Library Document B 155/b.
26. Emily Anderson, editor and translator, 1961, Vol. 1, Letter No. 199, pp. 217–18, note 6.
27. Wayne M. Senner, Robin Wallace and William Meredith editors, *The Critical Reception of Beethoven's Compositions by his German contemporaries*, 1999, Vol.1, p. 59.
28. Emily Anderson editor and translator, 1961, Vol. 2, Letter No. 594a, p. 546.
29. Wayne M. Senner, et al. (see above), pp. 67–68.
30. Quoted by Peter Clive, 2001, pp. 210–11.
31. Alan Walker, *Reflections on Liszt*, 2005.
32. Elliot Forbes editor, *Thayer's Life of Beethoven*, 1967 pp. 361–62.
33. Sebastian Hensel, *The Mendelsohn Family*, 1881, p. 333.
34. Percy M. Young, *The Concert Tradition: From the Middle Ages to the Twentieth Century*, 1965, pp. 162–63.
35. Quoted by Leo Schrade, *Beethoven in France: The Growth of an Idea*, 1942, pp. 28–29.
36. *Ibid*.
37. Adam von Ahnen Carse, *The Orchestra from Beethoven to Berlioz: A History of the Orchestra in the First Half of the 19th Century, and of the Development of Orchestral Baton-Conducting*, 1948, p. 90.
38. Robin Wallace, *Beethoven's Critics: Aesthetic Dilemmas and Resolutions during the Composer's Lifetime*, 1986, p. 108.
39. François Castil-Blaze quoted by Leo Schrade, *Beethoven in France: The Growth of an Idea*, 1942, pp. 28–29.
40. Michel Austin, translator, *Berlioz, Predecessors and Contemporaries*, The Hector Berlioz website. Originally published in: Hector Berlioz, *The Art of Music and other Essays* (A travers chants).
41. Adam von Ahnen Carse, *The Orchestra from Beethoven to Berlioz: A History of the Orchestra in the First Half of the 19th Century, and of the
42. Alec Hyatt King, *Musical Pursuits: Selected Essays*, 1987, pp. 126–36.

hands of Haydn and Mozart. In treatment too, it has the attributes of the lighter and more humorous style, especially in the use made of the opening idea of the violins. More allied to the older minuet is the section labelled trio, a somewhat long one, which leads to a return of the *Minuet*, and then both trio and minuet are repeated in their entirety — an unusual procedure which Beethoven also employed in his Seventh Symphony.'

'For Finale we have a busy bustling movement on running passages of semiquavers which seldom cease, forming a figure of accompaniment when they are no longer subject matter ... The whole Finale is of the most genial type, and forms a fitting ending to the gaiety and spontaneous delight of the entire movement.'

Ernest Markham Lee, *The Story of the Symphony*. London: Scott Publishing Co., 1916, pp. 61–63.

ROMAIN ROLLAND

Notwithstanding his celebrity as a philosopher, dramatist, novelist, essayist, art historian and Nobel Laureate (prize for literature in 1915) Romain Rolland wrote extensively on music and was appointed to the first chair of music history at the Sorbonne in 1903. His passion for music — he was an accomplished pianist — found expression in several studies of Beethoven who for Rolland was 'the universal musician above all the others'. His writings about the composer and his works include: *Beethoven and Handel* (1917); *Goethe and Beethoven* (1930); and *Beethoven the creator* (1937). His *Essays on Music* (1915) also includes a study of

Beethoven in his thirtieth year. Typical of Rolland's word-imagery is:

> 'The music of Beethoven is the daughter of the same forces of imperious Nature that had just sought an outlet in the man of Rousseau's *Confessions*. Each of them is the flowering of a new season'.

Rolland is here making reference to the autobiographical work *The Confessions of his fellow countryman Jean-Jacques Rousseau — published in 1782.*

Writing of the Fourth Symphony in *Beethoven and Handel*, Rolland described the work as being 'happy and serene' but considered it to be 'overshadowed by its two towering neighbours' — reference, of course, to the *Eroica* Symphony that preceded it and the Fifth Symphony that followed it. In his analysis of the Fourth Symphony he observes:

> 'The opening adagio sounds the only dark mood in the Symphony. It is lashed on to the allegro by some powerful violin scales. The flute, oboe and bassoon converse sportively over the second subject. A strange sequential passage in unison upon the strings in three-bar phrases following a happy little canon on the woodwind instruments and some powerful syncopations lead in to the development. An atmosphere of humour permeates the movement.
>
> 'The lovely melody which forms the chief theme of the adagio is given to the violins. It is accompanied by a strong persistent rhythmic figure, which is transferred later on to the drums

with great effect. The woodwind work and the horn passages are exquisite.

'The Third movement *allegro vivace* is full of fun, lively syncopations and duple-time effects giving it more of the nature of a *scherzo*. It has a charmingly tender trio and a coda of exquisite poetry ending with Schumann's "Just one more question for the horn to put" before the final crash. This is one of the longest movements which Beethoven has written in this form.

'The bright, sunny mood of the opening movements increases in the radiant finale. There, the modulations are surprising and the touches of humour delightful. The little skirmish on the part of the bassoon just before the return, the whimsical little notes on the flutes and the violins, the augmentation of the subject as it fades away into the stealthy questionings between the violins and bassoons near the end, are but a few of the many little quips and sallies.'

Romain Rolland, *Beethoven and Handel*. London: Waverley Book Co., 1917, pp. 116–17.

PAUL BEKKER

Paul Bekker was one of the most articulate and influential of German music critics of the early 20th century who imparted to his musicology the insights gained as a professional violinist with the Berlin Philharmonic Orchestra. Later, he was chief music critic for the F*rankfurter Zeitung*. Placing Beethoven in the context of other composers, Bekker states:

'Compared with the works of other musicians of the first rank, Beethoven's compositions are few in number and restricted in kind; a glance at the collected works of Bach, Handel, Haydn and of the short-lived Mozart and Schubert confirms this. But to deduce that Beethoven was, therefore, less creatively fertile would be wrong. The explanation lies in the peculiar nature of his genius as an artist. He was first a thinker and poet, and secondarily a musician.'

In his analysis of Beethoven's Fourth Symphony Bekker remarks:

'Like the Second Symphony the Fourth opens no clearly marked mood, yet the plan of the introduction in each of these works is strikingly different. In the earlier work we have an aimless, fantastic sequence of ideas, in the later, this indecisiveness of mood is part of the imaginative scheme of the whole work. The dreamy and romantic introduction is, however, no mere transitional device for arousing expectancy, but is based on the same pensive emotions which animate the *allegro* and their exercising a restraining effect upon the lively violin theme ... For a time, all elements of strife give way to an idyllic peaceful mood, but they reassert themselves in the recapitulatory section and their play becomes almost earnest till, in the coda, joy and peace are finally enthroned.

'The movement is conceived clearly in the romantic vein, hitherto only worked by the composer in the D major Symphony.

> 'The adagio is even more distinctly sentimental, and shows Beethoven in a light so unusual that several attempts have been made to connect this Symphony with some [emotional] adventure. The "Immortal Beloved" [Bekker is making reference to the composer's emotional attachments] is frequently seen as the source of the most intimate of all Beethoven's symphonic *adagios*; but ... we may well ascribe the work to the stimulation of some tense emotion such as the love-letter, whether aroused by the "Immortal Beloved", or some other, beloved. It is an expression of deep, absorbed happiness, and even the interruption of threatening minor keys cannot break the song. Mozart-like in its clear beauty and precision, and truly Beethoven-like in its breadth and depth of emotion ... With Haydn, the secondary themes are almost too luxuriant and the significance of the main theme is somewhat lost in consequence; but in the adagio of Beethoven's B-flat major Symphony, the first theme retains its predominance throughout.'

At this point in his text Bekker gives expression to reflections of a wider nature:

> 'These improvements in technique are all due to Beethoven's imaginative advance, his strict unity of conception, the highly individual character of his themes and the careful economy of construction, despite his overflowing wealth of ideas. In addition to these beauties, exquisite shading of tone, the skill with which the contrasts of strings and wind are utilised, the poetic *soli* for wind

instruments and kettledrums, all work together to produce an atmosphere of deep quiet happiness, which makes this adagio Beethoven's most perfect composition in lyrical vein.'

Turning to the other movements of the Fourth Symphony, Bekker continues:

'The third movement is entitled "Minuet", but this is no more than a title. It is not, indeed (like the corresponding movement in the *Eroica*), a *scherzo*, but it is not a minuet in the traditional manner. The violent alterations, the fury and intensity of emotion, the touch of weird fantasy make it highly characteristic of its composer, a new form, superficially resembling a blend of minuet and scherzo ... It is drama in a highly compressed form ...

'The finale possesses little of that variety of light and shade that characterises the preceding portions. It is full of everyday joyousness and points very clearly to Haydn's London Symphony (in B-flat major), which served as a model for the complete work.'

Bekker concludes his essay on the Fourth Symphony with a summative reflection:

'Regarded apart from its context, this movement would seem no more than a piece of light original humour, but its significance is heightened by its position within the symphonic organism. The course of the work hitherto shows an undercurrent of pensive gravity, melancholy, dreamy depression, but cheerful, even playful thoughts, a desire for the love of life and action make themselves felt. This conflict with the darker powers is reflected in the first movement and echoed in the third. In the adagio these opportunities are in some degree reconciled in a romanticism at once cheerful and melancholy. In the finale, the gay and active forces triumph; the opposing powers are reconciled, rather than defeated, through the sense of humour. The conflict is forgotten, and humour dances over hidden precipices. This development with its gay laughing changes at the end is, indeed, in the nature of an evasion; but it was a successful one and gave the work a roundness and completeness unattained in Beethoven's earlier symphonies.'

Paul Bekker, *Beethoven*. London: J. M. Dent & Sons, 1925, pp.166–69.

DONALD FRANCIS TOVEY*

Professor Sir Donald Francis Tovey, to give him his full title, espoused his scholarly views concerning Beethoven's music at length in his *Essays in Musical Analysis* (1935–41). Writing of the Fourth Symphony in the first of these he expatiates — in his characteristically uncompromising manner:

'The sky-dome vastness of the dark introduction is evident at the outset; but it is first fully understood in the daylight of the opening of the allegro ... The "spin" of the whole movement, tremendous as it is, depends entirely on the variety, the contrasts, and the order of themes and sequences, varying in length from odd fractions of bars ... to the 32-bar and even longer processes in the development ... The development keeps up the spin by moving on lines far broader than any yet indicated by the exposition. The delightful cantabile added as a counterpoint to the entries (in various keys) of the main theme, is one of the salient features ... The recapitulation is quite normal, and the coda is no longer than one of Mozart's usual final expansions.

'The slow movement is a full-sized rondo, a form which is extremely spacious when worked out in a slow tempo ... The main theme returns in a florid variation; and the middle episode, which follows is one of the most imaginative anywhere in Beethoven ... The coda consists of a final allusion to the main theme, dispersing itself mysteriously over the orchestra, till the drums make an early end by recalling the opening stoke of genius.

'[The] double repetition of scherzo and trio makes everything as clear as any dance, in spite of the numerous rhythmic whims ... Never have three short bars contained more meaning than the coda in which the two horns blow the whole movement away.

'The finale represents Beethoven's full maturity in that subtlest of all disguises, his discovery of the true inwardness of Mozart and Haydn; a discovery inaccessible to him whenever, as in a few early works (notably the Septet), he seemed or tried to imitate them, but possible as soon as he obtained full freedom in handling his own

> resources ... Everything is present in this unsurpassably adroit and playful finale; and it is all pure Beethoven ...'.

Donald Francis Tovey, *Essays in Musical Analysis*. London: Oxford University Press, H. Milford, 7 Vols., 1935—41; derived from Vol.1, pp. 36—37.

MARION SCOTT

Marion Scott studied violin and piano at the Royal College of Music and after graduating founded *The Marion Scott String Quartet*. Her great enthusiasm was to introduce contemporary music to London audiences, particularly that of Frank Bridge, Hubert Parry and Charles Villiers Stanford. However, Scott is primarily remembered today for her contribution to musicology. Her early writings were for such publications as *Music and Letters* and *The Musical Times* with her later, more substantial, researches appearing in *Grove's Dictionary of Music and Musicians*. She became a respected authority on the lives of Haydn and Mendelssohn but it is for her pioneering study of Beethoven with which Marion Scott's name will forever be most associated. This was published in 1934 by J. M. Dent & Sons, Ltd. as part of their *Music Masters Series*. In its later form *The Master Musicians*, Scott has the following to say about Beethoven's Symphony, Op. 60:

> '[With] his next Symphony No. 4 in B-flat major, Op. 60 ... [Beethoven] returned to the form — but not the spirit — of the symphony as Haydn knew it. The slow introduction leading to a bright *allegro, a cantabile* slow movement, a minuet and trio, [and] a dancing finale — all are here, but

suffused with colours, felicitous, emotion, beyond anything in Haydn. Yet I think Beethoven was not unmindful of Haydn's introduction to the E Flat *Drum Roll* Symphony, perhaps even the *Chaos* prelude in the *Creation*, when he composed the marvellous introduction to the B flat Symphony. Mysterious, immense, it would not be hard to find in it Beethoven's vision of 'the earth without form' [quotation marks added], and the Spirit of God moving on the face of the waters. But Beethoven gave no programme and we only know that the first allegro is the one by Beethoven which grows out of the material of the introduction.

'The adagio of the Fourth Symphony is so touchingly beautiful that few listeners realise it is a supreme technical achievement ... [If] the difficulty of the task which Beethoven set himself were fully realised, with the necessary consequences of his wonderful solution of it being appreciated, the inclination would be to regard this work as the finest example among all Beethoven's symphonies of delicate and tasteful treatment.

'The main theme is a magnificent example of Beethoven's *cantabile* conjunct melodies, and the rhythmic figure of the accompaniment produces an effect which, when properly played, unites with one's heart-beats. Berlioz always felt this movement intensely. He says: "One is seized, from the first bars, with an emotion that by the end becomes shattering in its intensity! ... The impression produced is like that one experiences on reading the touching episode of Francesca da

Rimini in the *Divina Commedia*, of which Virgil could not hear the recital without sobbing and weeping, and which, at the last verse, made Dante fall as dead".'

'But in Beethoven's adagio there is no tragedy; only the extreme beauty and happiness that bring one near to tears. If there be a heartache it is engendered by the sense of exile in ourselves.

'For the minuet the emotional tension is reduced, the music broken up by cross rhythms and sudden changes, and the trio with its wistful charm is most loveable. The finale is in effect, though not in name, a *perpetuum mobile*, where the instruments swirl and flush in an endless ring, into the centre of which each in turn runs out to do a little solo and then retires in favour of the next. The moment when the bassoon does his is an inimitable bit of clowning.'

Marion M. Scott, *Beethoven: The Master Musicians*. London: Dent, 1940, pp. 169–70.

ARTURO TOSCANINI

Although the interpretation of Beethoven in the form recordings falls outside our terms of reference, we make an exception here to include selected observations of the British composer and musician Spike Hughes. He made a close study of the records Arturo Toscanini made of Beethoven's symphonies with the NBC Orchestra. The following extracts derive from what Hughes has to say about Toscanini's recording of the Fourth Symphony which he made in 1951 on HMV ALP 1145:

ADAGIO — ALLEGRO VIVACE

'The idea that Beethoven's "even-numbered" can in any way be automatically regarded as of a more docile nature than his "odd numbered" symphonies was never more strongly dispelled by Toscanini in the slow introduction to this Fourth Symphony. The sinisterly dramatic atmosphere of this whole remarkable passage was created not by any exaggeration of what Beethoven wrote but, on the contrary, by Toscanini's strictest possible, literal observance of note-values, the production of wonderfully balanced "marching dynamics" and an unwavering rhythm in a slow, dead-right tempo. The result was that an uncanny sense of tension, of apprehension and understatement was finally dispelled only by the outburst of the

ALLEGRO VIVACE.

'While the mood of the Fourth Symphony, once the first allegro has begun, is not so obviously intense as that of the *Eroica*, Toscanini never considered for a moment that its performance should be any less vigorous. He never made the mistake, made by so many conductors and encouraged by so many critics, of taking what is loosely called a "relaxed" view of the work because it is an "even-numbered" symphony. Toscanini saw the instruction "Allegro vivace" and observed it; and in so doing he avoided that miserably soft, emasculate performance which is generally tolerated as being "relaxed" and appropriate to Symphonies Nos. 2, 4, 6, and 8.

'The great emotional contrast in this movement does not occur until the development section when, after a beautiful all-in-one breath of phrasing for strings — which Toscanini made to sound as though it were played by one instrument with a compass from the E string of the violin to the C string of the violincello — the long episode in the extremely foreign key of B major at last modulates and the movement returns to the parent key of B flat.'

ADAGIO

'The word "cantabile" appears in the first violin part as soon as the tune starts in the second bar of this movement; it provides the listener with an immediate clue to the kind of performance he might expect to hear from Toscanini ... Perhaps even more remarkable than the "singing" which Toscanini drew from his orchestra was the extraordinary feeling he created of breadth, of phrases effortlessly stretching apparently to eternity, so that a Beethoven's slow movement had the majesty of some great and noble river ... A Beethoven slow movement played by Toscanini as he played one, was an experience of unending enchantment, every single bar offered some novel and intriguing aspect of what one had been brought up to regard as a fairly well-worn and familiar piece of music.'

SCHERZO: ALLEGRO VIVACE

'The scherzo, as performed by Toscanini in this recording, will hold no surprises for the pedant. The conductor took the trio slower than the scherzo (as the composer told him to) and the performance was deprived neither of vigour nor of the playful charm characteristic of a Beethoven scherzo.'

ALLEGRO MA NON TROPPO

'Toscanini had a particularly tender spot in his heart for this Fourth Symphony, and he inclined to include it in his concert programmes — that is, in non-Beethoven programmes — more than one would expect. The *Eroica*, the Fifth, the Sixth, the Seventh — these were regularly heard in ordinary programmes as natural "high spots". But the Fourth would be comparatively tucked away, usually to end the first half of a programme ... Toscanini's ability to influence the whole style of an individual instrumentalist, to such a degree that it sounded almost as though Toscanini himself were playing the instrument, was shown to great effect in the famous solo bassoon entry in this last movement ... This little touch was typical of Toscanini's attention to detail which made all the difference between a pedestrian and an inspired performance, and his finale of the Fourth Symphony of Beethoven was an inspired performance which always stood out as a model of characteristic Beethoven vitality and good humour.'

Spike Hughes, *The Toscanini Legacy: A Critical Study of Arturo Toscanini's Performances of Beethoven, Verdi, and other Composers.* London: Putnam, 1959, pp. 48–54.

RICHARD STRAUSS

In 1904 the Austrian pianist, conductor and writer on music August Göllerich published a collection of illustrated musical studies, the first volume of which was titled *Beethoven* (Bard, Marquart & Co., 1953). Richard Strauss was invited to contribute an introduction. In responding, although Strauss did not refer directly to Beethoven's Fourth Symphony, his opening remarks provide insights into his views on the nature of art, taken in the widest sense of the meaning:

> 'Art is a product of civilisation. It is not its "calling" to lead a self-sufficient, isolated existence in accordance with "laws" which are first arbitrarily formulated or designed to meet the needs of the moment and then proclaimed to be "eternal": its natural calling is to bear witness to the civilisation of an age and of a people.'

Turning to his attention to music, Strauss comments:

> 'We observe in the history of music, as in the development of the other arts, an evolution from the representation of indefinite or general and typical concepts to the expression of an orbit of ideas which become increasingly more definite, individual and intimate.'

In commending Göllerich's study of Beethoven, Strauss enthused:

> 'A monograph on Beethoven would appear to be best suited to form the first volume of such a collection, because the appreciation of

> Beethoven's position with regard to our civilisation may well offer today the largest field of agreement between friend and foe. It may be hoped that more-or-less general agreement on this interpretation of Beethoven's life and work will form a sure foundation for agreement on greater and more hotly disputed issues of musical aesthetics.'

Willi Schuh editor: *Richard Strauss: Recollections and Reflections*, London; New York: Boosey & Hawkes, 1953, pp. 10–11.

Towards the end of his long life Strauss reflected on the art of conducting in his essay *On Conducting Classical Masterpieces*. He first cites the precepts of Richard Wagner:

> 'It was Richard Wagner who demanded that conductors should grasp the fundamental tempo correctly, since this is all-important for the proper performance of the music; especially in slow movements.'

Strauss was fond of Beethoven's Fourth Symphony, once describing it to his close friend Ludwig Thuille as 'the splendid Symphony', and had particular views as to how it should be performed (see: Bryan Gilliae editor. *Richard Strauss and his World*, 1992, p. 197). Concerning performance, Strauss maintained:

> 'A conductor who interprets aright the adagio theme of Beethoven's Fourth Symphony will never allow himself to be led by the rhythmical figure accompanying the first bar into chopping

> this fine melody up into quavers. Always conduct periods. Never scan bars.'

Strauss next remarked on the need to control fast tempi.

> 'That good old conductor Franz Lachner ... once remarked to my farther [an accomplished horn player]: "In fast movements, when conductor and orchestra have become all too excited, the conductor's art consists in guessing with accuracy the point at which the mad rush can be stopped either by gradual slowing down to the *tempo primo* or even by well-motivated sudden retardation".'

This disposed Strauss to elucidate:

> 'I myself have known so-called gentlemen geniuses of the baton to rush headlong into ... Beethoven and Mozart finales as if their horse had shied and was pulling the reins. I would also mention in connection with [the] finale of Beethoven's B flat Symphony, which is always played far too fast and should be a comfortable allegretto, that *heiter* [cheerful] does not mean a speed record!'

As recounted in: Willi Schuh editor, *Richard Strauss: Recollections and Reflections*. London; New York: Boosey & Hawkes, 1953, pp. 44– 46.

DONALD NIVISON FERGUSON*

In his *Masterworks of the Orchestral Repertoire* (1954),

Donald Nivison Ferguson discusses the musicology of the Fourth Symphony:

> 'Tension, not joy, firsts sets the tone of the music. The first dark phrases descend into what seems a kind of harmonic abyss, although it is only B flat major. But the hesitant, detached notes of the ensuing figure in the violins, above the tense interval of the diminished third (G flat–E natural) in the bassoon and the basses, retain the sense of awe but somehow release us from its usual concomitant of fear.
>
> 'The quality of serenity, as Albert Spalding [American violinist] noted in his interesting Autobiography, *Rise to Follow*, [1943], pervades other works of the same period – the *Waldstein Sonata*, which has an approach to the recapitulation almost identical with that of this movement; the G major Piano Concerto; and the great Violin Concerto.
>
> 'The development is not strained or learnedly difficult. In it the lyrical sense is heightened by the introduction of a new theme, in octaves in violins and 'celli, to which the main subject in the bassoon makes a counterpoint. This new theme, after being heard five times in succession, never recurs but its contribution is immeasurable. So is the expansion of the woodwind phrase in sixths that completed the principle theme, which now begins after a hushed enharmonic modulation to the dominant of B major. The tympani, here and in the similarly coloured return to B flat, have a singularly impressive role to play – as they will have in the adagio.

'The adagio ... like the opening *allegro* of the Violin Concerto, presents at the outset a rhythmic figure whose true value will be revealed only as the movement proceeds ... The theme is immediately repeated by the flute, with its harmony now also in the winds; and the crescendo of its last strain provokes ejaculations of strong sonority in the strings — passionate outbursts, without thematic design, that alternate with brief lyrical phrases which at their peak are first accompanied and then supplanted by figurations of their own colour ...The spacious exposition is here somewhat shortened and is differently coloured; and just before the end, as if to sum up the sense of the whole movement in a single gesture, there is again the hushed beating of the drum. In all Beethoven — indeed, in all the literature of music — there are few movements like this.

'The scherzo begins with a succession of upward leaps, most compelling to the muscles of the imagination; but just as in the first movement the initial excitement that followed the erupting scales was quieted into song, this hint of boisterousness is at once subdued to quiet legato phrases, and in the development, quietness is imposed even upon the leaping figures. The tang of the sardonic and the sense of the uncouth, often apparent in Beethoven scherzi, are here wholly banished.

'Berlioz describes the finale as "one animated swarm of sparkling notes, presenting a continual babble". His image is just, but it is not always realised in performance, perhaps because Beethoven's superscription, A*llegro ma non*

> *troppo*, is startlingly at variance with his metronome mark, minim = 80 [added years later after the music's composition], a speed at which the notes yield only an inarticulate scrambling instead of the sparkle of which Berlioz speaks.'

Donald Nivison Ferguson, *Masterworks of the Orchestral Repertoire: A Guide for Listeners.* Minneapolis: University of Minnesota Press, 1954, pp. 54–59.

WILFRID HOWARD MELLERS*

In his wide-ranging survey of *The Sonata Principle* (1957) in music, Wilfrid Howard Mellers makes reference to the Fourth Symphony:

> 'Intense levity we may certainly find in the Fourth Symphony. It opens in archaistic fashion with a slow introduction, solemn, veiled in tonality and orchestration. This heroic sublimity is then abruptly debunked by a burst of Beethoven's raucous mirth — a tootling, footling allegro theme like those of the *buffa* overture or the early rococo symphony. During the development, however, the most weird things happen to this frivolous tune; and the recapitulation is approached by a mysterious passage of enharmonic moderation, in which a pianissimo pedal note on the timpani gradually changes its significance from A sharp to the tonic B flat. This is a musical pun, and puns are supposed to be funny. But the effect of the passage as a whole is far from comic; it is dramatic and, still more, strange. And its strangeness was already implicit in the myste-

rious equivocations of the slow introduction: so that, as things turn out, it is not the sublime but the debunker who is debunked. Things are not what they seem. There are no clear-cut barriers between the varieties of human experience. The solemn may be absurd, the absurd sinister, the simple mysterious, the mystery an illumination.'

Wilfrid Howard Mellers, *The Sonata Principle (from c. 1750)*, London: Rockliff, 1957, pp. 66—67.

ROBERT SIMPSON*

Alongside his accomplishments as a prolific composer. Robert Simpson was known to the classical, musically-minded public for his scholarly and informed BBC Radio Broadcasts. In 1970 he published a monograph — *Beethoven Symphonies* — in which he discussed the delight that he found in the Fourth Symphony:

'Joy is expressed in abundance, but its point is surely that light is no longer light when darkness in inconceivable; so the music emerges from an impenetrable blackness into gleaming sunlight whose vividness is thereafter constantly preserved by passing patches of cloud. The light is never again obscured but if it is sometimes dimmed, as in the development of the first movement, some passages in the adagio, and in momentary gusty threats in the otherwise irrepressibly gay finale. It always shines out again, brighter than ever. This is as much a drama as the heroics of the Third and Fifth Symphonies, albeit of a more elusive kind; to appreciate it is not to indulge in mystery-mongering, but to feel the richness and limitless sensitivity of the composer's mind.

'In a sense the Fourth Symphony is a study in subtlety of movement such as aptly expressed delight. It is many other things besides, but there is something curiously fascinating in the way the scherzo, after the vast syncopation of the period structures of the adagio, takes obvious pleasure in the deliberate disruption of the smaller-scaled rhythms.

'The trio by contrast spreads itself with grand regularity; it is often played too slowly — the marking is *un poco meno allegro*, which does not mean the rheumatic *andantino* we frequently hear, making the second repetition intolerable. This is the first of Beethoven's scherzos that brings in its trio twice; anyone who is impatient with this device misses the point; Beethoven is not merely filling up the space allowed him by the quicker speed of a scherzo as opposed to a minuet. It is all a matter of momentum, if the music is properly played we should feel that the second appearance of the trio has come spinning round before it can be halted. It can be halted, and the rotation could go on until Beethoven, like a *deus ex machine*, chooses to stop it.

'[The] final movement contains as many rhythmic ingenuities as the rest of the Symphony, though its directions and its character of a *moto perpetuo* tend to deceive the ear into supposing it to be simpler than it is. The *moto perpetuo* aspect often leads conductors into excessive speed, which destroys its natural grace, breadth, and even leisure.'

Robert Simpson, *Beethoven Symphonies*. London: British Broadcasting Corporation, 1970, p. 25 and pp. 32–33.

IGOR STRAVINSKY

As a child Stravinsky showed an aptitude for the piano and by the age of fifteen he had mastered Mendelssohn's Piano Concerto in G minor. In his student days he had lessons in orchestration with Rimsky-Korsakov. He was required to set passages of Beethoven sonatas and Schubert quartets, which the master then criticised and corrected. In his *Autobiography*, Stravinsky pays homage to Beethoven's piano music: 'I recognized in him [Beethoven] the indisputable monarch of the instrument. It is the instrument that inspires his thought and determines its substance.'

Reflecting more generally on Beethoven, Stravinsky summed up his feelings in relation to him:

> 'I did not hero-worship Beethoven, nor have I ever done so, and the nature of Beethoven's talent and work are more "human" and more comprehensible to me than are, say the talents and works of more "perfect" composers like Bach and Mozart; I think I know how Beethoven composed. I have little enough Beethoven in me, alas, but some people have found I have some.'

Igor Stravinsky and Robert Craft, *Memories and Commentaries*, London: Faber and Faber, 2002, p. 23, and p. 39.

In September 1970, the music correspondent of *The York Review* interviewed Igor Stravinsky and discussed his musical preferences. He propositioned the composer:

'You have shared your views on the Beethoven sonatas and quartets [see Stravinsky, *Selected Correspondence,* 1982–85 and Stravinsky, *Memories and commentaries,* 2002] but not those of the symphonies.'

Stravinsky responded:

'Because we have no perspective on music *that* popular. Also, while negative criticism does not interest me, the affirmative kind is too difficult ... [In addition] because the symphonies are public statements, [whereas] the sonatas and quartets — especially the later examples — [are] private, or at least more intimate ones, in which I am more drawn.'

Despite his reservations, Stravinsky ventured the following observations:

'The Fourth (with the Eighth) is the most sustained of the symphonies, but conductors generally miss the point that one measure in the introduction equals two measures of the allegro (just as the sixteenths at the end of the introduction to the First Symphony equals the sixteenths of the allegro, i.e. should be played as sixty-fourths). Yet the first tempo is taken so slowly, as a rule, that an *accelerando* is needed to accommodate the chords at the end. The incomprehension of Weber [see 'Reception History'] before this introduction, is that the clarinet *cantabile* in the second movement is so close to his own music.'

Igor Stravinsky, *Themes and Conclusions*. London: Faber and Faber, 1972, p. 165 and p. 168.

LOUISE ELVIRA CUYLER*

In her survey *The Symphony* (1973), the American musicologist Louise Elvira Cuyler gives an abbreviated, musicological description of the Fourth Symphony:

'The adagio begins full orchestra on the note B flat, but turns, at the second measure, to the key of B-flat major, with a profusion of the minor-oriented pitches C flat and D flat. At about the midpoint of the introduction (measure 181), a division into two parts is suggested when the note C flat changes enharmonically to F sharp, initiating a series of colourful modulations.

'The *Allegro vivace* is cast in the usual sonata-allegro design, a less devious and more conventional one than that found in the first movement of the *Eroica* ... The mid-section is skilfully wrought, deriving interest from vividly juxtaposed harmonies (for example, the C major and A major triads at measures 202–03), louvred texture, and finally, a persistent tonic (B flat) pedal point in the kettledrum, beginning at measure 283 ... The recapitulation is an orthodox one.

'[The Second] movement uses another hybrid form — the sonata-variation ... The movement is marked by long, unbroken lyric lines and by the pervasive trochaic rhythms of the accompaniment.

'[The third] movement is a scherzo and trio, distinguished by the invigorating metric displacement found in the opening strain especially. As

> was the case in the two preceding symphonies, the reprise of the scherzo (*da capo*) is varied and extended.
>
> 'Sonata-allegro is probably the proper designation for [the fourth] movement, since two sonata-allegro "signals" are present – the double bar at the end of the exposition (measure 100) and a sizable mid-section (measures 101–88). The conspicuous and protracted recall of [pervious themes] gives the exposition a flavour of the rondo.'

Louise Elvira Cuyler, *The Symphony*. New York: Harcourt Brace Jovanovich, 1973, pp. 63–64.

BASIL DEANE

The Irish musicologist and academic Samuel Basil Deane, known as Basil Deane, introduced his study of the Fourth Symphony (1973) by making reference to the writings of the German musicologist Ludwig Mische. Mische served for a time as music critic to the *Allgemeine musikalische Zeitung* and was author of *Neue Beethoven-Studien und andere Themen* (Bonn, 1967). Deane writes:

> '[Mische] suggests that the prime unifying factor in the [Fourth] Symphony is a harmonic one: the relatively frequent occurrence of the diminished seventh, and of the dominant ninth and leading-note chords, throughout the work. Other unifying factors include rhythmic similarities and interconnections between themes; and the character of the instrumentation. All of these contribute to create the specific "style" of the work. Although

this concept of unity, as arising out of a complex of relationships of different kinds — occurring almost at random through the work — has not the logical attraction of the thematic unity-theory, it does correspond more closely to the composer's methods of composition.

'The introductory adagio combines in a remarkable way the apparently contradictory function of the two earlier introductions. Like that of the Second Symphony, it establishes the keynote firmly at the beginning. Like that of the First, it leads forward to a resolution in the fifth bar of the *Allegro vivace* by avoiding a cadence on to B flat, with the defining major third ... In the development section, Beethoven again uses his favourite descending sequence leading to a strong subdominant statement. The main arpeggio theme gives birth at bar 221 to a lyrical counter-subject of great charm, which disappears during the shadowy transition, but returns in outline in wind and first violins at bar 351 in the recapitulation.

'The adagio, in E flat, resumes the lyrical vein of the Second Symphony, but with greater concentration and correspondingly richer meaning. The intensely expressive melodic line is set against an impersonal background conjured up by the martial drum-like figure heard in the first bar ... Just as the martial figure begins the movement, so too, it has the last word. Its presence leads to a poignancy to the music almost unequalled before the works of the [composer's] last period. The texture is a delicate tapestry of instrumental colours, in which each strand is distinctly perceived, giving it the special quality of chamber music on an orchestral scale.

'The third movement, also marked *Allegro vivace*, although different from its *Eroica* predecessor in so many ways, shares with it the interplay of duple groupings within triple time as a source of rhythmic energy. Just as the dominance of the horns in the *Eroica's* trio symbolizes the character of the whole work, so, too, the trio of the Fourth, with its emphasis on the woodwind as graceful soloists and their interplay with lightly scored strings, sums up the spirit of the whole Symphony, which is confirmed by the alternating exuberance of the finale.'

Basil Deane, *The Orchestral Music* in: Denis Arnold and Nigel Fortune editors. *The Beethoven Companion*. London: Faber and Faber, 1973.

JOSEPH BRAUNSTEIN*

In his capacity as music critic to the *New York Times*, the Viennese-born, American musicologist Joseph Braunstein imbued his writings about music with the insights of a professional musician gained during his time as a violinist with the Vienna State Opera Orchestra. Writing of Beethoven's Fourth Symphony in his programme notes for *Musica Aeterna*, that covered the period 1971–76, he first remarked on the work's affinities with other of the composer's contemporary compositions:

'The first allegro is prefaced by a sombre adagio in which harmonic vagueness does not presage the pleasant things to come, particularly the sudden vanishing of the misty atmosphere and the abrupt entry of the allegro in a brilliant mood. The harmonic vagueness parallels the *Introduzione* to the String Quartet in C major, Op. 59, No. 3. The Quartet and the Symphony are chronological neighbours.

'A mistiness develops that seems to duplicate that of the introductory adagio, yet it is solved differently. The fog is not lifted suddenly, but gradually, and an extended *crescendo* passage finally brings about the re-entry of the main idea. Berlioz appropriately compared this passage to "a peaceful flowing river, which disappears and [then] leaves the subterranean bed in a foaming cascade which falls down roaringly".'

'According to Berlioz, the adagio defies any analysis. It is an immensely broad *cantabile* containing expressive motifs with small note values. The melody is, to quote Berlioz again, "angelic and irresistible tenderness". It is pushed aside only once, about midway, by the rhythmically intensive motif of the accompaniment in the measures that precede the recapitulation. The melodic thread is spun over the entire orchestra, and nearly all the instruments share the melodic contour.

'This technique is conspicuous in the frolicsome scherzo, where the melodic line jumps from instrument to instrument and from section to section. This movement offers a novelty: the scherzo and trio are repeated — the scherzo is played three times and the trio twice; this occurs in the Sixth and Seventh Symphonies. The trio is the domain of the woodwinds and horns, which form septets in different combinations.

> 'The speedy finale is akin to some of Haydn's witty last movements and to that of the Second Symphony. There is no juxtaposition of darkness and light as there is in the first movement; the gaiety is never seriously threatened ... At the very end ... Beethoven smiles at us good-naturedly and dismisses us tersely with a hearty laugh.'

Joseph Braunstein, *Musica Aeterna, Program* Notes for 1971–1976. New York: *Musica Aeterna*, 1978, Vol. 3, pp. 52–53.

WILLIAM PRESTON STEDMAN

William Preston Stedman is an American musicologist who has held a number of important positions during his long life – at the time of writing he is now in his 99th year. As a music educator, he taught at the Eastman School of Music and held the post of Professor of music at California State University. He was also Director of Western Opera, San Francisco Opera and Vice president of the executive board of the Pacific Symphony Orchestra. As author, he published a wide-ranging survey of the symphony (1979) in which in discussed Beethoven's Fourth Symphony in the following terms:

> 'The opening movement has a slow introduction which sustains the tonic (B-flat major) tonality and routes itself through B major before finally regaining its tonal bearings near the introduction's final half-cadence. The thematic materials of the introduction are related to the materials in the exposition through the motives based on chord outlines which appear in both sections.

'The beginning of the development section is intriguing as it winds down the frenzy of the closing measures of the exposition by having the first tune repeated on successively lower pitches (diatonic) until the tonal level of the development has been reached (measures 189–200) ... The development section continues to work with the first in a flexible tonal environment until the section begins to migrate homeward in a grace-note-studded passage.

'The adagio second movement is broader and more lyric than are the slow movements of the first and second symphonies, apparently reaching for the more noble cantabile style of the composer's later works. The emphasis of the woodwinds to carry much of the melodic material of the movement shows advances in orchestral writing beyond that in the scores of Haydn and Mozart. The woodwinds are used in over half of the exposition alone to state thematic materials.

'The scherzo continues the developmental concepts Beethoven adopted for many of his symphonies' third movements ... Both the trio and the scherzo are repeated in the *da capo*, with an abbreviated scherzo added to complete a five-part form. The woodwind section applies most of the thematic materials of the trio.

'The finale (*Allegro ma non troppo*) is closely aligned with the early classical style in its multi-sectioned thematic groupings. The movement is also reminiscent of the style *galant* with its incessant rush of sixteenth notes. The closing section (measures 70–100) is especially rococo.

'Beethoven was very faithful to the air of

informality and near frivolity that infects many
finales in symphonies between 1710 and 1810.
In the Fourth Symphony's finale, this off-the-cuff
attitude is further compounded by starting the
recapitulation with the solo bassoon playing the
demanding principal theme, with only a soft
pizzicato accompaniment in the strings (measures
184–87) ... The Symphony preserves the best of
Haydn and Mozart conceptions of the symphony
and yet infuses just enough of the expansive style
of Beethoven to maintain both stylistic integrity
and individuality.'

William Preston Stedman, *The Symphony*. Englewood
Cliffs, New Jersey; London: Prentice-Hall, 1979, pp. 70–71.

ANTHONY HOPKINS

Antony Hopkins was something of a musical polymath being
variously a composer, pianist, conductor, writer, and radio
broadcaster. In the latter capacity he endeared himself in the
late 1950s to many radio listeners – the present writer
included – when he discussed classical music in his BBC
Third Programme broadcasts *Talking About Music.* In these
he explored a particular piece of music with what has been
described as 'a judicious mix of analysis and vivid metaphor'
– nothing less than 'a listener's Baedeker'. Writing of the
B-flat major Symphony in 1984, he shared with the reader
what the music meant to him. As we read what he has to say,
we have to imagine him illustrating his remarks at the piano
– as he did so effectively in his radio broadcasts:

> '[The] Fourth [Symphony] has always tended to
> be overshadowed by its two mighty neighbours.

Nevertheless, the Fourth has magical qualities, and is perhaps the best orchestrated of the nine. The opening in particular is unforgettable for the liberty of its sound. During the slow introduction, the music seems to be feeling its way towards a destination only dimly perceived. At last, after long deferment, a series of brief ascending scale-fragments, crisp and sharp as the crack of a whip, leads us into the main theme allegro.

'The principal theme alternates swift detached notes on the strings with a smooth *legato* phrase on the woodwind. It is like emerging into bright sunlight after the mysterious shadows of the introduction.

'The second movement begins with an important rhythmic figure against which the violins unfold a deeply expressive melody, later to be elaborately decorated. After a second main theme has been introduced by a solo clarinet, and then taken up by the full woodwind choir, the double-basses remind us of the initial rhythmic figure; in due course it comes to dominate the scene leading to an astonishingly dramatic descent with each note heavily accented by explosive cannon-shots from the tympani ... Soon a solo bassoon reminds us of the opening rhythm, though Beethoven might have preferred a horn at this point (The notes would have been unobtainable on the instruments used in his time.) The closing pages of the movement have a romantic beauty that is virtually unsurpassed in the whole canon of the nine symphonies.

'The next movement is vigorous in its rhythmic drive, alternating strongly accented chords with strange ribbons of unison notes in woodwind and strings. As a contrast, the central Trio is mincingly elegant, a parody of the refined conventions Beethoven had clearly lost patience with.'

Hopkins concludes:

'The finale is as exuberant a movement as he ever wrote, almost a study in perpetual motion. Like Mozart and Haydn before him, Beethoven was a more than adequate violinist [?] and there are passages in this Symphony that suggest that he was recalling hours of technical practice spent in mastering the instrument. There are also notoriously difficult passages for the double basses as well as a famous bassoon solo. The whole movement bubbles over with good humour and high spirits.'

Anthony Hopkins appears here to have regarded Beethoven as being a more accomplished violinist than perhaps was the case. Although he possessed a fine set of string instruments, at least one contemporary described Beethoven's violin playing as 'excruciating'. And back in his youthful days in Bonn, it was the viola he played in the Elector's orchestra, not the violin. Moreover, when composing his Violin Concerto, he consulted with Franz Clement — who premiered the work — when writing out certain passages for the soloist.

Antony Hopkins, *The Concertgoer's Companion*. London: J.M. Dent & Sons Ltd., 1984, pp. 59—60.

DENIS MATTHEWS

Denis Matthews is remembered today primarily for being a concert pianist with a particular liking for the music of the first Viennese school — notably that of Haydn, Mozart, Beethoven and Schubert. His many writings on music, however, reveal his knowledge of, and affinity for, the keyboard music of their contemporaries such as Hummel and Clementi. Matthews outlined his thoughts about music in his Autobiography *In Pursuit of Music* (1968) and reached a wide audience in his study of Beethoven, published in the *Master Musicians* series (1985). In his role as professor of music at the University of Newcastle (1971–81) Matthews wrote extensively about Beethoven, inspiring a younger generation thereby. Writing of Beethoven's Fourth Symphony, in his 1985 study of the composer, he states:

> 'The Fourth Symphony ... opens with a slow introduction of minor-key darkness and mysteriously measured tread, which invoked the scorn of Weber through its sparseness of notes [see 'Reception History']. Yet its sense of space is immense. The opening moves, having established the key of B-flat major, are then diverted by a semitonal rise into remote regions, giving the unexpected outburst of dominant-seventh harmony, preceding the allegro, the alarmingly dramatic effect of a sudden sunrise at midnight ... The exposition pursues its varied course with confidence and humour, incorporating a clarinet-and-bassoon canon in the second group and rounding off the whole section with a brilliant syncopated theme deriving from an earlier idea.
>
> 'Though the development is based entirely on the figures of the first subject, two features deserve

mention: the melodious counterpoint that blossoms in sequences and in smooth contrast to the detached quavers; and the enharmonic use of the tympani's B flat as A sharp when the music, as in the introduction, has wandered into distant keys ... The exciting crescendo leading to the recapitulation resembles a parallel one in the *Waldstein* Sonata, though being based entirely on tonic-harmony effect in the Symphony is more original, simpler and stronger.

'The slow movement, doubtless admired by Schumann, the lyric grace of the first of theme is introduced by a rhythmic figure that hints at the latent strength underlying the outward tenderness. It flares up from time-to-time, but is also heard in the forlorn high registers of a bassoon and appears quietly on the timpani at the end. The most dramatic contrast in this sonata-rondo comes in the middle episode where a forceful minor-key version of the subject yields to a delicate interweaving of arabesques in first and second violins in the region of G-flat major.

'The scherzo is the first of the symphonies to bring round its trio-section a second time, and the third statement of the scherzo itself is accordingly abridged. It makes great play with cross-rhythms, alternating with unison phrases and minor key inflections, and these elements are expanded with a wider modulating scheme in the second part. The trio, however, is carried through smoothly on a tonic pedal, and its *poco meno mosso* allows more room for its lyrical but playful exchanges between wind and strings.

'As for the finale, it is an extrovert affair with

many glimpses at the past, as in the Mozartian *Alberti bass* treatment of the clarinet in the second group. Its main topic is the opening semiquaver subject and its tendency to build up sequences in perpetual motion: it taxes the bassoon in the recapitulation and the bases in the coda, and is eventually handed round at half-speed being whisked away in a surprise ending. The brusque treatment of dynamics should temper any lingering notions of Schumann's "Greek maiden".'

Denis Matthews, *Beethoven, Master Musicians*. London: J. M. Dent, 1985, pp. 157–59.

MICHAEL BROYLES*

In his discussion of *The Emergence and Evolution of Beethoven's Heroic Style* (1987), the American musicologist Michael Broyles outlined his views on the musicology of the Fourth Symphony in the context of its predecessor the *Eroica* Symphony:

'In some ways the Fourth Symphony represents Beethoven's most intense use of syncopation as a structural device. It does not exceed the syncopation of the *Eroica* in magnitude, as the syncopations are not projected upon such a vast scale, but in a number of places they are even more biting and direct than the *Eroica*. The second half of the exposition of the first movement consists of a series of syncopations which propel the movement with great intensity toward a particularly strong closing accent for the entire exposition.

'Other movements of the Fourth Symphony reflect a greater freedom and flexibility of rhythm. This is particularly true of the finale, where the question of tempo is critical. Beethoven's marking of minim = 80, is contradicted by his own designation, *allegro ma non troppo*. This metronome marking has been justified by a perceived *perpetuum mobile* character to the movement.

'Another important aspect of the Fourth Symphony that is related to the style change of 1804–07 is the use of orchestral colour. Writers have frequently described the Symphony in chiaroscuric [*chiaroscuro*] terms. Metaphors of light and dark abound. [The German musicologist] August Kretzschmar speaks of "a romantic tendency, the dusk, in which the imagination loves to linger in all movements except the last".' [*Symphonies and Suites*, Leipzig: Breitkopf & Härtel 1921]

'Part of the effect has to do with Beethoven's handling of orchestral sonority. The score is rich in subtle details, such as in the first movement, the opening wind sound against the string pizzicato, the fluidity with which one theme in the development passes through winds to strings, or the use of the tympani. Similar examples could be cited in all of the movements, but there is another aspect to Beethoven's use of the orchestra which is closely related to a specifically chiaroscuric quality; a greater flexibility and contrast in the overall richness or body of the sonority. Beethoven defines various musical spaces or ranges in a freer way and varies much more the degree of fullness or transparency of the sounds within them.'

Michael Broyles, *Beethoven: The Emergence and Evolution of Beethoven's Heroic Style*. New York: Excelsior Music Publishing Co., 1987, p. 174, p. 177 and p. 184.

ALEC HARMAN, ANTHONY MILNER, AND WILFRID MELLERS*

In their study *Man and his Music* (1988), Alec Harman, Anthony Milner, and Wilfrid

The authors remind us that humour is to be found in Beethoven's music:

> 'Beethoven is a composer of strife, and strife between wildly conflicting kinds of experience may sometimes not be tragic, but comic. We are apt to forget that Beethoven's music is often funny, and we have excuse for forgetting, since his humour is a disruptive force, like his passion. Both his humour and his self-assertions are dramatic, a threat to complacency ... Perhaps humour is not the word, and we may rather find in Beethoven's music an exaggerated form of the intense levity which we [discover] in Haydn and Mozart, but which disappears in the age of romanticism.'

The authors follow these generalisations with reference to the Fourth Symphony:

> 'Intense levity we may certainly find in the Fourth Symphony. It opens in archaic fashion with a slow introduction, solemn, veiled in tonality and orchestration. This heroic sublimity is then abruptly debunked by a burst of Beethoven's raucous mirth

> — a tootling, footling allegro like those of the *buffa* overture or the early rococo symphony. During the development, however, the most weird things happen to this frivolous tune, and the recapitulation is approached by a mysterious passage of enharmonic modulation, in which a pianissimo pedal note on the tympani gradually changes its significance from A sharp to the tonic B flat. This is a musical pun, and puns are supposed to be funny. But the effect of the passage as whole is far from comic; it is dramatic and, still more, strange. And its strangeness was already implicit in the mysterious equivocations of the slow introduction: so that, as things turn out, it is not the sublime but the debunker who is debunked. Things are not what they seem. There are no clear-cut barriers between the varieties of human experience. The solemn may be absurd, the absurd sinister; the simple mysterious, the mystery an illumination.'

Alec Harman, Anthony Milner and Wilfrid Mellers. *Man and his Music: The Story of Musical Experience in the West.* London: Barrie & Jenkins, 1988, pp. 644–45.

RICHARD OSBORNE*

In his contribution *Beethoven*, to Robert Layton's *A Guide to the Symphony* (1995), Richard Osborne pays tribute to Beethoven's musicological craftmanship, as evidenced in the Fourth Symphony:

> 'Strange as [the] opening is, the ascent to the light is gradual and the transition of the *Allegro vivace* almost staid, with so gradual increase of tempo

and only a handful of unvarnished dominant sevenths to announce that B-flat major will, after all, be the tonic key. It is often said that the Fourth Symphony breaks no new ground, that it is a tribute to Haydn by a composer who now wears his own nose and who has absolutely nothing to fear from being thought old-fashioned.

'The Symphony's outer movements are richly various, expansive and abrupt, playful yet controlled, exuberant yet given to moments of hypnotic quiet.

'Everywhere in this Symphony the craft is consummate, not least in areas we perhaps too often take for granted with Beethoven — the use of dynamics (often there in the originating sketches) and orchestration. The wonderfully terse coda to the first movement would be nothing without the simple allure of the *subito piano* in bar 483 prefacing the *fortissimo* roar eight bars later. And how wonderfully the wind choir is used in this Symphony, with Beethoven lavishing special craft and affection on the writing for flute, clarinet and bassoon. This is especially to the fore in what is the loveliest of Beethoven's adagios. Among other things, the Adagio is an essay in the interplay of stillness and motion.'

Richard Osborne, *Beethoven* in: Robert Layton editor. *A Guide to the Symphony*. Oxford: Oxford University Press, 1995, pp. 93–95.

PETER HAUSCHILD

Writing in 1996, the German musicologist Peter Hauschild considered some of the affinities and contrasts that the

Fourth Symphony has with its two musical neighbours the *Eroica* Symphony and the Fifth Symphony:

'While Beethoven's Fifth is the concentrated example of an instance of the supreme exercise of will power and energy as a precondition for the powerful depiction of extreme musical drama, the comparatively more relaxed Fourth Symphony is, so to speak, the result of a "creative pause" during the process of that exercise of power. The apodictically compressed "fate motif" of the Fifth is contrasted in the Fourth by the pianissimo opening of an adagio introduction in which the music guardedly emerges from the silence ... In contrast to the *Eroica* and the Fifth, in which Beethoven expands the orchestral resources through additional wind instruments, in the Fourth he reduces the scoring and brings it back to the level of Haydn and Mozart. In the score, he even does without the second flute. This helps enhance the chamber character of the work.

'The second movement is an adagio ... The opening motif outlining a fourth, repeated in staccato, is followed by the heartfelt song of a cantabile melody ... In filigree, finely chiselled variants of the melodic theme, Beethoven once again reduces the sound to form a one- and two-part texture.

'Beethoven gave the third movement the traditional designation "Menuetto", even though it can be regarded as a full-fledged scherzo. The movement is laid out in a large-scale five-part form (A—B—A—B—A) while the main *Allegro vivace* section of the movement evidences a typical Scherzo character with its powerful, driving dictus, its brusque dynamic contrasts and the occasionally abrupt alternation of keys ... the sphere of cantabile introspection is conjured up in the slower Trio section.

'In the closing *Allegro ma non troppo*, the contrasts of the preceding movements are "fused" into a flowing current of chiefly uninterrupted 16th-note figurations, whereby the dynamics are intensified alternatingly from a scurrying pianissimo to a blustery, raging fortissimo ... Developments, build-ups, climaxes — they are all carried out here primarily in the parameters of sound and harmony. As the piece rushes down and back up within its modulatory circle of keys, we are treated to a number of mesmerising "endurance tests" which remind us of the extent to which drama and latent tragedy bubble under the surface of this work too, which is so often undervalued as "cheerful" and light-weight.'

Peter Hauschild, *Ludwig van Beethoven, Symphonie Nr.4*. Breitkopf & Härtel. *Preface to Miniature Score*.1996.

WILLIAM KINDERMAN

In his *Beethoven* (1997) the American pianist and musicologist William Kinderman cites a passage from the writings of the British philosopher Isaiah Berlin on early Romantic aesthetics:

'All creation is in some sense creation out of nothing. It is the only fully autonomous activity of man. It is self-liberation from causal laws, the

> mechanism of the external world, from tyrants, or environmental influences, or the passions, which govern me — factors in relation to which I am as much an object in nature as trees, or stones, or animals.'

Kinderman responds:

> 'Beethoven, a pivotal figure in this reassessment of artistic creation as original, autonomous activity, left an incomparable documentary record of the process itself, in the form of thousands of pages of sketches and drafts for his musical works.'

William Kinderman, *Contrast and Continuity in Beethoven's Creative Process.* In: Scott G. Burnham, and Michael P. Steinberg, editors: *Beethoven and his World.* Princeton, New Jersey; Oxford: Princeton University Press, 2000. p. 193).

In his *Beethoven*, Kinderman draws attention to the composer's innovative use of the tympani in the Fourth Symphony:

> 'The first movement of the Fourth Symphony in B-flat major, Op. 60 offers another example of Beethoven's extraordinary use of the tympani, here in connection with an unorthodox approach to the recapitulation. The general character of the *Allegro vivace* is energetic and even boisterous, but Beethoven withdraws into subdued *pianissimo* towards the end of the development. Mysterious drum rolls are heard in B, and the music lingers for some moments in the remote key of

B major, as hushed, transparent descending scales unfold in the strings, while the tympani are silent. Beethoven then returns to the harmony of the B-flat major while maintaining the enigmatic *pianissimo*. The drum rolls recur, first intermittently, then as a sustained tonic pedal held for 23 bars until the beginning of the recapitulation.

'A fascinating aspect of this passage is that the drum roll sounds on B can be heard, at least in retrospect, as a subtle foreshadowing of the actual recapitulation, which is ushered in by the long tympani roll in the tonic.

'This passage may have helped inspire the remarkable approach to the recapitulation in the first movement of Schubert's last Piano Sonata, in B-flat major, in which analogous "drum rolls" in the form of low trills introduce a foreshadowing of the main theme on (but not in) the tonic, moments before the actual recapitulation is reached.'

William Kinderman, *Beethoven*. Oxford: Oxford University Press, 1997, pp. 118–19.

THEODORE W. ADORNO*

Amidst his many *Fragments and Texts* (1998) bearing on the music of Beethoven, the German philosopher, sociologist and composer Theodor W. Adorno discusses the musicology of the Fourth Symphony — styled in his characteristically cryptic-aphoristic manner:

'[The] Fourth Symphony, a splendid much underrated work. Regarding harmony and form:

the crux of the immensely precise and economical introduction (compare the First and Second [Symphonies]) is the reinterpretation of G flat as F sharp (B minor). By contrast, the turning point of the development interprets F sharp as G flat, as a retransition to B flat. The tension of the introduction is resolved only here: "functional harmony". How unschematically Beethoven thinks: the last few bars of the transition to the second subject group; the following theme of the second subject-group itself and the later melodic idea (canon of clarinet and bassoon), are "too alike", especially the last two, and yet *entirely* compelling: Syncopation *as such* is used thematically in the movement as a linking element, somewhat as chords accented off the beat in the first movement of the *Eroica* and the closing section ... The *magnificent* treatment of the of the development ... has a quasi-new theme, though still as a counterpoint, so that it is wholly absorbed into the intrinsic flow of the movement.'

At this point in his text, Adorno writes in a more personal manner:

'I could not get much out of the slow movement when reading the score, but saw it quite differently through a not particularly good recording under Furtwängler (too slow and sentimental). Especially the short, development-like section ... I could *not* properly imagine the force of the underlying voice in B flat, or the dynamic contrasts in the last movements. The danger of *reading*. By contrast, I can effortlessly imagine the harmonic proportions over the longer passages.'

Theodor W. Adorno, *Beethoven: The Philosophy of Music; Fragments and Texts*. Cambridge: Polity Press, 1998, pp. Article No. 239, pp. 106–07.

MICHAEL P. STEINBERG*

The American scholar-musicologist Michael P. Steinberg opens his account of Beethoven's Fourth Symphony (1998) by recalling the acute musical perceptions possessed by the members of an audience of Beethoven's time:

'The key signature says B-flat major, but the music is really in B-flat minor. The most musical of the guests at the Lobkowitz Palace in 1807 [see 'Creation Origins'] would have been more aware than most of us today of just how slowly this music moves — not so much in terms of notes per minute (which most conductors today ration out more slowly than Beethoven's signature and metronome mark indicate) as in the passage of events. The harmony nearly stands still, and the effect of suspended motion is underlined by the pianissimo that lasts — as Beethoven reminds us four times — unbroken through the first twelve measures.

'The material in the *Allegro vivace* is of almost studied neutrality. (The same could be said of the introduction.) The life of this ebullient music resides in the contrast between those passages where the harmonies change slowly (as they mostly do) and others where harmonic territory is traversed at a great rate, in the syncopations, in the sudden *fortissimo* outbursts, and in such colourful details as the stalking half-notes. The development ventures a few moments of lyrical song, but most of the orchestra is impatient with that sort of thing, impatient to get on and to get back ... Beethoven concludes the movement with an exceptionally long and emphatic assertion of the tonic.

'The adagio is an expansive, rapt song; rarely does Beethoven insist so often on the direction *cantabile* ... Not until the Ninth [Symphony] would Beethoven again write a symphony with a really slow "slow movement".

'In the finale, a comedy worthy of Haydn, certain characters from the first movement reappear, newly costumed, but this *Allegro ma non troppo* is a more relaxed kind of movement than the first *Allegro vivace* ... Beethoven learned more from Haydn's scores than from Haydn's lessons: the Symphony No. 4, for which Haydn's Symphony No. 102 clearly served as a model, is a case in point.'

Michael P. Steinberg, *The Symphony: A Listener's Guide*, Oxford University Press; reprint edition, 1998, pp. 21 – 22.

ALFRED PETER BROWN*

In his expansive two-volume survey *The Symphonic Repertoire* (2002), the American musicologist Alfred Peter Brown situates the Fourth Symphony within the wider context of Beethoven's contemporaneous works and that of his former teacher Haydn:

'Previously Beethoven commenced his symphonies with traditional models and gestures; however, the Fourth Symphony's introduction does not parody tradition, but a single piece, "Chaos" from Haydn's *The Creation*, which, since its first performance in 1798, had overwhelmed Continental musical life. The success and content of this work seems to have obsessed Beethoven. Among others "Chaos", and its ultimate movement to light, reappeared in such works as the String Quartet, Op. 59/3. The Piano Concerto No. 4 [second movement], and Symphonies Nos. 5, 6, and 9. The Fourth Symphony was perhaps the first after Haydn to fully exploit the "Chaos" topic, with its flattened sixth degree at the opening, tonal uncertainty, rhythmic inactivity, and multiple flashes of light at the exposition's beginning in the bright key of B-flat major.

'The second movement, adagio, provides a wonderful contrast to the muscular rhythms of the first, delicate melodies and fragile timbres treated in an expansive rondo form ...'.

'In the placid — almost pastoral — context, the second episode, a mere four measures, is a shocker. The one-measure upbeat leads not to the refrain, as we have been led to expect, but to a bare-bones version of its outline in the tonic minor played tutti and *fortissimo*; it is reharmonized with descending bass moving to quarter notes than the more sustained bass line of the beginning. This passage is the most dramatic utterance of the entire Symphony.

'This wonderful piece is one of Beethoven's most sensitively orchestrated works. The beginning with its interweaving of the four string parts, could just as well have been part of a string quartet movement. The first episode could belong to a clarinet quintet. A chamber-music quality is further underlined when a single line results from soloistic fragments heard in several instruments.

'The third movement continues on the same track as the three previous symphonic scherzos: a diminutive first strain with conflicts of meter and melody; an expanded second strain — here beginning with a tertian relationship followed by a *development* and recapitulation; and a more metrically and here tempo-relaxed Trio featuring the winds with the strings providing background activity. The most important innovation is the expansion of the form; added to the usual scherzo-trio-scherzo are a repeat of the trio and another of the scherzo. Special note should be made of the four-measure horn-coloured coda, a compositional afterthought, which rhymes in sound with the conclusion of the adagio.

'For the finale, Beethoven reverts to the structure of the First and Second Symphonies: a sonata-form ... however, we have a *perpetuum mobile*; only a fraction of the coda [is] not saturated in sixteenth notes. As a result, these passages gain their utmost not only from the surface activity but also from the action of the harmonic rhythm ... The recapitulation considerably abbreviates the first part of the exposition by excluding seventeen measures ... It is often forgotten that the tempo marking for this finale is *Allegro ma non troppo* with a metronome indication of minim = 80. Many present-day conductors opt for the faster of these contradictory instructions. Perhaps *a ma non troppo* tempo would result in greater clarity in the melodic-rhythmic as well as the harmonic-rhythmic profile of this extraordinarily well-paced piece.'

Alfred Peter Brown, *The Symphonic Repertoire*. Vol. 2, *The First Golden Age of the Viennese Symphony: Haydn, Mozart, Beethoven, and Schubert*. Bloomington, Indiana: Indiana University Press, 2002, pp. 476–80.

TERRY BARFOOT

Terry Barfoot was a music educator and founder of *Arts in Residence* that provided music appreciation courses at country-house venues in rural England. He also contributed to summer schools at The Royal Opera House and Oxford. In June 2005 the BBC devoted a whole week to performances of Beethoven's music. Each broadcast was accompanied with specially commissioned programme notes for which Barfoot contributed on 7 and 8 June when the Fourth Symphony was broadcast. He introduced these programmes by remarking:

> 'Although the adagio introduction is not lengthy it is spacious and impressive, and provides the ideal foil for the main body of the first movement, which develops at tempo *Allegro vivace* ... Delight and vivacity feature predominantly, and there are some splendid opportunities for the wind instruments. These various ideas are developed with considerable ingenuity and presented with imaginative orchestration. One example is the deploy-

ment of a prolonged tympani roll to herald the recapitulation of the principal theme.

'The slow movement is spacious and serene, though dramatic gestures make their impact too ... The principal theme is a gloriously lyrical inspiration, sustaining many presentations of its song-like contour. The closing bars emphasise these subtleties, as the drums tap out the basic rhythm.

'The harmonic range of the scherzo is surprisingly wide, but more interesting still is the music's rhythmic energy. The complex textures enhance the vivacious approach, while the central trio takes the form of a long crescendo, at the climax of which the double basses add their weight.

'The finale has abundant high spirits, the music propelled by the introductory phrase that sets the agenda ... The development is chiefly concerned with the lively first theme, however, until the solo bassoon heralds the recapitulation, while even during the coda it is this same material that holds centre stage. Here, Beethoven also employs one of Haydn's favourite devices, slowly spelling out the contour of what has been a lively theme before suddenly resuming that rhythmic vitality which is ultimately this symphony's prime concern.'

Terry Barfoot, *Symphony No.4 in B-flat major, Op. 60: Notes to the BBC Radio Three Beethoven Experience,* Tuesday 7 and Wednesday 8 June 2005, https://www.bbc.co co.uk/programmes/p08gdjbs

BIBLIOGRAPHY

The author has individually consulted all the publications listed in this bibliography and can confirm that each makes reference, in some way or other, to Beethoven and his works. It will be evident from their titles which of these are publications devoted exclusively to the composer. Others that make only passing reference to Beethoven and his compositions, nevertheless unfailingly bear testimony to his genius and humanity. The diversity of the titles listed testifies to the centrality of Beethoven to western culture and beyond; the mere survey of these should be of itself a rewarding experience for a lover of so-called classical music. The entries are confined to book publications, reflecting the scope of the author's researches. The cut-off date for this was 2007; no works after this date are listed, notwithstanding the author is mindful that Beethoven musicology, and related publication, continue to be a major field of endeavour.

Abraham, Gerald. *Beethoven's second-period quartets*. London: Oxford University Press: Humphrey Milford, 1944.

Abraham, Gerald. *Essays on Russian and East European music*. Oxford: Clarendon Press: New York: Oxford University Press, 1985.

Abraham, Gerald, Editor. *The age of Beethoven, 1790-1830*. London: Oxford University Press, 1982.

Abraham, Gerald. *The tradition of Western music*. London: Oxford University Press, 1974.

Abse, Dannie and Joan. *The Music lover's literary companion*. London: Robson Books, 1988.

Adorno, Theodor W., Translator. *Alban Berg: master of the smallest link*. Cambridge: Cambridge University Press, 1991.

Adorno, Theodor W. *Beethoven: the philosophy of music; fragments and texts*. Cambridge: Polity Press, 1998.

Albrecht, Daniel, Editor. *Modernism and music: an anthology of sources*. Chicago; London: University of Chicago Press, 2004.

Albrecht, Theodore, Translator and Editor. *Letters to Beethoven and other correspondence*. Lincoln, New England: University of Nebraska Press, 3 vols., 1996.

Allsobrook, David Ian. *Liszt: my travelling circus life*. London: Macmillan, 1991.

Anderson, Christopher, Editor and Translator. *Selected writings of Max Reger*. New York; London: Routledge, 2006.

Anderson, Emily, Editor and Translator. *The letters of Beethoven*. London: Macmillan, 3 vols., 1961.

Anderson, Martin, Editor. *Klemperer on music: shavings from a musician's workbench*. London: Toccata Press, 1986.

Antheil, George. *Bad boy of music*. London; New York: Hurst & Blackett Ltd., 1945.

Appleby, David P. *Heitor Villa-Lobos: a bio-bibliography*. New York: Greenwood Press, 1988.

Aprahamian, Felix, Editor. *Essays on music: an anthology from The Listener*. London, Cassell, 1967.

Armero, Gonzalo and Jorge de Persia. *Manuel de Falla : his life & works*. London: Omnibus Press, 1999.

Arnold, Ben, Editor. *The Liszt companion*. Westport, Connecticut; London: Greenwood Press, 2002.

Arnold, Denis and Nigel Fortune, Editors. *The Beethoven companion*. London: Faber and Faber, 1973.

Ashbrook, William. *Donizetti*. London: Cassell, 1965.

Auner, Joseph Henry. *A Schoenberg reader: documents of a life*. New Haven Connecticut; London: Yale University Press, 2003.

Avins, Styra, Editor. *Johannes Brahms: life and letters*. Oxford: Oxford University Press, 1997.

Azoury, Pierre H. *Chopin through his contemporaries: friends, lovers, and rivals*. Westport, Connecticut: Greenwood Press, 1999.

Badura-Skoda, Paul. *Carl Czerny: On the Proper Performance of all Beethoven's Works for the Piano*. Universal Edition: A. G. Wien, 1970.

Bailey, Cyril. *Hugh Percy Allen*. London: Oxford University Press, 1948.

Bailey, Kathryn. *The life of Webern*. Cambridge: Cambridge University Press, 1998.

Barenboim, Daniel. *A life in music*. London: Weidenfeld & Nicolson, 1991.

Barlow, Michael. *Whom the gods love: the life and music of George Butterworth*. London: Toccata Press, 1997.

Barrett-Ayres, Reginald. *Joseph Haydn and the string quartet*. New York: Schirmer Books, 1974.

Bartos, Frantisek. *Bedrich Smetana: Letters and reminiscences*. Prague: Artia, 1953.

Barzun, Jacques. *Pleasures of music: an anthology of writing about music and musicians*. London: Cassell, 1977.

Bauer-Lechner, Natalie. *Recollections of Gustav Mahler*. London: Faber Music, 1980.

Bazhanov, N. Nikolai. *Rakhmaninov*. Moscow: Raduga, 1983.

Beaumont, Antony, Editor. *Ferruccio Busoni: Selected letters*. London: Faber and Faber, 1987.

Beaumont, Antony, Editor. *Gustav Mahler, letters to his wife*. London: Faber and Faber, 2004.

Beecham, Thomas. *A mingled chime: an autobiography*. New York: Da Capo Press, 1976.

Bekker, Paul. *Beethoven*. London: J. M. Dent & Sons, 1925.

Bellasis, Edward. *Cherubini: memorials illustrative of his life*. London: Burns and Oates, 1874.

Bennett, James R. Sterndale. *The life of William Sterndale Bennett*. Cambridge: University Press, 1907.

Benser, Caroline Cepin. *Egon Wellesz (1885–1974): chronicle of twentieth-century musician*. New York: P. Lang, 1985.

Berlioz, Hector. *Evenings in the orchestra*. Harmondsworth: Penguin Books, 1963.

Berlioz, Hector. *The musical madhouse (Les grotesques de la musique)*. Rochester, New York: University of Rochester Press, 2003.

Bernard, Jonathan W., Editor. *Elliott Carter: collected essays and lectures, 1937-1995*. Rochester, New York; Woodbridge: University of Rochester Press, 1998.

Bernstein, Leonard. *The joy of music*. New York: Simon and Schuster, 1959.

Bertensson, Sergei. *Sergei Rachmaninoff: a lifetime in music*. London: G. Allen & Unwin, 1965.

Biancolli, Louis. *The Flagstad manuscript*. New York: Putnam, 1952.

Bickley, Nora, Editor. *Letters from and to Joseph Joachim*. London: Macmillan, 1914.

Bie, Oskar. *A history of the pianoforte and pianoforte players*. New York: Da Capo Press, 1966.

Blaukopf, Herta. *Mahler's unknown letters*. London: Gollancz, 1986.

Blaukopf, Kurt and Herta. *Mahler: his life, work and world*. London: Thames and Hudson, 1991.

Bliss, Arthur. *As I remember*. London: Thames Publishing, 1989.

Block, Adrienne Fried. *Amy Beach, passionate Victorian: the life and work of an American composer, 1867–1944*. New York: Oxford University Press, 1998.

Bloch, Ernst. *Essays on the philosophy of music*. Cambridge: Cambridge University Press, 1985.

Blocker, Robert. *The Robert Shaw reader*. New Haven; London: Yale University Press, 2004.

Blom, Eric. *A musical postbag*. London: J. M. Dent, 1945.

Blom, Eric. *Beethoven's pianoforte sonatas discussed*. London: J. M. Dent, 1938.

Blom, Eric. *Classics major and minor: with some other musical ruminations*. London: J. M. Dent, 1958.

Blum, David. *The art of quartet playing: the Guarneri Quartet in conversation with David Blum*. London: Gollancz, 1986.

Blume, Friedrich. *Classic and Romantic music: a comprehensive survey*. London: Faber and Faber, 1972.

Boden, Anthony. *The Parrys of the Golden Vale: background to genius*. London: Thames Publishing, 1998.

Bonavia, Ferruccio. *Musicians on music*. London: Routledge & Kegan Paul, 1956.

Bonds, Mark Evan *After Beethoven: imperatives of originality in the symphony*. Cambridge, Massachusetts; London: Harvard University Press, 1996.

Bonis, Ferenc, Editor. *The selected writings of Zoltán Kodály*. London; New York: Boosey & Hawkes, 1974.

Bookspan, Martin. *André Previn: a biography*. London: Hamilton, 1981.

Boros, James and Richard Toop, Editors. *Brian Ferneyhough: Collected writings*. Amsterdam: Harwood Academic, 1995.

Boulez, Pierre. *Stocktakings from an apprenticeship*. Oxford: Clarendon Press, 1991.

Boult, Adrian. *Boult on music: words from a lifetime's communication*. London: Toccata Press, 1983.

Boult, Adrian. *My own trumpet*. London, Hamish Hamilton, 1973.

Boult, Adrian with Jerrold Northrop Moore. *Music and friends: seven decades of letters to Adrian Boult from Elgar, Vaughan Williams, Holst, Bruno Walter, Yehudi Menuhin and other friends*. London: Hamish Hamilton, 1979.

Bovet, Marie Anne de. *Charles Gounod: his life and his works*. London: S. Low, Marston, Searle & Rivington, Ltd., 1891.

Bowen, Catherine Drinker. *Beloved friend: the story of Tchaikowsky and Nadejda von Meck*. London: Hutchinson & Co., 1937.

Bowen, Meiron, Editor. *Gerhard on music: selected writings*. Brookfield, Vermont: Ashgate, 2000.

Bowen, Meirion. *Michael Tippett*. London: Robson Books, 1982.

Bowen, Meiron, Editor. *Music of the angels: essays and sketchbooks of Michael Tippett*. London: Eulenburg, 1980.

Bowen, Meiron, Editor. *Tippett on music*. Oxford: Clarendon Press, 1995.

Bowers, Faubion. *Scriabin: a biography*. Mineola: Dover; London: Constable, 1996.

Boyden, Matthew. *Richard Strauss*. London: Weidenfeld & Nicolson, 1999.

Bozarth, George S., Editor. *Brahms*

studies: analytical and historical perspectives; papers delivered at the International Brahms Conference, Washington, DC, 5-8 May 1983. Oxford: Clarendon Press, 1990.

Brand, Juliane, Christopher Hailey and Donald Harris, Editors. *The Berg-Schoenberg correspondence: selected letters.* Basingstoke: Macmillan, 1987.

Brandenbugh, Sieghard, Editor. *Haydn, Mozart, & Beethoven: studies in the music of the classical period: essays in honor of Alan Tyson.* Oxford: Clarendon Press, 1998.

Braunstein, Joseph. *Musica Æterna, program notes for 1961–1971.* New York: Musica Æterna, 1972.

Braunstein, Joseph. *Musica Æterna, program notes for 1971–1976.* New York: Musica Æterna, 1978.

Brendel, Alfred. *Alfred Brendel on music: collected essays.* Chicago, Iliinois: A Cappella Books, 2001.

Brendel, Alfred. *The veil of order: Alfred Brendel in conversation with Martin Meyer.* London: Faber and Faber, 2002.

Breuning, Gerhard von. *Memories of Beethoven: from the house of the black-robed Spaniards.* Cambridge: Cambridge University Press, 1992.

Briscoe, James R., Editor. (Brief Description): *Debussy in performance.* New Haven: Yale University Press, 1999.

Brott, Alexander Betty Nygaard King. *Alexander Brott: my lives in music.* Oakville, Ontario; Niagara Falls, New York: Mosaic Press, 2005.

Brown, Alfred Peter. *The symphonic repertoire. Vol. 2, The first golden age of the Viennese symphony: Haydn, Mozart, Beethoven, and Schubert.* Bloomington, Indiana: Indiana University Press, 2002.

Brown, Maurice John Edwin. *Schubert: a critical biography.* London: Macmillan; New York: St. Martin's Press, 1958.

Broyles, Michael. *Beethoven: the emergence and evolution of Beethoven's heroic style.* New York: Excelsior Music Publishing Co., 1987.

Brubaker, Bruce and Jane Gottlieb, Editors. *Pianist, scholar, connoisseur: essays in honor of Jacob Lateiner.* Stuyvesant, N.Y., Pendragon Press, 2000.

Buch, Esteban. *Beethoven's Ninth: a political history.* Chicago; London: University of Chicago Press, 2003.

Burk, John N., Editor. *Letters of Richard Wagner: the Burrell collection.* London: Gollancz, 1951.

Burnham, Scott G. *Beethoven hero.* Princeton, New Jersey: Princeton University Press, 1995.

Burnham, Scott G and Michael P. Steinberg, Editors. *Beethoven and his world.* Princeton, New Jersey; Oxford: Princeton University Press, 2000.

Burton, William Westbrook, Editor. *Conversations about Bernstein.* New York; Oxford: Oxford University Press, 1995.

Busch, Fritz. *Pages from a musician's life.* London: Hogarth Press, 1953.

Busch, Hans, Editor. *Verdi's Aida: the history of an opera in letters and documents.* Minneapolis: University of Minnesota Press, 1978.

Busch, Hans, Editor. *Verdi's Falstaff in letters and contemporary reviews.* Bloomington: Indiana University Press, 1997.

Busch, Marie, Translator. *Memoirs of Eugenie Schumann.* London: W. Heinemann, 1927.

Bush, Alan Dudley. *In my eighth decade and other essays.* London: Kahn & Averill, 1980.

Busoni, Ferruccio. *Letters to his wife.* Translated by Rosamond Ley. New York: Da Capo Press, 1975.

Byron, Reginald. *Music, culture, & experience: selected papers of John Blacking.* Chicago: University of Chicago Press, 1995.

Cairns, David. *Responses: musical essays and reviews.* New York: Da Capo Press, 1980.

Cardus, Neville. *Talking of music.* London: Collins, 1957.

Carley, Lionel. *Delius: a life in letters.* London: Scolar Press in association with the Delius Trust, 1988.

Carley, Lionel. *Grieg and Delius: a chronicle of their friendship in letters.* London: Marion Boyars, 1993.

Carner, Mosco. *Major and minor.* London: Duckworth, 1980

Carner, Mosco. *Puccini: a critical biography.* London: Duckworth, 1958.

Carroll, Brendan G. *The last prodigy: a biography of Erich Wolfgang Korngold.* Portland, Oregon: Amadeus Press, 1997.

Carse, Adam von Ahn. *The life of Jullien: adventurer, showman-conductor and establisher of the Promenade Concerts in England, together with a history of those concerts up to 1895.* Cambridge England: Heffer, 1951.

Carse, Adam von Ahn. *The orchestra from Beethoven to Berlioz: a history of the orchestra in the first half of the 19th century, and of the development of orchestral baton-conducting.* Cambridge: W. Heffer, 1948.

Casals, Pablo. *Joys and sorrows: reflections by Pablo Casals as told to Albert E. Kahn.* London: Macdonald, 1970.

Casals, Pablo. *The memoirs of Pablo Casals as told to Thomas Dozier.* London: Life en Español, 1959.

Chappell, Paul. *Dr. S. S. Wesley, 1810–1876: portrait of a Victorian musician.* Great Wakering: Mayhew-McCrimmon, 1977.

Chasins, Abram. *Leopold Stokowski, a profile.* New York: Hawthorn Books, 1979.

Charlton, Davi, Editor and Martyn Clarke Translator. *E.T.A. Hoffmann's musical writings: Kreisleriana, The Poet and the Composer.* Cambridge: Cambridge University Press, 1989.

Chávez, Carlos. *Musical thought.* Cambridge: Harvard University Press, 1961.

Chesterman, Robert, Editor. *Conversations with conductors: Bruno Walter, Sir Adrian Boult, Leonard Bernstein, Ernest Ansermet, Otto Klemperer, Leopold Stokowski.* Totowa, New Jersey: Rowman and Littlefield, 1976.

Chissell, Joan. *Clara Schumann: a dedicated spirit; a study of her life and work.* London: Hamilton, 1983.

Chua, Daniel K. L. *The "Galitzin" quartets of Beethoven: Opp.127, 132, 130.* Princeton: Princeton University Press, 1995.

Citron, Marcia, Editor. *The letters of Fanny Hensel to Felix Mendelssohn.* Stuyvesant, New York: Pendragon Press, 1987.

Clark, Walter Aaron. *Enrique Granados: poet of the piano.* Oxford, England; New York, N.Y.: Oxford University Press, 2006.

Clark, Walter Aaron. *Isaac Albéniz: portrait of a romantic.* Oxford; New York: Oxford University Press, 1999.

Clive, Peter. *Beethoven and his world.* Oxford University Press, 2001.

Closson, Ernest. *History of the piano.* Translated by Delano Ames and edited by Robin Golding. London: Paul Elek, 1947.

Cockshoot, John V. *The fugue in Beethoven's piano music.* London: Routledge & Kegan Paul, 1959.

Coe, Richard N, Translator. *Life of Rossini by Stendhal.* London: Calder & Boyars, 1970.

Coleman, Alexander, Editor. *Diversions & animadversions: essays from The new criterion.* New Brunswick, New Jersey; London: Transaction Publishers, 2005.

Colerick, George. *From the Italian girl to Cabaret: musical humour, parody and burlesque.* London: Juventus, 1998.

Coleridge, A. D. *Life of Moscheles, with selections from his diaries and correspondence by his wife.* London: Hurst & Blackett, 1873.

Colles, Henry Cope. *Essays and lectures.* London: Humphrey Milford, Oxford University Press, 1945.

Cone, Edward T., Editor. *Roger Sessions on music: collected essays.* Princeton, New Jersey: Princeton University Press, 1979.

Cone, Edward T. *The composer's voice.* Berkeley; London: University of California Press, 1974.

Cook, Susan and Judy S. Tsou, Editors. *Cecilia reclaimed: feminist perspectives on gender and music.* Urbana: University of Illinois Press, 1994.

Cooper, Barry. *Beethoven:* The master musicians series. Oxford: Oxford University Press, 2000.

Cooper, Barry. *Beethoven and the creative process.* Oxford: Clarendon Press, 1990.

Cooper, Barry. *Beethoven's folksong settings: chronology, sources, style.* Cambridge: Cambridge University Press, 1991.

Cooper, Barry. *The Beethoven compendium: a guide to Beethoven's life and music.* London: Thames and Hudson, 1991.

Cooper, Martin. *Beethoven: the last decade, 1817–1827.* London: Oxford University Press, 1970.

Cooper, Martin. *Judgements of value: selected writings on music.* Oxford; New York: Oxford University Press, 1988.

Cooper, Martin. *Ideas and music.* London: Barrie and Rockliff, 1965.

Cooper, Victoria L. *The house of Novello: the practice and policy of a Victorian music publisher, 1829–1866.* Aldershot, Hants: Ashgate, 2003.

Coover, James. *Music at auction: Puttick and Simpson (of London), 1794–1971: being an* annotated, chronological list of sales of musical materials. Warren, Michigan: Harmonie Park Press, 1988.

Copland, Aaron. *Copland on music*. London: Deutsch, 1961.

Corredor, J. Ma. *Conversations with Casals*. London: Hutchinson, 1956.

Cott, Jonathan. *Stockhausen: conversations with the composer*. London: Picador, 1974.

Cottrell, Stephen. *Professional music making in London: ethnography and experience*. Aldershot: Ashgate, 2004.

Cowell, Henry. *Charles Ives and his music*. New York: Oxford University Press, 1955.

Cowling, Elizabeth. *The cello*. London: Batsford, 1983.

Crabbe, John. *Beethoven's empire of the mind*. Newbury: Lovell Baines, 1982.

Craft, Robert. *An improbable life: memoirs*. Nashville: Vanderbilt University Press, 2002.

Craft, Robert, Editor. *Stravinsky: selected correspondence*. London: Faber and Faber, 3 Vols. 1982–1985.

Craw, Howard Allen. *A biography and thematic catalog of the works of J. L. Dussek: 1760–1812*. Ann Arbor: Michigan, 1965.

Crawford, Richard, R. Allen Lott and Carol J. Oja, Editors. *A Celebration of American music: words and music in honor of H. Wiley Hitchcock*. Ann Arbor: University of Michigan Press, 1990.

Craxton, Harold and Tovey, Donald Francis. *Beethoven: Sonatas for Pianoforte*. London: The Associated Board, [1931].

Crichton, Ronald: Editor. *The memoirs of Ethel Smyth*. New York: Viking, 1987.

Crist, Stephen A. and Roberta M. Marvin, Editors. *Historical musicology: sources, methods, interpretations*. Rochester, New York: University of Rochester Press, 2004.

Crofton, Ian and Donald Fraser, Editors. *A dictionary of musical quotations*. London: Croom Helm, 1985.

Crompton, Louis, Editor. *Shaw, Bernard: The great composers: reviews and bombardments*. Berkeley; London: University of California Press, 1978.

Csicserry-Ronay, Elizabeth, Translator and Editor. *Hector Berlioz: The art of music and other essays: (A travers chants)*. Bloomington: Indiana University Press, 1994.

Curtiss, Mina Kirstein. *Bizet and his world*. London: Secker & Warburg, 1959.

Cuyler, Louise Elvira. *The symphony*. New York: Harcourt Brace Jovanovich, 1973.

Dahlhaus, Carl. *Ludwig van Beethoven: approaches to his music*. Oxford: Clarendon Press, 1991.

Dahlhaus, Carl. *Nineteenth-century music*. Translated by J. Bradford Robinson. Berkeley; London: University of California Press, 1989.

Daniels, Robin. *Conversations with Cardus*. London: Gollancz, 1976.

Daniels, Robin. Conversations with Menuhin. London: Macdonald General Books, 1979.

Day, James. *Vaughan Williams*. London: Dent, 1961.

Davies, Peter Maxwell. *Studies from two decades*. Selected and introduced by Stephen Pruslin. London: Boosey & Hawkes, 1979.

Dean, Winton. *Georges Bizet: his life and work*. London: J.M. Dent, 1965.

Deas, Stewart. *In defence of Hanslick*. London: Williams and Norgate, 1940.

Debussy, Claude. *Debussy on music*. London: Secker & Warburg, 1977.

Delbanco, Nicholas. *The Beaux Arts Trio*. London: Gollancz, 1985.

Demény, Janos, Editor. *Béla Bartók: letters*. London: Faber and Faber, 1971.

Dent, Edward Joseph. *Selected essays*. Edited by Hugh Taylor. Cambridge; New York: Cambridge University Press, 1979.

Deutsch, Otto Erich. *Mozart: a documentary biography*. London: Adam & Charles Black, 1965.

Deutsch, Otto Erich. *Schubert: a documentary biography*. London: J.M. Dent, 1946

Deutsch, Otto Erich. *Schubert: memoirs by his friends*. London: Adam & Charles Black, 1958.

Dibble, Jeremy. *C. Hubert H. Parry: his life and music*. Oxford: Clarendon Press, 1992.

Dibble, Jeremy. *Charles Villiers Stanford: man and musician*. Oxford: Oxford University Press, 2002.

Donakowski, Conrad L. *A muse for the masses: ritual and music in an age of democratic revolution, 1770–1870*. Chicago: University of Chicago Press, 1977.

Dower, Catherine. *Alfred Einstein on music: selected music criticisms*. New York: Greenwood Press, 1991.

Downs, Philip G. *Classical music: the era of Haydn, Mozart, and Beethoven*. New York: W.W. Norton, 1992.

Drabkin, William. *Beethoven: Missa Solemnis*. Cambridge: Cambridge University Press, 1991.

Dreyfus, Kay. *The farthest north of humanness: letters of Percy Grainger, 1901–1914*. South Melbourne; Basingstoke: Macmillan, 1985.

Dubal, David, Editor. *Remembering Horowitz: 125 pianists recall a legend*. New York: Schirmer Books, 1993.

Dubal, David. *The world of the concert pianist*. London: Victor Gollancz, 1985.

Dvorák, Otakar. *Antonín Dvorák, my father*. Spillville, Iowa: Czech Historical Research Center, 1993.

Dyson, George. *The progress of music*. London: Oxford University Press, Humphrey Milford, 1932.

Eastaugh, Kenneth. *Havergal Brian: the making of a composer*. London: Harrap, 1976.

Edwards, Allen. *Flawed words and stubborn sounds: a conversation with Elliott Carter*. New York: Norton & Company, 1971.

Edwards, Frederick George. *Musical haunts in London*. London: J. Curwen & Sons, 1895.

Ehrlich, Cyril. *First philharmonic: a history of the Royal Philharmonic Society*. Oxford: Clarendon Press, 1995.

Einstein, Alfred. *A short history of music*. London: Cassell and Company Ltd., 1948.

Einstein, Alfred. *Essays on music*. London: Faber and Faber, 1958.

Einstein, Alfred. *Mozart: his character, his work*. London: Cassell and Company Ltd., 1946.

Einstein, Alfred. *Music in the Romantic era*. London: J.M. Dent Ltd., 1947.

Ekman, Karl. *Jean Sibelius, his life and personality*. New York: Tudor Publishing. Co., 1945.

Elgar, Edward. *A future for English music: and other lectures*, Edited by Percy M. Young. London: Dobson, 1968.

Elkin, Robert. *Queen's Hall, 1893–1941*. London: Rider, 1944.

Ella, John. *Musical sketches, abroad and at home: with original music by Mozart, Czerny, Graun, etc., vocal cadenzas and other musical illustrations*. London: Ridgway, Vol. 1., 1869.

Ellis, William Ashton. *The family letters of Richard Wagner*. Edited and translated by William Ashton Ellis and enlarged with introduction and notes by John Deathridge. Basingstoke: Macmillan, 1991.

Ellis, William Ashton. *Richard Wagner's prose works: Vol. 1, The art-work of the future*. Edited and translated by William Ashton Ellis. London: Kegan Paul, Trench, Trübner, 1895.

Ellis, William Ashton. *Richard Wagner's prose works: Vol. 2, Opera and drama*. Edited and translated by William Ashton Ellis. London: Kegan Paul, Trench, Trübner, 1900.

Ellis, William Ashton. *Richard Wagner's prose works: Vol. 3, The theatre*. Edited and translated by William Ashton Ellis. London: Kegan Paul, Trench, Trübner, 1907.

Ellis, William Ashton. *Richard Wagner's prose works: Vol. 4, Art and politics*. Edited and translated by William Ashton Ellis. London: Kegan Paul, Trench, Trübner, 1895.

Ellis, William Ashton. *Richard Wagner's prose works: Vol. 5, Actors and singers*. Edited and translated by William Ashton Ellis. London: Kegan Paul, Trench, Trübner, 1896.

Ellis, William Ashton. *Richard Wagner's prose works: Vol. 6, Religion and art*. Edited and translated by William Ashton Ellis. London: Kegan Paul, Trench, Trübner, 1897.

Ellis, William Ashton. *Richard Wagner's prose works: Vol. 7, In Paris and Dresden*. Edited and translated by William Ashton Ellis. London: Kegan Paul, Trench, Trübner, 1898.

Ellis, William Ashton. *Richard Wagner's prose works: Vol. 8, Posthumous*. Edited and translated by William Ashton Ellis. London: Kegan Paul, Trench, Trübner, 1899.

Elterlein, Ernst von. *Beethoven's pianoforte sonatas: explained for the lovers of the musical art*. London: W. Reeves, 1898.

Engel, Carl. *Musical myths and facts*. London: Novello, Ewer & Co.; New York: J.L. Peters, 1876.

Eosze, László. *Zoltán Kodály: his life and work*. London: Collet's, 1962.

Etter, Brian K. *From classicism to modernism: Western musical culture and the metaphysics of order*. Aldershot: Ashgate, 2001.

Ewen, David. *From Bach to Stravinsky: the history of music by its *foremost critics*. New York, Greenwood Press, 1968.

Ewen, David. *Romain Rolland's Essays on music*. New York: Dover Publications, 1959.

Fay, Amy. *Music-study in Germany: from the home correspondence of Amy Fay*. New York: Dover Publications, 1965.

Fenby, Eric. *Delius as I knew him*. London: Quality Press, 1936.

Ferguson, Donald Nivison. *Masterworks of the orchestral repertoire: a guide for listeners*. Minneapolis: University of Minnesota Press, 1954.

Fétis, François-Joseph. *Curiosités historiques de la musique: complément nécessaire de la Musique mise à la portée de tout le monde*. Paris: Janet et Cotelle, 1830.

Fifield, Christopher. *Max Bruch: his life and works*. London: Gollancz, 1988.

Fifield, Christopher. *True artist and true friend: a biography of Hans Richter*. Oxford: Clarendon Press, 1993.

Finson, Jon and R. Larry Todd, Editors. *Mendelssohn and Schumann: essays on their music and its context*. Durham, N.C.: Duke University Press, 1984.

Fischer, Edwin. *Beethoven's pianoforte sonatas: a guide for students & amateurs*. London: Faber and Faber, 1959.

Fischer, Edwin. *Reflections on music*. London: Williams and Norgate, 1951.

Fischer, Hans Conrad and Erich Kock. *Ludwig van Beethoven: a study in text and pictures*. London: Macmillan; New York, St. Martin's Press, 1972.

Fischmann, Zdenka E. *Janác̆ek-Newmarch correspondence. 1st limited and numbered edition*. Rockville, MD: Kabel Publishers, 1986.

Fitzlyon, April. *Maria Malibran: diva of the romantic age*. London: Souvenir Press, 1987.

FitzLyon, April. *The price of genius: a life of Pauline Viardot*. London: John Calder, 1964.

Forbes, Elliot, Editor. *Thayer's life of Beethoven*. Princeton, New Jersey: Princeton University Press, 1967.

Foreman, Lewis. *Bax: a composer and his times*. London: Scolar Press, 1983.

Foreman, Lewis, Editor. *Farewell, my youth, and other writings by Arnold Bax*. Aldershot: Scolar Press, 1992.

Foster, Myles Birket. *History of the Philharmonic Society of London, 1813–1912: a record of a hundred years' work in the cause of music*. London: Bodley Head, 1912.

Foulds, John. *Music today: its heritage from the past, and legacy to the future*. London: I. Nicholson and Watson, limited, 1934.

Frank, Mortimer H. *Arturo Toscanini: the NBC years*. Portland, Oregon: Amadeus Press, 2002.

Fraser, Andrew Alastair. *Essays on music*. London: Oxford University Press, H. Milford, 1930.

Frohlich, Martha. *Beethoven's Appassionata' sonata*. Oxford: Clarendon Press, 1991.

Gal, Hans. *The golden age of Vienna*. London: Max Parrish & Co. Limited, 1948.

Gal, Hans. *The musician's world:*

Galatopoulos, Stelios. *Bellini: life, times, music.* London: Sanctuary, 2002.

Garden, Edward and Nigel Gottrei, Editors. *'To my best friend': correspondence between Tchaikovsky and Nadezhda von Meck, 1876–1878.* Oxford: Clarendon Press, 1993.

Geck, Martin. *Beethoven.* London: Haus, 2003.

Gerig, Reginald. *Famous pianists & their technique.* Washington: R. B. Luce, 1974.

Gilliam, Bryan. *The life of Richard Strauss.* Cambridge: Cambridge University Press, 1999.

Gilliam, Bryan, Editor. *Richard Strauss and his world.* Princeton, New Jersey: Princeton University Press, 1992.

Gillies, Malcolm and Bruce Clunies Ross, Editors. *Grainger on music.* Oxford; New York: Oxford University Press, 1999.

Gillies, Malcolm and David Pear, Editors. *The all-round man: selected letters of Percy Grainger, 1914–1961.* Oxford: Clarendon Press, 1994.

Gillies, Malcolm, Editor. *The Bartók companion.* London: Faber and Faber, 1993.

Gillmor, Alan M. *Erik Satie.* Basingstoke: Macmillan Press, 1988.

Glehn, M. E. *Goethe and Mendelssohn : (1821–1831).* London: Macmillan, 1874.

Glowacki, John, Editor. *Paul A. Pisk: Essays in his honor.* Austin, Texas: University of Texas, 1966

Gollancz, Victor. *Journey towards music: a memoir.* London: Victor Gollancz Ltd., 1964.

Good, Edwin Marshall. *Giraffes, black dragons, and other pianos: a technological history from Cristofori to the modern concert grand.* Stanford, California: Stanford University Press, 1982.

Gordon, David. *Musical visitors to Britain.* London: Routledge, 2005.

Gordon, Stewart. *A history of keyboard literature: music for the piano and its forerunners.* Schirmer Books: New York: London : Prentice Hall International, 1996.

Gorrell, Lorraine. *The nineteenth-century German lied.* Portland, Oregon: Amadeus Press, 1993.

Goss, Glenda D. *Jean Sibelius: the Hämeenlinna letters: scenes from a musical life, 1875–1895.* Esbo, Finland: Schildts, 1997.

Goss, Madeleine. *Bolero: the life of Maurice Ravel.* New York: Tudor, 1945.

Gotch, Rosamund Brunel, Editor. *Mendelssohn and his friends in Kensington: letters from Fanny and Sophy Horsley, written 1833–36.* London: Oxford University Press, 1938.

Gounod, Charles. *Charles Gounod; autobiographical reminiscences: with family letters and notes on music; from the French.* London: William Heinemann, 1896.

Grabs, Manfred, Editor. *Hanns Eisler: a rebel in music; selected writings.* Berlin: Seven Seas Publishers, 1978.

Grace, Harvey. *A musician at large.* London: Oxford University Press, H. Milford, 1928.

(La) Grange, Henry-Louis de. *Gustav Mahler*. Oxford: Oxford University Press, 1995.

Graves, Charles L. *Hubert Parry: his life and works*. London: Macmillan, 1926.

Graves, Charles L. *Post-Victorian music: with other studies and sketches*. London: Macmillan and Co., limited, 1911.

Graves, Charles L. *The life & letters of Sir George Grove, Hon. D.C.L. (Durham), Hon. LL.D. (Glasgow), formerly director of the Royal college of music*. London: Macmillan and Co., Ltd.; New York: The Macmillan Co., 1903.

Gray, Cecil. *Musical chairs, or, between two stools: being the life and memoirs of Cecil Gray*. London: Home & Van Thal, 1948.

Gregor-Dellin and Dietrich Mack, Editors. *Cosima Wagner's diaries.: Vol. 1, 1869 - 1877*. London: Collins, 1978-1980.

Griffiths, Paul. *Modern music: the avant-garde since 1945*. London: J. M. Dent & Sons Ltd., 1981.

Griffiths, Paul. *Olivier Messiaen and the music of time*. London: Faber and Faber, 1985.

Griffiths, Paul. *Peter Maxwell Davies*. London: Robson Books, 1988.

Griffiths, Paul. *The sea on fire: Jean Barraqué*. Rochester, New York: Woodbridge: University of Rochester Press, 2003.

Griffiths, Paul. *The string quartet*. London: Thames and Hudson, 1983.

Grout, Donald Jay and Claude V. Palisca, Editors. *A history of Western music*. London: J. M. Dent, 1988.

Grove, George. *Beethoven and his nine symphonies*. London: Novello, Ewer, 1896.

Grover, Ralph Scott. *Ernest Chausson: the man and his music*. London: The Athlone Press, 1980.

Grover, Ralph Scott. *The music of Edmund Rubbra*. Aldershot: Scolar Press, 1993.

Grun, Bernard. *Alban Berg: letters to his wife*. Edited and translated by Bernard Grun. London: Faber and Faber, 1971.

Gutman, David. *Prokofiev*. London: Omnibus Press, 1990.

Hadow, William Henry. *Collected essays*. London: H. Milford at the Oxford University Press, 1928.

Hadow, William Henry. *Beethoven's Op. 18 Quartets*. London: H. Milford at the Oxford University Press, 1926.

Haggin, Bernard H. *Music observed*. New York: Oxford University Press, 1964.

Hailey, Christopher. *Franz Schreker, 1878–1934: a cultural biography*. Cambridge: Cambridge University Press, 1993.

Hall, Michael. *Leaving home: a conducted tour of twentieth-century music with Simon Rattle*. London: Faber and Faber, 1996.

Hall, Patricia and Friedemann Sallis, Editors. (Brief Description): *A handbook to twentieth-century musical sketches*. Cambridge: Cambridge University Press, 2004.

Hallé, C. E. *Life and letters of Sir Charles Hallé: being an autobiography (1819–1860) with correspondence and diaries*. London: Smith, Elder & Co., 1896.

Halstead, Jill. *The woman composer: creativity and the gendered politics of musical composition*. Aldershot: Ashgate, 1997.

Hamburger, Michael, Editor and Translator. *Beethoven letters, journals, and conversations*. New York: Thames and Hudson, 1951.

Hammelmann, Hanns A. and Ewald Osers. *The correspondence between Richard Strauss and Hugo von Hofmannsthal*. London: Collins, 1961.

Hanson, Lawrence and Elisabeth Hanson. *Tchaikovsky: the man behind the music*. New York: Dodd, Mead & Co, 1967.

Harding, James. *Massenet*. London: J. M. Dent & Sons Ltd., 1970.

Harding, James. *Saint-Saëns and his circle*. London: Chapman & Hall, 1965.

Harding, Rosamond E. M. *Origins of musical time and expression*. London: Oxford University Press, 1938.

Harman, Alec with Anthony Milner and Wilfrid Mellers. *Man and his music: the story of musical experience in the West*. London: Barrie & Jenkins, 1988.

Harper, Nancy Lee. *Manuel de Falla: his life and music*. Lanham, Maryland; London: The Scarecrow Press, 2005.

Hartmann, Arthur. *'Claude Debussy as I knew him' and other writings of Arthur Hartmann*. Edited by Samuel Hsu, Sidney Grolnic, and Mark Peters. Rochester, New York; Woodbridge: University of Rochester Press, 2003.

Haugen, Einar and Camilla Cai. *Ole Bull: Norway's romantic musician and cosmopolitan patriot*. Madison: The University of Wisconsin Press, 1993.

Headington, Christopher. *The Bodley Head history of Western music*. London: The Bodley Head, 1974.

Heartz, Daniel. *Music in European capitals: the galant style, 1720-1780*. New York; London: W. W. Norton, 2003.

Hedley, Arthur, Editor. *Selected correspondence of Fryderyk Chopin: abridged from Fryderyk Chopin's correspondence*. London: Heinemann, 1962.

Heiles, Anne Mischakoff. *Mischa Mischakoff: journeys of a concertmaster*. Sterling Heights, Michigan: Harmonie Park Press, 2006.

Henderson, Sanya Shoilevska. *Alex North, film composer: a biography, with musical analyses of a Streetcar named desire, Spartacus, The misfits, Under the volcano, and Prizzi's honor*. Jefferson, N.C.; London: McFarland, 2003.

Henschel, George. *Personal recollections of Johannes Brahms: some of his letters to and pages from a journal kept by George Henschel*. Boston: R G. Badger, 1907.

Henze, Hans Werner. *Bohemian fifths: an autobiography*. London: Faber and Faber, 1998.

Henze, Hans Werner. *Music and politics: collected writings 1953-81*. London: Faber and Faber, 1982.

Herbert, May, Translator. *Early letters of Robert Schumann*. London: George Bell and Sons, 1888.

Heyman, Barbara B. *Samuel Barber:*

Heyworth, Peter. *Otto Klemperer, his life and times.* Cambridge: Cambridge University Press, 2 Vols. 1983–1996.

Hildebrandt, Dieter. *Pianoforte: a social history of the piano.* London: Hutchinson, 1988.

Hill, Peter. *The Messiaen companion.* London: Faber and Faber, 1995.

Hill, Peter and Nigel Simeone. *Messiaen.* New Haven Connecticut; London: Yale University Press, 2005.

Hiller, Ferdinand. *Mendelssohn: Letters and recollections.* New York: Vienna House, 1972.

Hines, Robert Stephan. *The orchestral composer's point of view: essays on twentieth-century music by those who wrote it.* Norman: University of Oklahoma Press, 1970.

Ho, Allan B. *Shostakovich reconsidered.* London: Toccata Press, 1998.

Hodeir, André. *Since Debussy: a view of contemporary music.* New York: Da Capo Press, 1975.

Holmes, Edward. *The life of Mozart: including his correspondence.* London: Chapman and Hall, 1845.

Holmes, John L. *Composers on composers.* New York: Greenwood Press, 1990.

Hopkins, Anthony. *The concertgoer's companion.* London: J.M. Dent & Sons Ltd., 1984.

Hopkins, Anthony. *The seven concertos of Beethoven.* Aldershot: Scolar Press, 1996.

Holt, Richard. *Nicolas Medtner (1879–1951): a tribute to his art and personality.* London: D. Dobson, 1955.

Honegger, Arthur. *I am a composer.* London: Faber and Faber, 1966.

Hoover, Kathleen and John Cage. *Virgil Thomson: his life and music.* New York; London: T. Yoseloff, 1959.

Horgan, Paul. *Encounters with Stravinsky: a personal record.* London: The Bodley Head, 1972.

Horowitz, Joseph. *Conversations with Arrau.* London: Collins, 1982.

Horowitz, Joseph. Understanding Toscanini. London: Faber and Faber, 1987.

Horwood, Wally. *Adolphe Sax, 1814–1894: his life and legacy.* Bramley: Bramley Books, 1980.

Howie, Crawford. *Anton Bruckner: a documentary biography.* Lewiston, N.Y.; Lampeter: Edwin Mellen Press, 2002.

Hueffer, Francis. *Correspondence of Wagner and Liszt.* New York: Greenwood Press, 2 Vols.1969.

Hughes, Spike. *The Toscanini legacy: a critical study of Arturo Toscanini's performances of Beethoven, Verdi, and other composers.* London: Putnam, 1959.

Hullah, Annette. *Theodor Leschetizky.* London and New York: J. Land & Co., 1906.

Le Huray, Peter and James Day, Editors. *Music and aesthetics in the eighteenth and early-nineteenth centuries.* Cambridge: Cambridge University Press, 1988.

D' Indy, Vincent. *César Franck.* New York: Dover Publications, 1965.

Jacobs, Arthur. *Arthur Sullivan: A*

Victorian musician. Aldershot: Scolar Press, 1992.

Jahn, Otto. *Life of Mozart*. London: Novello, Ewer & Co., 1882.

Jefferson, Alan. *Sir Thomas Beecham: a centenary tribute*. London: World Records Ltd., 1979.

Jezic, Diane. *The musical migration and Ernst Toch*. Ames: Iowa State University Press, 1989.

Johnson, Douglas Porter, Editor. *The Beethoven sketchbooks: history, reconstruction, inventory*.

Oxford: Clarendon, 1985.

Johnson, Stephen. *Bruckner remembered*. London: Faber and Faber, 1998.

Jones, David, Wyn. *Beethoven: Pastoral symphony*. Cambridge: Cambridge University Press, 1995.

Jones, David Wyn. *The life of Beethoven*. Cambridge: Cambridge University Press, 1998.

Jones, David Wyn. *The symphony in Beethoven's Vienna*. Cambridge: Cambridge University Press, 2006.

Jones, J. Barrie, Editor. *Gabriel Fauré: a life in letters*. London: Batsford, 1989.

Jones, Peter Ward, Editor and Translator. *The Mendelssohns on honeymoon: the 1837 diary of Felix and Cécile Mendelssohn Bartholdy, together with letters to their families*. Oxford: Clarendon Press, 1997.

Jones, Timothy. *Beethoven, the Moonlight and other sonatas, Op. 27 and Op. 31*. Cambridge; New York, N.Y.: Cambridge University Press, 1999.

Kalischer, A. C., Editor. *Beethoven's letters: a critical edition*. London: J. M. Dent, 1909.

Kárpáti, János. *Bartók's chamber music*. Stuyvesant, New York: Pendragon Press, 1994.

Keefe, Simon P. *The Cambridge companion to the concerto*. Cambridge, New York, N.Y.: Cambridge University Press, 2005.

Keller, Hans. *The great Haydn quartets: their interpretation*. London: J. M. Dent, 1986.

Keller, Hans, Editor. *The memoirs of Carl Flesch*. New York: Macmillan, 1958.

Keller, Hans, and Christopher Wintle. *Beethoven's string quartets in F minor, Op. 95 and C minor, Op. 131: two studies*. Nottingham: Department of Music, University of Nottingham, 1995.

Kelly, Thomas Forrest. *First nights at the opera: five musical premiers*. New Haven: Yale University Press, 2004.

Kennedy, Michael. *Adrian Boult*. London: Hamish Hamilton, 1987.

Kennedy, Michael. *Barbirolli, conductor laureate: the authorised biography*. London: Hart-Davis, MacGibbon, 1973.

Kennedy, Michael, Editor. *The autobiography of Charles Hallé; with correspondence and diaries*.

London: Paul Elek, 1972.

Kennedy, Michael. *Hallé tradition: a century of music*. Manchester: Manchester University Press, 1960.

Kennedy, Michael. *The works of Ralph Vaughan Williams*. London: Oxford University Press, 1964.

Kemp, Ian. *Tippett: the composer and his music*. London; New York: Eulenburg Books, 1984.

Kerman, Joseph. *The Beethoven quartets.* London: Oxford University Press, 1967, c1966.

Kerman, Joseph. *Write all these down: essays on music.* Berkeley, California; London: University of California Press, 1994.

Kildea, Paul, Editor. *Britten on music.* Oxford: Oxford University Press, 2003.

Kinderman, William. *Beethoven.* Oxford: Oxford University Press, 1997.

Kinderman, William. *Beethoven's Diabelli variations.* Oxford: Clarendon Press; New York: Oxford University Press, 1987.

Kinderman, William, Editor. *The string quartets of Beethoven.* Urbana, Ilinois: University of Illinois Press, 2005.

King, Alec Hyatt. *Musical pursuits: selected essays.* London: British Library, 1987.

Kirby, F. E. *Music for piano: a short history.* Amadeus Press: Portland, 1995.

Kirkpatrick, John, Editor. *Charles E. Ives: Memos.* New York: W.W. Norton, 1972.

Knapp, Raymond. *Brahms and the challenge of the symphony.* Stuyvesant, N.Y.: Pendragon Press, c.1997.

Knight, Frida. *Cambridge music: from the Middle Ages to modern times.* Cambridge, England.: New York: Oleander Press, 1980.

Knight, Max, Translator. *A confidential matter: the letters of Richard Strauss and Stefan Zweig, 1931–1935.* Berkeley; London: University of California Press, 1977.

Kok, Alexander. *A voice in the dark: the philharmonia years.* Ampleforth: Emerson Edition, 2002.

Kopelson, Kevin. *Beethoven's kiss: pianism, perversion, and the mastery of desire.* Stanford, California: Stanford University Press, 1996.

Kostelanetz, Richard, Editor. *Aaron Copland: a reader; selected writings 1923–1972.* New York; London: Routledge, 2003.

Kostelanetz, Richard. *Conversing with Cage.* New York; London: Routledge, 2003.

Kostelanetz, Richard. *On innovative musicians.* New York: Limelight Editions, 1989.

Kostelanetz, Richard, Editor. *Virgil Thomson: a reader ; selected writings, 1924–1984.* New York; London: Routledge, 2002.

Kowalke, Kim H. *Kurt Weill in Europe.* Ann Arbor, Michigan: UMI Research Press, 1979.

Krehbiel, Henry Edward. *The pianoforte and its music.* New York: Cooper Square Publishers, 1971.

Kruseman, Philip, Editor. *Beethoven's own words.* London: Hinrichsen Edition, 1948.

Kurtz, Michael. *Stockhausen: a biography.* London: Faber and Faber, 1992.

Lam, Basil. *Beethoven string quartets.* Seattle: University of Washington Press, 1975.

Lambert, Constant. *Music ho!: a study of music in decline.* London: Faber and Faber, Ltd. 1934.

Landon, H. C. Robbins. *Beethoven: a documentary study.* London: Thames and Hudson, 1970.

Landon, H. C. Robbins. *Beethoven: his life, work and world.*

London: Thames and Hudson, 1992.

Landon, H. C. Robbins. *Essays on the Viennese classical style: Gluck, Haydn, Mozart, Beethoven*. London: Barrie & Rockliff The Cresset Press, 1970.

Landon, H. C. Robbins. *Haydn: chronicle and works/Haydn, the late years, 1801–1809*. Bloomington: Indiana University Press, 1977.

Landon, H. C. Robbins. *Haydn: his life and music*. London: Thames and Hudson, 1988.

Landon, H. C. Robbins. *Haydn in England, 1791–1795*. London: Thames and Hudson, 1976.

Landon, H. C. Robbins. *Haydn: the years of 'The creation', 1796–800*. London: Thames and Hudson, 1977.

Landon, H. C. Robbins. *Mozart: the golden years, 1781–1791*. New York: Schirmer Books, 1989.

Landon, H. C. Robbins. *1791, Mozart's last year*. London: Thames and Hudson, 1988.

Landon, H. C. Robbins *The collected correspondence and London notebooks of Joseph Haydn*. London: Barrie and Rockliff, 1959.

Landon, H. C. Robbins: Editor. *The Mozart companion*. London: Faber, 1956.

Landowska, Wanda. *Music of the past*. London: Geoffrey Bles, 1926.

Lang, Paul Henry. *Musicology and performance*. New Haven: Yale University Press, 1997.

Lang, Paul Henry. *The creative world of Beethoven*. New York: W. W. Norton 1971.

Laurence, Dan H., Editor. *Shaw's music: the complete musical criticism in three volumes*. London: Max Reinhardt, the Bodley Head, 1981.

Lawford-Hinrichsen, Irene. *Music publishing and patronage: C. F. Peters, 1800 to the Holocaust*. Kenton: Edition Press, 2000.

Layton, Robert, Editor. *A guide to the concerto*. Oxford: Oxford University Press, 1996.

Layton, Robert, Editor. *A guide to the symphony*. Oxford: Oxford University Press, 1995.

Lebrecht, Norman. *The maestro myth: great conductors in pursuit of power*. London: Simon & Schuster, 1991.

Lee, Ernest Markham. *The story of the symphony*. London: Scott Publishing Co., 1916.

Leibowitz, Herbert A., Editor. *Musical impressions: selections from Paul Rosenfeld's criticism*. London: G. Allen & Unwin, 1970.

Lenrow, Elbert, Editor and Translator. *The letters of Richard Wagner to Anton Pusinelli*. New York: Vienna House, 1972.

Leonard, Maurice. *Kathleen: the life of Kathleen Ferrier: 1912–1953*. London: Hutchinson, 1988.

Lesure, François and Roger Nichols, Editors. *Debussy, letters*. London: Faber and Faber, 1987.

Letellier, Robert Ignatius, Editor and Translator. *The diaries of Giacomo Meyerbeer*. Madison: Fairleigh Dickinson University Press; London: Associated University Presses, 4 Vols., 1999–2004.

Levas, Santeri. *Sibelius: a personal portrait*. London: J. M. Dent, 1972.

Levy, Alan Howard. *Edward MacDowell, an American master.* Lanham, Md. & London: Scarecrow Press, 1998.

Levy, David Benjamin. *Beethoven: the Ninth Symphony.* New Haven, Connecticut; London: Yale University Press, 2003.

Leyda, Jay and Sergi Bertensson. *The Musorgsky reader: a life of Modeste Petrovich Musorgsky in letters and documents.* New York: W.W. Norton, 1947.

Lewis, Thomas P., Editor. *Raymond Leppard on music: an anthology of critical and personal writings.* White Plains, N.Y.: Pro/Am Music Resources, 1993.

Liébert, Georges. *Nietzsche and music.* Chicago: University of Chicago Press, 2004.

Liszt, Franz. *An artist's journey: lettres d'un bachelier ès musique, 1835–1841.* Chicago: University of Chicago Press, 1989.

Litzmann, Berthold, Editor. *Clara Schumann: an artist's life, based on material found in diaries and letters.* London: Macmillan; Leipzig: Breitkopf & Härtel, 2 Vols. 1913.

Litzmann, Berthold, Editor. *Letters of Clara Schumann and Johannes Brahms, 1853–1896.* New York, Vienna House. 2 Vols. 1971.

Lloyd, Stephen. *William Walton: muse of fire.* Woodbridge, Suffolk: The Boydell Press, 2001.

Locke, Ralph P. and Cyrilla Barr, Editors. *Cultivating music in America: women patrons and activists since 1860.* Berkeley: University of California Press, 1997.

Lockspeiser, Edward. *Debussy: his life and mind.* London: Cassell. 2 Vols. 1962–1965.

Lockspeiser, Edward. *The literary clef: an anthology of letters and writings by French composers.* London: J. Calder. 1958.

Lockwood, Lewis, Editor. *Beethoven essays: studies in honor of Elliot Forbes.* Cambridge, Massachusetts: Harvard University Department of Music: Distributed by Harvard University Press, 1984.

Lockwood, Lewis and Mark Kroll, Editors. *The Beethoven violin sonatas: history, criticism, performance.* Urbana: University of Illinois Press, 2004.

Loft, Abram. *Violin and keyboard: the duo repertoire.* New York: Grossman Publishers. 2 Vols. 1973.

Longyear, Rey Morgan. *Nineteenth-century romanticism in music.* Englewood Cliffs: Prentice-Hall, 1969.

Lowe, C. Egerton. *Beethoven's pianoforte sonatas: hints on their rendering, form, etc., with appendices on definition of sonata, music forms, ornaments, pianoforte pedals, and how to discover keys.* London: Novello, 1929.

Macdonald, Hugh, Editor. *Berlioz: Selected letters.* London: Faber and Faber, 1995.

Macdonald, Malcolm, Editor. *Havergal Brian on music: selections from his journalism: Volume One, British music.* London: Toccata Press, 1986.

MacDonald, Malcolm. *Varèse: astronomer in sound.* London: Kahn & Averill, 2003.

MacDowell, Edward. *Critical and historical essays: lectures delivered at Columbia University.* Edited by W. J. Baltzell. London: Elkin; Boston: A.P. Schmidt, 1912.

MacFarren, Walter. Memories: an autobiography. London: Walter Scott Publishing Co.,1905.

Mackenzie, Alexander Campbell. *A musician's narrative.* London: Cassell and company, Ltd, 1927.

McCarthy, Margaret William, Editor. *More letters of Amy Fay: the American years, 1879–1916.* Detroit: Information Coordinators, 1986.

McClary, Susan. *Feminine endings: music, gender, and sexuality.* Minneapolis: University of Minnesota Press, 1991.

McClatchie, Stephen, Editor and Translator. *The Mahler family letters.* Oxford: Oxford University Press, 2006.

McVeigh, Simon. *Concert life in London from Mozart to Haydn.* Cambridge: Cambridge University Press, 1993.

Mahler, Alma. *Gustav Mahler: memories and letters.* Enlarged edition revised and edited and with and introduction by Donald Mitchell. London: John Murray, 1968.

Mai, François Martin. *Diagnosing genius: the life and death of Beethoven.* Montreal; London: McGill-Queen's University Press, 2007.

Del Mar, Norman. *Orchestral variations: confusion and error in the orchestral repertoire.* London: Eulenburg, 1981.

Del Mar, Norman. *Richard Strauss: a critical commentary on his life and works.* London: Barrie & Jenkins. 3 Vols. 1978.

(La) Mara [pseudonym]. *Letters of Franz Liszt.* London: H. Grevel & Co., 2 Vols. 1894.

Marek, George Richard. *Puccini.* London: Cassell & Co., 1952.

Marek, George Richard. *Toscanini.* London: Vision, 1976.

(De) Marliave, Joseph. *Beethoven's quartets.* New York: Dover Publications (reprint), 1961.

Martin, George Whitney. *Verdi: his music, life and times.* London: Macmillan, 1965.

Martner, Knud, Editor. *Selected letters of Gustav Mahler.* London; Boston: Faber and Faber, 1979.

Martyn, Barrie. *Nicolas Medtner: his life and music.* Aldershot: Scolar Press, 1995.

Martyn, Barrie. *Rachmaninoff: composer, pianist, conductor.* Aldershot: Scolar, 1990.

Massenet, Jules. *My recollections.* Westport, Connecticut: Greenwood Press.1970.

Matheopoulos, Helena. *Maestro: encounters with conductors of today.* London: Hutchinson, 1982.

Matthews, Denis. *Beethoven.* London: J. M. Dent, 1985.

Matthews, Denis. *Beethoven piano sonatas.* London: British Broadcasting Corporation, 1967.

Matthews, Denis. *In pursuit of music.* London: Victor Gollancz Ltd., 1968.

Matthews, Denis. *Keyboard music.* Newton Abbot: London David & Charles, 1972.

Mellers, Wilfrid Howard. *Caliban reborn: renewal in twentieth-century music.* London: Victor Gollancz, 1967.

Mellers, Wilfrid Howard. *The sonata principle (from c. 1750)*. London: Rockliff, 1957.

Mendelssohn Bartholdy. *Letters from Italy and Switzerland*. London: Longman, Green, Longman, and Roberts, 1862.

Mendelssohn Bartholdy, Paul. *Letters of Felix Mendelssohn Bartholdy, from 1833 to 1847*. London: Longman, Green, Longman, Roberts, & Green, 1864.

Menuhin, Yehudi and Curtis W. Davis. *The music of man*. London: Macdonald and Jane's, 1979.

Menuhin, Yehudi. *Theme and variations*. London: Heinemann Educational Books Ltd., 1972.

Menuhin, Yehudi. *Unfinished journey*. London: Macdonald and Jane's, 1977.

Messian, Olivier. *Music and color: conversations with Claude Samuel*. Portland, Oregon: Amadeus, 1994.

Miall, Anthony. *Musical bumps*. London: J.M. Dent & Sons Ltd, 1981.

Michotte, Edmond. *Richard Wagner's visit to Rossini (Paris 1860): and, An evening at Rossini's in Beau-Sejour (Passy), 1858*. Chicago; London: University of Chicago Press, 1982.

Mies, Paul. *Beethoven's sketches: an analysis of his style based on a study of his sketchbooks.*
New York: Johnson Reprint, 1969.

Milhaud, Darius. *My happy life*. London: Boyars, 1995.

Miller, Mina. *The Nielsen companion*. London: Faber and Faber, 1994.

Milsom, David. *Theory and practice in late nineteenth-century violin performance: an examination of style in performance, 1850–1900*. Aldershot: Ashgate, 2003.

Mitchell, Donald, Editor. *Letters from a life: the selected letters and diaries of Benjamin Britten 1913–1976*. London: Faber and Faber. 3 Vols., 1991.

Mitchell, Donald and Hans Keller, Editors. *Music survey: new series 1949–1952*. London: Faber Music in association with Faber & Faber, 1981.

Mitchell, Jon C. *A comprehensive biography of composer Gustav Holst, with correspondence and diary excerpts: including his American years*. Lewiston, New York: Edwin Mellen Press, 2001.

Moldenhauer, Hans. *Anton von Webern: a chronicle of his life and work*. London: Victor Gollancz, 1978.

Monrad-Johansen. Edvard Grieg. New York: Tudor Publishing Co., 1945.

Moore, Gerald. *Am I too loud?: memoirs of an accompanist*. London: Hamish Hamilton, 1962.

Moore, Gerald. *Farewell recital: further memoirs*. Harmondsworth: Penguin Books, 1979.

Moore, Gerald. *Furthermoore: interludes in an accompanist's life*. London: Hamish Hamilton, 1983.

Moore, Jerrold Northrop. *Edward Elgar: a creative life*. Oxford: Oxford University Press, 1984.

Moore, Jerrold Northrop. *Elgar, Edward. The windflower letters: correspondence with Alice Caroline Stuart Wortley and her family*. Oxford: Clarendon

Press; New York: Oxford University Press, 1989.

Moore, Jerrold Northrop. *Elgar, Edward. Edward Elgar: letters of a lifetime.* Oxford: Clarendon Press; New York: Oxford University Press, 1990.

Moore, Jerrold Northrop. *Elgar, Edward. Elgar and his publishers: letters of a creative life.* Oxford: Clarendon, 1987.

Moreux, Serge. *Béla Bartók.* London: Harvill Press, 1953.

Morgan, Kenneth. *Fritz Reiner, maestro and martinet.* Urbana: University of Illinois Press, 2005.

Cone, Edward T., Editor. *Music, a view from Delft: selected essays.* Chicago: University of Chicago Press, 1989.

Morgan, Robert P. *Twentieth-century music: a history of musical style in modern Europe and America.* New York: Norton, 1991.

Morgenstern, Sam., Editor. *Composers on music: an anthology of composers' writings.* London: Faber & Faber, 1956.

Morrow, Mary Sue. *Concert life in Haydn's Vienna: aspects of a developing musical and social institution.* Stuyvesant, New York: Pendragon Press, 1989.

Moscheles, Felix, Editor and Translator. *Letters from Felix Mendelssohn-Bartholdy to Ignaz and Charlotte Moscheles.* London: Trübner and Co., 1888.

Mudge, Richard B., Translator. *Glinka, Mikhail Ivanovich: Memoirs.* Norman: University of Oklahoma Press, 1963.

Munch, Charles. *I am a conductor.* New York: Oxford University Press, 1955.

Mundy, Simon. *Bernard Haitink: a working life.* London: Robson Books, 1987.

Musgrave, Michael. *The musical life of the Crystal Palace.* Cambridge: Cambridge University Press, 1995.

Music & Letters. *Beethoven: special number.* London: Music & Letters, 1927.

Musical Times. *Special Issue.* John A. Fuller-Maitland London: Vol. VIII, No. 2, 1927.

Myers, Rollo H., Editor. *Twentieth-century music.* London: Calder and Boyars, 1960.

National Gallery (Great Britain). *Music performed at the National Gallery concerts, 10th October 1939 to 10th April 1946.* London: Privately printed, 1948.

Nattiez, Jean-Jacques, Editor. *Orientations: collected writings – Pierre Boulez.* London: Faber and Faber, 1986.

Nauhaus, Gerd, Editor. *The marriage diaries of Robert & Clara Schumann.* London: Robson Books, 1994.

Nectoux, Jean Michel. *Gabriel Fauré: a musical life.* Translated by Roger Nichols. Cambridge: Cambridge University Press, 1991.

Nettl, Paul. *Beethoven handbook.* Westport, Connecticut: Greenwood Press, 1975.

Neumayr, Anton. *Music and medicine.* Bloomington, Illinois: Medi-Ed Press, 1994–1997

Newbould, Brian. *Schubert and the symphony: a new perspective.* Surbiton: Toccata Press, 1992.

Newlin, Dika. *Schoenberg remembered: diaries and recollections (1938–76).* New York: Pendragon Press, 1980.

Newman, Ernest. *From the world of music: essays from 'The Sunday Times'*. London: J. Calder, 1956.

Newman, Ernest. Hugo Wolf. New York: Dover Publications, 1966.

Newman, Ernest, Annotated and Translated. *Memoirs of Hector Berlioz from 1803 to 1865, comprising his travels in Germany, Italy, Russia, and England*. New York: Knopf, 1932.

Newman, Ernest. *More essays from the world of music: essays from the 'Sunday Times'*. London: John Calder, 1958.

Newman, Ernest. *Musical studies*. London; New York: John Lane, 1910.

Newman, Ernest. *Testament of music: essays and papers*. London: Putnam, 1962.

Newman, Richard. *Alma Rosé: Vienna to Auschwitz*. Portland, Oregon: Amadeus Press, 2000.

Newman, William S. *The sonata in the classic era*. Chapel Hill: University of North Carolina Press 1963.

Newman, William S. *The sonata in the Classic era*. New York; London: W.W. Norton, 1983.

Newmarch, Rosa Harriet. *Henry J. Wood*. London & New York: John Lane, 1904.

Nicholas, Jeremy. *Godowsky: the pianists' pianist; a biography of Leopold Godowsky*. Hexham: Appian Publications & Recordings, 1989.

Nichols, Roger. *Debussy remembered*. London: Faber and Faber, 1992.

Nichols, Roger. *Mendelssohn remembered*. London: Faber and Faber, 1997.

Nichols, Roger. *Ravel remembered*. London: Faber and Faber, 1987.

Niecks, Frederick. *Robert Schumann*. London: J. M. Dent, 1925.

Nielsen, Carl. *Living music*. Copenhagen, Wilhelm Hansen, 1968.

Nielsen, Carl. *My childhood*. Copenhagen, Wilhelm Hansen, 1972.

Nikolska, Irina. *Conversations with Witold Lutoslawski, (1987–92)*. Stockholm: Melos, 1994.

Nohl, Ludwig. *Beethoven depicted by his contemporaries*. London: Reeves, 1880.

De Nora, Tia. *Beethoven and the construction of genius: musical politics in Vienna, 1792–1803*. Berkeley: University of California Press, 1997.

Norton, Spencer, Editor and Translator. *Music in my time: the memoirs of Alfredo Casella*. Norman: University of Oklahoma Press, 1955.

Nottebohm, Gustav. *Two Beethoven sketchbooks: a description with musical extracts*. London: Gollancz, 1979.

Oakeley, Edward Murray. *The life of Sir Herbert Stanley Oakeley*. London: George Allen, 1904.

Lucas, Brenda and Michael Kerr. *Virtuoso: the story of John Ogdon*. London: H. Hamilton, 1981.

Oliver, Michael, Editor. *Settling the score: a journey through the music of the twentieth century*. London: Faber and Faber, 1999.

Olleson, Philip. *Samuel Wesley: the man and his music*. Woodbridge: Boydell Press, 2003.

Olleson, Philip, Editor. *The letters of Samuel Wesley: professional and social correspondence, 1797–1837.* Oxford; New York: Oxford University Press, 2001.

Olmstead, Andrea. *Conversations with Roger Sessions.* Boston: Northeastern University Press, 1987.

Orenstein, Arbie, Editor. *A Ravel reader: correspondence, articles, interviews.* New York: Columbia University Press, 1990.

Orenstein, Arbie. *Ravel: man and musician.* New York: Columbia University Press, 1975.

Orledge, Robert. *Charles Koechlin (1867–1950): his life and works.* New York: Harwood Academic Publishers, 1989.

Orledge, Robert. *Gabriel Fauré.* London: Eulenburg Books, 1979.

Orledge, Robert. *Satie remembered.* London: Faber and Faber, 1995.

Orledge, Robert. *Satie the composer.* Cambridge: Cambridge University Press, 1990.

Orlova, Alexandra. *Glinka's life in music: a chronicle.* Ann Arbor: UMI Research Press, 1988.

Orlova, Alexandra. *Musorgsky's days and works: a biography in documents.* Ann Arbor: UMI Research Press, 1983.

Orlova, Alexandra. *Tchaikovsky: a self-portrait.* Oxford: Oxford University Press, 1990.

Osborne, Charles, Editor and Translator. *Letters of Giuseppe Verdi.* London: Victor Gollancz, 1971.

Osmond-Smith David, Editor and Translator. *Luciano Berio: Two interviews with Rossana Dalmonte and Bálint András Varga.* New York; London: Boyars, 1985.

Ouellette, Fernand. *Edgard Varèse.* London: Calder & Boyars, 1973.

Paderewski, Ignacy Jan and Mary Lawton. *The Paderewski memoirs.* London: Collins, 1939.

Page, Tim: Editor. *The Glenn Gould reader.* London: Faber and Faber, 1987.

Page, Tim. *Music from the road: views and reviews, 1978–1992.* New York; Oxford: Oxford University Press, 1992.

Page, Tim and Vanessa Weeks, Editors. *Selected letters of Virgil Thomson.* New York: Summit Books, 1988.

Page, Tim. *Tim Page on music: views and reviews.* Portland, Oregon: Amadeus Press, 2002.

Palmer, Christopher. *Herbert Howells, (1892–1983): a celebration.* London: Thames, 1996.

Palmer, Christopher, Editor. *Sergei Prokofiev: Soviet diary 1927 and other writings.* London: Faber and Faber, 1991.

Palmer, Fiona M. *Domenico Dragonetti in England (1794–1846): the career of a double bass virtuoso.* Oxford: Clarendon, 1997.

Palmieri, Robert, Editor. *Encyclopedia of the piano.* New York: Garland, 1996.

Panufnik, Andrzej. *Composing myself.* London: Methuen, 1987.

Parsons, James, Editor. *The Cambridge companion to the Lied.* Cambridge: Cambridge University Press, 2004.

Paynter, John, Editor. *Between old worlds and new: occasional writings on music by Wilfrid Mellers.* London: Cygnus Arts, 1997.

Pestelli, Giorgio. *The age of Mozart and Beethoven.* Cambridge:

Cambridge University Press, 1984.

Peyser, Joan. *Bernstein: a biography: revised & updated.* New York: Billboard Books, 1998.

Phillips-Matz, Mary Jane. *Verdi: a biography.* Oxford: Oxford University Press, 1993.

Piggott, Patrick. *The life and music of John Field, 1782–1837: creator of the nocturne.* London: Faber and Faber, 1973.

Plantinga, Leon. *Beethoven's concertos: history, style, performance.* New York: Norton, 1999.

Plantinga, Leon. *Clementi: his life and music.* London: Oxford University Press, 1977.

Plantinga, Leon. *Romantic music: a history of musical style in nineteenth-century Europe.* New York; London: Norton, 1984.

Plaskin, Glenn. *Horowitz: a biography of Vladimir Horowitz.* London: Macdonald, 1983.

Pleasants, Henry, Editor and Translator. *Hanslick, Eduard: Music criticisms, 1846–99.* Baltimore: Penguin Books, 1963.

Pleasants, Henry, Editor and Translator. *Hanslick's music criticisms.* New York: Dover Publications, 1988.

Pleasants, Henry, Editor and Translator. *The music criticism of Hugo Wolf.* New York: Holmes & Meier Publishers, 1978.

Pleasants, Henry, Editor and Translator. *The musical journeys of Louis Spohr.* Norman: University of Oklahoma Press, 1961.

Pollack, Howard. *Aaron Copland: the life and work of an uncommon man.* New York: Henry Holt, 1999.

Poulenc, Francis. *My friends and myself.* London: Dennis Dobson, 1978.

Powell, Richard, Mrs. *Edward Elgar: memories of a variation.* Aldershot, Hants, England: Scolar Press; Brookfield, Vermont, USA: Ashgate Publishing. Co., 1994.

Poznansky, Alexander, Editor. *Tchaikovsky through others' eyes.* Bloomington: Indiana University Press, 1999.

Praeger, Ferdinand. *Wagner as I knew him.* London; New York: Longmans, Green, 1892.

Previn, Andre. *Anthony Hopkins. Music face to face.* London, Hamish Hamilton, 1971.

Prieberg, Fred K. *Trial of strength: Wilhelm Furtwängler and the Third Reich.* London: Quartet, 1991.

Procter-Gregg, Humphrey. *Beecham remembered.* London: Duckworth, 1976.

Prokofiev, Sergey. *Prokofiev by Prokofiev: a composer's memoir.* London: Macdonald and Jane's, 1979.

Rachmaninoff, Sergei. *Rachmaninoff's recollections told to Oskar von Riesemann.* London: George Allen & Unwin, 1934.

Radcliffe, Philip. *Beethoven's string quartets.* Cambridge: Cambridge University Press, 1978.

Radcliffe, Philip. *Piano Music in: The Age of Beethoven, The New Oxford History of Music, Vol. VIII.* Gerald Abraham, (Editor), 1988, p. 340.

Ratner, Leonard G. *Romantic music: sound and syntax.* New York: Schirmer Books, 1992.

Raynor, Henry. *A social history of music: from the middle ages to*

Beethoven. London: Barrie & Jenkins, 1972.

Rees, Brian. *Camille Saint-Saëns: a life*. London: Chatto & Windus, 1999.

Reich, Willi, Editor. *Anton Webern: The path to the new music*. London; Bryn Mawr: Theodore Presser in association with Universal Edition, 1963.

Reid, Charles. *John Barbirolli: a biography*. London, Hamish Hamilton, 1971.

Reid, Charles. *Malcolm Sargent: a biography*. London: Hamilton, 1968.

Rennert, Jonathan. *William Crotch (1775–1847): composer, artist, teacher*. Lavenham: Terence Dalton, 1975.

Rice, John A. *Antonio Salieri and Viennese Opera*. Chicago, Illinois: University of Chicago Press, 1998.

Rice, John A. *Empress Marie Therese and music at the Viennese court, 1792–1807*. Cambridge: Cambridge University Press, 2003.

Richards, Fiona. *The Music of John Ireland*. Aldershot: Ashgate, 2000.

Rigby, Charles. *Sir Charles Hallé: a portrait for today*. Manchester: Dolphin Press, 1952.

Ringer, Alexander, Editor. *The early Romantic era: between Revolutions; 1789 and 1848*. Basingstoke: Macmillan, 1990.

Roberts, John P.L. and Ghyslaine Guertin, Editors. *Glenn Gould: Selected letters*. Toronto; Oxford: Oxford University Press, 1992.

Robertson, Alec. *More than music*. London: Collins, 1961.

Robinson, Harlow, Editor and Translator. *Selected letters of Sergei Prokofiev*. Boston: Northeastern University Press, 1998.

Robinson, Harlow. *Sergei Prokofiev: a biography*. London: Hale, 1987.

Robinson, Paul A. *Ludwig van Beethoven, Fidelio*. Cambridge: Cambridge University Press, 1996.

Robinson, Suzanne, Editor. *Michael Tippett: music and literature*. Aldershot: Ashgate, 2002.

Rochberg, George. *The aesthetics of survival: a composer's view of twentieth-century music*. Ann Arbor, Michigan: University of Michigan Press, 2004.

Rodmell, Paul. *Charles Villiers Stanford*. Aldershot: Ashgate, 2002.

Roeder, Michael Thomas. *A history of the concerto*. Portland, Oregon: Amadeus Press, 1994.

Rohr, Deborah Adams. *The careers of British musicians, 1750–1850: a profession of artisans*. Cambridge: Cambridge University Press, 2001.

Rolland, Romain. *Goethe and Beethoven*. New York; London: Blom, 1968.

Rolland, Romain. *Beethoven and Handel*. London: Waverley Book Co., 1917.

Rolland, Romain. *Beethoven the creator*. Garden City, New York: Garden City Pub., 1937.

Roscow, Gregory, Editor. *Bliss on music: selected writings of Arthur Bliss, 1920–1975*. Oxford: Oxford University Press, 1991.

Rosen, Charles. *Beethoven's piano sonatas: a short companion*. New Haven, Connecticut:

London: Yale University Press, 2002.

Rosen, Charles. *Critical entertainments: music old and new.* Cambridge, Massachusetts; London: Harvard University Press, 2000.

Rosen, Charles. *The classical style: Haydn, Mozart, Beethoven.* London: Faber and Faber, 1976.

Rosen, Charles. *The romantic generation.* Cambridge, Massachusetts: Harvard University Press, 1995.

Rosenthal, Albi. *Obiter scripta: essays, lectures, articles, interviews and reviews on music, and other subjects.* Oxford: Offox Press; Lanham: Scarecrow Press, 2000.

Rostal, Max. *Beethoven: the sonatas for piano and violin; thoughts on their interpretation.* London: Toccata Press, 1985.

Rostropovich, Mstislav and Galina Vishnevskaya. *Russia, music, and liberty.* Portland, Oregan: Amadeus Press, 1995.

Rubinstein, Arthur. *My many years.* London: Jonathan Cape, 1980.

Rubinstein, Arthur. *My young years.* London: Jonathan Cape, 1973.

Rumph, Stephen C. *Beethoven after Napoleon: political romanticism in the late works.* Berkeley; London: University of California Press, 2004.

Rye, Matthew Rye. *Notes to the BBC Radio Three Beethoven Experience, Friday 10 June 2005,* www.bbc.co.uk/radio3/Beethoven.

Sachs, Harvey. *Toscanini.* London: Weidenfeld and Nicholson, 1978.

Sachs, Joel. *Kapellmeister Hummel in England and France.* Detroit: Information Coordinators, 1977.

Saffle, Michael, Editor. *Liszt and his world: proceedings of the International Liszt Conference held at Virginia Polytechnic Institute and State University, 20–23 May 1993.* Stuyvesant, New York: Pendragon Press, 1998.

Safránek, Milos. *Bohuslav Martinu, his life and works.* London: Allan Wingate, 1962.

Saint-Saëns, Camille. *Outspoken essays on music.* Westport, Connecticut: Greenwood Press, 1970.

Saussine, Renée de. *Paganini.* Westport, Connecticut: Greenwood Press, 1976.

Sayers, W. C. Berwick. *Samuel Coleridge-Taylor, musician: his life and letters.* London; New York: Cassell and Co., 1915.

Schaarwächter, Jürgen. *HB: aspects of Havergal Brian.* Aldershot: Ashgate, 1997.

Schafer, R. Murray. *E.T.A. Hoffmann and music.* Toronto: University of Toronto Press, 1975.

Schafer, R. Murray, Editor. *Ezra Pound and music: the complete criticism.* London: Faber and Faber, 1978.

Schat, Peter. *The tone clock.* Chur, Switzerland; Langhorne, Pa.: Harwood Academic Publishers, 1993.

Schenk, Erich. *Mozart and his times.* Edited and Translated by Richard and Clara Winstin. London: Secker & Warburg, 1960.

Schindler, Anton Felix. *Beethoven as I knew him.* Edited by Donald W. MacArdle and Translated by Constance S. Jolly from the

German edition of 1860 London: Faber and Faber, 1966.

Schlosser, Johann. *Beethoven: the first biography, 1827.* Edited by Barry Cooper. Portland, Oregon: Amadeus Press, 1996.

Schnabel, Artur. *My life and music.* London: Longmans, 1961.

Schnittke, Alfred. *A Schnittke reader.* Bloomington: Indiana University Press, 2002.

Scholes, Percy Alfred. *Crotchets: a few short musical notes.* London: John Lane, 1924.

Schonberg, Harold C. *The great pianists.* London: Victor Gollancz, 1964.

Schrade, Leo. *Beethoven in France: the growth of an idea.* New Haven; London: Yale University Press, H. Milford, Oxford University Press, 1942.

Schrade, Leo. *Tragedy in the art of music.* Cambridge, Massachusetts: Harvard University Press, 1964.

Schuh, Willi. *Richard Strauss: a chronicle of the early years 1864–1898.* Cambridge: Cambridge University Press, 1982.

Schuh, Willi, Editor. *Richard Strauss: Recollections and reflections.* London; New York: Boosey & Hawkes, 1953.

Schuller, Gunther. *Musings: the musical worlds of Gunther Schuller.* New York: Oxford University Press, 1986.

Schumann, Robert. *Music and musicians: essays and criticisms.* London: William Reeves, 1877.

Schuttenhelm, Editor. *Selected letters of Michael Tippett.* London: Faber and Faber, 2005.

Schwartz, Elliott. *Music since 1945: issues, materials, and literature.* New York: Schirmer Books, 1993.

Scott, Marion M. *Beethoven: (The master musicians).* London: Dent, 1940.

Scott-Sutherland, Colin. *Arnold Bax.* London: J. M. Dent, 1973.

Searle, Muriel V. *John Ireland: the man and his music.* Tunbridge Wells: Midas Books, 1979.

Secrest, Meryle. *Leonard Bernstein: a life.* London: Bloomsbury, 1995.

Seeger, Charles. *Studies in musicology II, 1929–1979.* Edited by Anne M. Pescatello. Berkeley; London: University of California Press, 1994.

Selden-Goth, Gisela, Editor. *Felix Mendelssohn: letters.* London: Paul Elek Publishers Ltd, 1946.

Senner, Wayne M., Robin Wallace and William Meredith, Editors. *The critical reception of Beethoven's compositions by his German contemporaries.* Lincoln: University of Nebraska Press, in association with the American Beethoven Society and the Ira F. Brilliant Center for Beethoven Studies, San José State University, 1999.

Seroff, Victor I. *Rachmaninoff.* London: Cassell & Company, 1951.

Sessions, Roger. *Questions about music.* Cambridge, Massachusetts: Harvard University Press, 1970.

Sessions, Roger. *The musical experience of composer, performer, listener.* New York: Atheneum, 1966, 1950.

Seyfried, Ignaz von. *Louis van Beethoven's Studies in thoroughbass, counterpoint and the art of scientific composition.* Leipzig; New-York: Schuberth and Company, 1853.

Sharma, Bhesham R. *Music and culture in the age of mechanical reproduction.* New York: Peter Lang, 2000.

Shaw, Bernard. *How to become a musical critic.* London: R. Hart Davis, 1960.

Shaw, Bernard. *London music in 1888–89 as heard by Corno di Bassetto (later known as Bernard Shaw): with some further autobiographical particulars.* London: Constable and Company, 1937.

Shaw, Bernard. *Music in London, 1890–1894.* London: Constable and Company Limited, 3 Vols., 1932.

Shedlock, John South. *Beethoven's pianoforte sonatas: the origin and respective values of various readings.* London: Augener Ltd., 1918.

Shedlock, John South. *The pianoforte sonata: its origin and development.* London: Methuen, 1895.

Shepherd, Arthur. *The string quartets of Ludwig van Beethoven.* Cleveland: H. Carr, The Printing Press, 1935.

Sheppard, Leslie and Herbert R. Axelrod. *Paganini: containing a portfolio of drawings by Vido Polikarpus.* Neptune City, New Jersey: Paganiniana Publications, 1979.

Short, Michael. *Gustav Holst: the man and his music.* Oxford: Oxford University Press, 1990.

Shostakovich, Dmitry. *Dmitry Shostakovich: about himself and his times.* Moscow: Progress Publishers, 1981.

Simpson, John Palgrave. *Carl Maria von Weber: the life of an artist, from the German of his son Baron, Max Maria von Weber.* London: Chapman and Hall, 1865.

Simpson, Robert. *Beethoven symphonies.* London: British Broadcasting Corporation, 1970.

Sipe, Thomas. *Beethoven: Eroica symphony.* Cambridge: Cambridge University Press, 1998.

Sitwell, Sacheverell. *Mozart.* Edinburgh: Peter Davies Limited, 1932.

Skelton, Geoffrey. *Paul Hindemith: the man behind the music; a biography.* London: Victor Gollancz, 1975.

Smallman, Basil. *The piano trio: its history, technique, and repertoire.* Oxford: Clarendon Press; Oxford; New York: Oxford University Press, 1990.

Smidak, Emil. *Isaak-Ignaz Moscheles: the life of the composer and his encounters with Beethoven, Liszt, Chopin, and Mendelssohn.* Aldershot, Hampshire, England: Scolar Press; Brookfield, Vermont, USA: Gower Publishing Co., 1989.

Smith, Barry. *Peter Warlock: the life of Philip Heseltine.* Oxford: Oxford University Press, 1994.

Smith, Joan Allen. *Schoenberg and his circle: a Viennese portrait.* New York: Schirmer Books, London: Collier Macmillan, 1986.

Smith, Richard Langham, Editor. *Debussy on music: the critical writings of the great French composer Claude Debussy.* London: Secker & Warburg, 1977.

Smith, Ronald. *Alkan.* London: Kahn and Averill, 1976.

Snowman, Daniel. *The Amadeus Quartet: the men and the music.* London: Robson Books, 1981.

Solomon, Maynard. *Beethoven.* New York: Schirmer, 1977.

Solomon, Maynard. *Beethoven essays.* Cambridge, Massachusetts; London: Harvard University Press, 1988.

Solomon, Maynard. *Late Beethoven: music, thought, imagination.* Berkeley; London: University of California Press, 2003.

Solomon, Maynard. *Mozart: a life.* London: Hutchinson, 1995.

Sonneck, Oscar George Theodore. *Beethoven: impressions of contemporaries.* London: Oxford University Press, 1927.

Spalding, Albert. *Rise to follow: an autobiography.* London: Frederick Muller Ltd., 1946.

Spohr, Louis. *Louis Spohr's autobiography.* London: Longman, Green, Longman, Roberts, & Green, 1865.

Stafford, William. *Mozart myths: a critical reassessment.* Stanford, California: Stanford University Press, 1991.

Stanford, Charles Villiers. *Interludes: records and reflections.* London: John Murray, 1922.

Stanley, Glen, Editor. *The Cambridge companion to Beethoven.* Cambridge; New York: Cambridge University Press, 2000

Stedman, Preston. *The symphony.* Englewood Cliffs, New Jersey; London: Prentice-Hall, 1979.

Stedron, Bohumír, Editor and Translator. *Leos Janácek: letters and reminiscences.* Prague: Artia, 1955.

Stein, Erwin, Editor. *Arnold Schoenberg: letters.* London: Faber and Faber, 1964.

Stein, Erwin. *Orpheus in new guises.* London: Rockliff, 1953.

Stein, Jack Madison. *Poem and music in the German lied from Gluck to Hugo Wolf.* Cambridge, Massachusetts: Harvard University Press, 1971.

Stein, Leonard, Editor. *Style and idea: selected writings of Arnold Schoenberg.* London: Faber and Faber, 1975.

Steinberg, Michael P. *Listening to reason: culture, subjectivity, and nineteenth-century music.* Princeton, New Jersey: Princeton University Press, 2004.

Steinberg, Michael. *The concerto: a listener's guide.* New York: Oxford University Press, 1998.

Steinberg, Michael. *The symphony: a listener's guide.* Oxford; New York: Oxford University Press, 1995.

Sternfeld, Frederick William. *Goethe and music: a list of parodies and Goethe's relationship to music; a list of references.* New York: Da Capo Press, 1979.

Stivender, David. *Mascagni: an autobiography compiled, edited and translated from original sources.* New York: Pro/Am Music Resources; London: Kahn & Averill, 1988.

Stone, Else and Kurt Stone, Editors. *The writings of Elliott Carter: an American composer looks at modern music.* Bloomington: Indiana University Press, 1977.

Stowell, Robin. *Beethoven: violin concerto.* Cambridge: Cambridge University Press, 1998.

Stowell, Robin: Editor. *The Cambridge companion to the cello.*

Cambridge: Cambridge University Press, 1999.

Stowell, Robin: Editor. *The Cambridge companion to the string quartet.* Cambridge: Cambridge University Press, 2003.

Stratton, Stephen Samuel. *Mendelssohn.* London: J.M. Dent & Co.; New York: E.P. Dutton & Co., 1901.

Straus, Joseph N. *Remaking the past: musical modernism and the influence of the tonal tradition.* Cambridge, Massachusetts: Harvard University Press, 1990.

Stravinsky, Igor. *An autobiography.* London: Calder and Boyars, 1975.

Stravinsky, Igor. *Themes and conclusions.* London: Faber and Faber, 1972.

Stravinsky, Igor and Robert Craft. *Conversations with Igor Stravinsky.* London: Faber and Faber, 1959.

Stravinsky, Igor and Robert Craft. *Dialogues and a diary.* London: Faber and Faber 1968.

Stravinsky, Igor and Robert Craft. *Memories and commentaries.* London: Faber and Faber, 2002.

Strunk, Oliver. *Source readings in music history, 4: The Classic era.* London: Faber and Faber 1981.

Sullivan, Blair, Editor. *The echo of music: essays in honor of Marie Louise Göllner.* Warren, Michigan: Harmonie Park Press, 2004.

Sullivan, Jack, Editor. *Words on music: from Addison to Barzun.* Athens: Ohio University Press, 1990.

Symonette, Lys and Kim H. Kowalke, Editors and Translators. *Speak low (when you speak love): the letters of Kurt Weill and Lotte Lenya.* London: Hamish Hamilton, 1996.

Swalin, Benjamin F. *The violin concerto: a study in German romanticism.* New York, Da Capo Press, 1973.

Szigeti, Joseph. *With strings attached: reminiscences and reflections.* London: Cassell & Co. Ltd, 1949.

Tanner, Michael, Editor. *Notebooks, 1924–1954: Wilhelm Furtwängler.* London: Quartet Books, 1989.

Taylor, Robert, Editor. *Furtwängler on music: essays and addresses.* Aldershot: Scolar, 1991.

Taylor, Ronald. *Kurt Weill: composer in a divided world.* London: Simon & Schuster, 1991.

Tchaikovsky, Peter Ilich. *Letters to his family: an autobiography.* Translated by Galina von Meck. London: Dennis Dobson, 1981.

Tertis, Lionel. *My viola and I: a complete autobiography; with, 'Beauty of tone in string playing', and other essays.* London: Paul Elek, 1974.

Thayer, Alexander Wheelock. *Salieri: rival of Mozart.* Edited by Theodore Albrecht. Kansas City, Missouri: Philharmonia of Greater Kansas City, 1989.

Thomas, Michael Tilson. *Viva voce: conversations with Edward Seckerson.* London: Faber and Faber 1994.

Thomson, Andrew. *Vincent d'Indy and his world.* Oxford: Clarendon Press, 1996.

Thomson, Virgil. *The musical scene.* New York: Greenwood Press, 1968.

Thomson, Virgil. Virgil Thomson.

Tillard, Françoise. *Fanny Mendelssohn*. Amadeus Press: Portland, 1996.

Tilmouth, Michael, Editor. *Donald Francis Tovey: The classics of music: talks, essays, and other writings previously uncollected.* Oxford: Oxford University Press, 2001

Tippett, Michael. *Moving into Aquarius.* London: Routledge and Kegan Paul, 1959.

Tippett, Michael. *Those twentieth century blues: an autobiography.* London: Hutchinson, 1991.

Todd, R. Larry, Editor. *Nineteenth-century piano music.* New York; London: Routledge, 2004.

Todd, R. Larry, Editor. *Schumann and his world.* Princeton: Princeton University Press, 1994.

Tommasini, Anthony. *Virgil Thomson: composer on the aisle.* New York: W.W. Norton, 1997.

Tortelier, Paul. *A self-portrait: in conversation with David Blum.* London: Heinemann, 1984.

Tovey, Donald Francis. *A Companion to Beethoven's Pianoforte Sonatas.* Revised by Barry Cooper. London: The Associated Board, [1931], 1998.

Tovey, Donald Francis. *Beethoven.* London: Oxford University Press, 1944.

Tovey, Donald Francis. *Essays and lectures on music.* London: Oxford University Press, 1949.

Tovey, Donald Francis. *Essays in musical analysis.* London: Oxford University Press, H. Milford, 7 Vols., 1935–41.

Tovey, Donald Francis. *The forms of music: musical articles from The Encyclopaedia Britannica.* London: Oxford University Press, 1944.

Toye, Francis. *Giuseppe Verdi: his life and works.* London: William Heinemann Ltd., 1931.

Truscott, Harold. *Beethoven's late string quartets.* London: Dobson, 1968.

Tyler, William R. *The letters of Franz Liszt to Olga von Meyendorff, 1871–1886, in the Mildred Bliss Collection at Dumbarton Oaks.* Translated by William R. Tyler. Washington: Dumbarton Oaks, Trustees for Harvard University; Cambridge, Massachusetts: distributed by Harvard University Press, 1979.

Tyrrell, John. *Janáček: years of a life. Vol. 1, (1854–1914) The lonely blackbird.* London: Faber and Faber, 2006.

Tyrrell, John, Editor and Translator. *My life with Janáček: the memoirs of Zdenka Janácková.* London: Faber and Faber, 1998.

Tyson, Alan, Editor. *Beethoven studies 2.* Cambridge: Cambridge University Press, 1977.

Tyson, Alan, Editor. *Beethoven studies 3.* Cambridge: Cambridge University Press, 1982.

Tyson, Alan. *Mozart: studies of the autograph scores.* Cambridge, Massachusetts; London: Harvard University Press, 1987.

Tyson, Alan. *The authentic English editions of Beethoven.* London: Faber and Faber, 1963.

Underwood, J. A., Editor. *Gabriel Fauré: his life through his letters.* London: Marion Boyars, 1984.

Vechten, Carl van, Editor. *Nikolay, Rimsky-Korsakov: My musical life*. London: Martin Secker & Warburg Ltd., 1942.

Vinton, John. *Essays after a dictionary: music and culture at the close of Western civilization*. Lewisburg: Bucknell University Press, 1977.

Volkov, Solomon, Editor. *Testimony: the memoirs of Dmitri Shostakovich*. London: Faber and Faber, 1981.

Volta, Ornella, Editor. *A mammal's notebook: collected writings of Erik Satie*. London: Atlas Press, 1996.

Wagner, Richard. Beethoven: *With [a] supplement from the philosophical works of A. Schopenhauer*. Translated by E. Dannreuther. London: Reeves, 1893.

Wagner, Richard. *My life*. London: Constable and Company Ltd., 1911.

Walden, Valerie. *One hundred years of violoncello: a history of technique and performance practice, 1740–1840*. Cambridge: Cambridge University Press, 1998.

Walker, Alan. *Franz Liszt. Volume 1, The virtuoso years: 1811–1847*. New York: Alfred A. Knopf, 1983.

Walker, Alan. *Franz Liszt. Volume 2, The Weimar years: 1848–1861*. London: Faber and Faber, 1989.

Walker, Alan. *Franz Liszt. Volume 3, The final years, 1861–1886*. London: Faber and Faber, 1997.

Walker, Bettina. *My musical experiences*. London: Richard Bentley and Son, 1890.

Walker, Ernest. *Free thought and the musician, and other essays*. London; New York: Oxford University Press, 1946.

Walker, Frank. *Hugo Wolf: a biography*. London: J. M. Dent, 1951.

Walker, Frank. *The man Verdi*. London: Dent, 1962.

Wallace, Grace, *[Lady Wallace]*. *Beethoven's letters (1790–1826): from the collection of Dr. Ludwig Nohl. Also his letters to the Archduke Rudolph, Cardinal-Archbishop of Olmutz, K.W., from the collection of Dr. Ludwig Ritter Von Kolchel*. London: Longmans, Green, 2 Vols., 1866.

Wallace, Robin. *Beethoven's critics: aesthetic dilemmas and resolutions during the composer's lifetime*. Cambridge; New York: Cambridge University Press, 1986.

Walter, Bruno. *Theme and variations: an autobiography*. London: H. Hamilton, 1948.

Warrack, John Hamilton. *Writings on music*. Cambridge: Cambridge University Press, 1981.

Wasielewski, Wilhelm Joseph von. *Life of Robert Schumann: with letters, 1833–1852*. London: William Reeves, 1878.

Watkins, Glenn. *Proof through the night: music and the Great War*. Berkeley: University of California Press, 2003.

Watkins, Glenn. *Pyramids at the Louvre: music, culture, and collage from Stravinsky to the postmodernists*. Cambridge, Massachusetts; London: Belknap Press of Harvard University Press, 1994.

Watkins, Glenn. *Soundings: music in the twentieth century*. New York: Schirmer Books London: Collier Macmillan, 1988.

Watson, Derek. *Liszt*. London: J. M. Dent, 1989.

Weaver, William, Editor. *The Verdi-Boito correspondence.* Chicago; London: University of Chicago Press, 1994.

Wegeler, Franz. *Remembering Beethoven: the biographical notes of Franz Wegeler and Ferdinand Ries.* London: Andre Deutsch, 1988.

Weingartner, Felix. *Buffets and rewards: a musician's reminiscences.* London: Hutchinson & Co., 1937.

Weinstock, Herbert. *Rossini: a biography.* New York: Limelight, 1987.

Weiss, Piero and Richard Taruskin. *Music in the Western World: a history in documents.* New York: Schirmer; London: Collier Macmillan, 1984.

Weissweiler, Eva *The complete correspondence of Clara and Robert Schumann.* New York: Peter Lang, 2 Vols., 1994.

Whittaker, William Gillies. *Collected essays.* London: Oxford University Press, 1940.

Whittall, Arnold. *Exploring twentieth-century music: tradition and innovation.* Cambridge; New York: Cambridge University Press, 2003.

Whittall, Arnold. *Music since the First World War.* London: J. M. Dent, 1977.

Whitton, Kenneth S. *Lieder: an introduction to German song.* London: Julia MacRae, 1984.

Wightman, Alistair, Editor. *Szymanowski on music: selected writings of Karol Szymanowski.* London: Toccata Press, 1999.

Wilhelm, Kurt. *Richard Strauss: an intimate portrait.* London: Thames and Hudson, 1999.

Will, Richard James. *The characteristic symphony in the age of Haydn and Beethoven.* Cambridge: Cambridge University Press, 2002.

Willetts, Pamela J. *Beethoven and England: an account of sources in the British Museum.* London: British Museum, 1970.

Williams, Adrian, Editor and Translator. *Liszt, Franz: Selected letters.* Oxford: Clarendon Press, 1998.

Williams, Adrian. *Portrait of Liszt: by himself and his contemporaries.* Oxford: Clarendon Press, 1990.

Williams, Ralph Vaughan. *Heirs and rebels: letters written to each other and occasional writings on music.* London; New York: Oxford University Press, 1959.

Williams, Ralph Vaughan. *Some thoughts on Beethoven's Choral symphony: with writings on other musical subjects.* London; Oxford University Press, 1953.

Williams, Ralph Vaughan. *The making of music.* Ithaca, New York: Cornell University Press, 1955.

Williams, Ursula Vaughan. *R.V.W.: a biography of Ralph Vaughan Williams.* London: Oxford University Press, 1964.

Wilson, Conrad. *Notes on Beethoven: 20 crucial works.* Edinburgh: Saint Andrew Press, 2003.

Wilson, Elizabeth. *Shostakovich: a life remembered.* Princeton, New Jersey: Princeton University Press, 1994.

Winter, Robert, Editor. *Beethoven, performers, and critics: the International Beethoven Congress, Detroit, 1977.* Detroit: Wayne State University Press, 1980.

Winter, Robert. *Compositional origins of Beethoven's opus 131.* Ann Arbor, Michigan: UMI Research Press, 1982.

Winter, Robert and Robert Martin, Editors. *The Beethoven quartet companion.* Berkeley: University of California Press, 1994.

Wolf, Eugene K. and Edward H. Roesner, Editors. *Studies in musical sources and style: essays in honor of Jan LaRue.* Madison, Wisconsin: A-R Editions, 1990.

Wolff, Christoph and Robert Riggs. *The string quartets of Haydn, Mozart and Beethoven: studies of the autograph manuscripts: a conference at Isham Memorial Library, March 15–17, 1979.* Cambridge, Massachusetts: Department of Music, Harvard University, 1980.

Wolff, Konrad. *Masters of the keyboard: individual style elements in the piano music of Bach, Haydn, Mozart, Beethoven, Schubert, Chopin, and Brahms.* Bloomington: Indiana University Press, 1990.

Wörner, Karl Heinrich. *Stockhausen: life and work.* London: Faber, 1973.

Wright, Donald, Editor. *Cardus on music: a centenary collection.* London: Hamish Hamilton, 1988.

Wyndham, Henry Saxe. *August Manns and the Saturday concerts: a memoir and a retrospect.* London and Felling-on-Tyne, New York, The Walter Scott Publishing Co., Ltd., 1909.

Yastrebtsev, V.V. Edited and Translated by Florence Jonas. *Reminiscences of Rimsky-Korsakov.* New York: Columbia University Press, 1985.

Yates, Peter. *Twentieth century music: its evolution from the end of the harmonic era into the present era of sound.* London: Allen & Unwin Ltd., 1968.

Young, Percy M. *Beethoven: a Victorian tribute based on the papers of Sir George Smart.* London: D. Dobson, 1976.

Young, Percy M. *George Grove, 1820–1900: a biography.* London: Macmillan, 1980.

Young, Percy M. *Letters of Edward Elgar and other writings.* London: Geoffrey Bles, 1956.

Young, Percy M., Editor. *Letters to Nimrod: Edward Elgar to August Jaeger, 1897–1908.* London: Dennis Dobson, 1965.

Young, Percy M. *The concert tradition: from the middle ages to the twentieth century.* London: Routledge and Kegan Paul, 1965.

Young, Rob, Editor. *(Brief Description): Undercurrents: the hidden wiring of modern music.* London; New York, N.Y.: Continuum, 2002.

Yourke, Electra Slonimsky, Editor. *Nicolas Slonimsky: writings on music.* New York, N.Y.; London: Routledge, 4 Vols. 2003-2005.

Slonimsky, Nicolas. *The great composers and their works.* Edited by Electra Slonimsky Yourke. New York: Schirmer Books, 2 Vols. 2000.

Ysaÿe, Antoine. *Ysaÿe: his life, work and influence.* London: W. Heinemann, 1947.

Zamoyski, Adam. *Paderewski.* London: Collins, 1982.

Zegers, Mirjam, Editor. *Louis Andriessen: The art of stealing time.* Todmorden: Arc Music, 2002.

Zemanova, Mirka, Editor. *Janácek's uncollected essays on music.* London: Marion Boyars, 1989.

INDEX

The order adopted for the listing of the individual entries in this index is chronological – according to the sequential unfolding of the events under discussion. Thereby, the reader is provided with both a guide to the contents discussed in the main text and a time-line of the principal events bearing on Beethoven's life and work.

SELECTED WRITINGS PP. 1-25
(Sir) George Grove
Ernest Markham Lee
Donald Francis Tovey
Donald Nivison Ferguson
Robert Simpson
Louise Elvira Cuyler
Joseph Braunstein
Michael Broyles
William Drabkin
Alec Harman, Anthony Milner and Wilfrid Mellers
Richard Osborne
Elizabeth Schwarm Glesner
Theodor Adorno
Michael P. Steinberg
Barry Cooper
Alfred Peter Brown

BEETHOVEN AND VIENNA:
   GESTATION OF THE B-FLAT
   MAJOR SYMPHONY PP. 26-53
Introduction
Opera Leonora revised

Work on String Quartets, Op,
    59 (Razumovsky); Violin
    Concerto Op. 61; Varia-
    tions for Piano WoO 16,
    and Symphony in C minor,
    Op. 67
Alexander Wheelock Thayer, views
    of
Maynard Solomon, views of

PORTRAITS OF BEETHOVEN PP. 28
Joseph Mähler
Isidor Neugass

PERSONAL IMPRESSIONS OF
    BEETHOVEN PP. 29-33
Ignaz von Seyfried, recollections of
Beethoven's Studien im General-
    basse
Beethoven's disposition to working
    with sketch sources
Beethoven's domestic circum-
    stances
Sir George Grove, views of
Theresa von Brunswick, reference
    to

POST HEILIGENSTADT PP. 33-35
Barry Cooper, views of
Heiligenstadt Testament
John Keats, reference to
Emmanuel Schikaneder
Mölkerbastei, Beethoven's resi-
    dence: Pasqualati House

ACHIEVEMENT AMIDST
    INSECURITY PP. 35-38
Beethoven's compositions of the
    period
Beethoven's negotiations with
    foreign publishers
Application for post of Director at
    the Royal Imperial Court
    Theatre
Carl Czerny, recollections of

JÉRÔME BONAPARTE: OFFER OF
    POST OF KAPELLMEISTER PP.
    38-40
Offer of post of Senior Kapell-
    meister at Kassel
Beethoven's disaffection with Vien-
    na's musicians

BEETHOVEN'S ANNUITY
    CONTRACT PP. 40-42
Countess Anna Maria Erdödy, role
    of
Archduke Rudolph, Prince Ferdi-
    nand Kinsky and Count Franz
    Joseph Lobkowitz, benefactors
Contract details

VIENNA: CONCERT VENUES AND
    MUSIC-MAKING PP. 42-47
Redoutensaal
Kärntnertortheater
Augarten
Tonkünstler-Societät
Liebhaber Concerte
Vienna University's Festsaal

BEETHOVEN'S ORCHESTRA PP. 47-
    51
Beethoven's personification of
    instruments
Debt to Haydn
Beethoven's adaptation of instru-
    ments to particular symphonies
Adam Von Ahnen Carse, views of
Domenico Dragonetti, influence of
Carl Maria von Weber, views of

CREATION ORIGINS PP. 54-84
Works contemporary with B-flat
    major Symphony
Franz Joachim Wenzel
    Oppersdorff
Kaspar Karl
Beethoven's sojourn in Silesia
Oppersdorf's commissioning a new
    symphony

Interrelationship with origins of Fifth Symphony
Sketch sources, scarcity of
Breitkopf and Härtel, negotiations with
Jonathan del Mar, study of Autograph Score, role of Mendelsohns' in history of
First public performance
Publication origins
Gottfried Christoph Härtel
George Thomson, Edinburgh negotiations
Muzio Clementi, London negotiations
William Frederick Collard
Nikolaus Simrock, contract with
Camille Pleyel, putative contract with
Ignaz von Gleichenstein, role of
Bureau des arts et d'Industrie
Joseph Schreyvogel
Count Oppersdorff, further negotiations with
Fifth and Sixth Symphonies, publication rights to Breitkopf and Härtel
Key significance to Beethoven
Johann Nepomuk Maelzel's metronome
Wiener Vaterländische Blätter
Sigmund Anton Steiner
Franz von Mosel
Sir Roger Norrington and authentic performance
1808, Fourth Symphony published
Title Page
Francesco Cianchettini and P. Sperati, London editions
The Harmonicon
Nikolaus Simrock, score edition
George Grove , views of Fourth Symphony
1862 Gesamtausgabe, complete publication of Beethoven's works
1902, C. F. Peters, miniature score
1923, Breitkopf & Härtel, Philharmonia publication series1

RECEPTION HISTORY PP. 85-139
RECEPTION IN BEETHOVEN'S LIFETIME: FIRST PERFORMANCES PP. 86-102
1807: Prince Lobkowitz, Journal des Luxus und der Modem, critical reception
1807—08: Musikalische Institut, Liebhaber-Concerte, Freunde der Tonkunst, or the Gesellschaft der Musikfreunden, Johann von Häring, role of, Mehlgrube and Festsaal performances, Carl Maria von Weber, views of
1808: Allgemeine musikalische Zeitung, critical reception, Liebhaber concerts
1811: Allgemeine musikalische Zeitung, critical impressions
1812: Mannheim winter concert season
1813: Vienna's Grosse Redoutensaal, Pierre Rode, role of, Joseph von Varena, charity concerts for The Society of Ursulines
1816: music-making in Kassel,
1819–21: Concerts Spirituels, Franz Xaver Gebauer, role of
1822: Lower Rhine Music Festival
1825: Ignaz Schuppanzigh, subscription concerts, Berliner Allgemeine musikalische Zeitung, critical reception
1826: Heinrich Carl Breidenstein, evaluation of Fourth Symphony — comparison with Haydn and Mozart

TRANSCRIPTIONS PP. 102-110
Donald Francis Tovey, views of

Beethoven, views of
Freidrich Stein
Friedrich Mockwitz
Allgemeine musikalische Zeitung, critical reception
1815, London transcriptions
Johann Nepomuk Hummel
Carl Czerny
Franz Liszt

BEETHOVEN-GEWANDHAUS-FELIX MENDELSOHN PP. 110-112
Performances at Berlin, Breslau, Brunswick, Dresden, Frankfurt-am-Main, and Munich
Gewandhaus Orchestra, support of
Felix Mendelsohn, role of

BEETHOVEN'S RECEPTION IN FRANCE PP. 117-122
Heinrich Simrock, publisher
Giuseppe Cambini
Allgemeine musikalische Zeitung
Tablettes de Polymnie
Concerts Français — Exercises Publics
François-Antoine Habeneck
Société des Concerts du Conservatoire
Concert Spirituel
François Castil-Blaze
Musical Chronicles
Journal des débats
Hector Berlioz
Revue et gazette musicale de Paris
Jean-François Le Sueur
Friedrich von Raumer

BEETHOVEN'S RECEPTION IN ENGLAND PP. 117-122
John Sterland
Harmonic Society
The Harmonicon
Sir George Smart
Johann Peter Salomon
The Philharmonic Society: record of performance of Beethoven's symphonies
Myles Birket Foster
Cipriani Potter
The Musical Times

LATER NINETEENTH-CENTURY RECEPTION PP. 122-131
Beiblatt der Kölnischen Zeitung
Cäcilia
Views of:
Adolf Bernhard Marx
Louis Spohr
Felix Mendelssohn
Carl Friedrich Zelter
Wilhelm Lampadius
George Hogarth
Cosima Wagner
George Bernard Shaw

RECEPTION NEARER TO OUR OWN TIME PP. 131-137
Views of:
Donald Francis Tovey
Neville Cardus
Felix Weingartner
Anthony Hopkins
Luciano Berio
Olivier Messiaen

LATER RECEPTION: MUSICOLOGY PP. 140-203
Heinrich Friedrich Rellstab
Hector Berlioz
Clara Schumann
Sir George Grove
Ernest Markham Lee
Romain Rolland
Paul Bekker
Donald Francis Tovey
Marion Scott
Arturo Toscanini
Richard Strauss
Donald Nivison Ferguson
Wilfrid Howard Mellers

Robert Simpson
Igor Stravinsky
Louise Elvira Cuyler
Basil Deane
Joseph Braunstein
William Preston Stedman
Anthony Hopkins
Denis Matthews
Michael Broyles

Alec Harman, Anthony Milner
  and Wilfrid Mellers
Richard Osborne
Peter Hauschild
William Kinderman
Theodore W. Adorno
Michael P. Steinberg
Alfred Peter Brown
Terry Barfoot

ABOUT THE AUTHOR

Terence M. Russell graduated with first class honours in architecture and was a nominee for the coveted Silver Medal of the Royal Institute of British Architects. He is a Fellow of the Royal Incorporation of Architects in Scotland (retired), was formerly Reader in the School of Arts, Culture and Environment at the University of Edinburgh, a Fellow of the British Higher Education Academy, and Senior Assessor to the Scottish Higher Education Funding Council. Alongside his professional work in the field of architecture – embracing practice, teaching and research – he has maintained a lifetime's interest in the music and musicology of Beethoven. He has an equal admiration for the work of Franz Schubert and was for many years an active member of the Schubert Institute, UK. His book writings in the field of architecture include the following:

The Built Environment: A Subject Index, Gregg Publishing (1989):
- Vol. 1: Town planning and urbanism, architecture, gardens and landscape design
- Vol. 2: Environmental technology, constructional engineering, building and materials
- Vol. 3: Decorative art and industrial design, international exhibitions and collections, recreational and performing arts
- Vol. 4: Public health, municipal services, community welfare

Architecture in the Encyclopédie of Diderot and D'Alemebert: The Letterpress Articles and Selected Engravings, Scolar Press (1993)

The Encyclopaedic Dictionary in the Eighteenth Century: Architecture, Arts and Crafts, Scolar Press (1997):
- Vol. 1: John Harris, Lexicon Technicum
- Vol. 2: Ephraim Chambers, Cyclopaedia
- Vol. 3: The Builder's Dictionary
- Vol. 4: Samuel Johnson, A Dictionary of the English Language
- Vol. 5: A Society of Gentlemen, Encyclopaedia Britannica

Gardens and Landscapes in the Encyclopédie of Diderot and D'Alemebert: The Letterpress Articles and Selected Engravings, 2 Vols., Ashgate (1999)

The Napoleonic Survey of Egypt: The Monuments and Customs of Egypt, 2 Vols., Ashgate (2001)

The Discovery of Egypt: Vivant Denon's Travels with Napoleon's Army, History Press (2005)

www.ingramcontent.com/pod-product-compliance
Lightning Source LLC
Chambersburg PA
CBHW010021130526
44590CB00047B/3753